DESIRE AFTER DARK

DESIRE AFTER DARK

Contemporary Queer Cultures and Occultly Marvelous Media

Andrew J. Owens

INDIANA UNIVERSITY PRESS

This book is a publication of

Indiana University Press
Office of Scholarly Publishing
Herman B Wells Library 350
1320 East 10th Street
Bloomington, Indiana 47405 USA

iupress.org

© 2021 by Andrew J. Owens

All rights reserved
No part of this book may be reproduced or utilized in any form or by any means, electronic or mechanical, including photocopying and recording, or by any information storage and retrieval system, without permission in writing from the publisher. The paper used in this publication meets the minimum requirements of the American National Standard for Information Sciences—Permanence of Paper for Printed Library Materials, ANSI Z39.48-1992.

Manufactured in the United States of America

Cataloging information is available from the Library of Congress.

ISBN 978-0-253-05380-0 (hardback)
ISBN 978-0-253-05382-4 (paperback)
ISBN 978-0-253-05384-8 (ebook)

First Printing 2021

CONTENTS

Acknowledgments vii

Introduction: Blood, Sulfur, Sex, Magick   1

1 Aquarian Alternatives: Midcentury Media and the Quest for Occultly Queer Histories   16

2 Le sexe qui parle du surnaturel: Supernatural Sexualities and Satanic Subcultures in the 1970s   57

3 The Blood Is the Life/Death: Queer Contagion and Viral Vampirism in the Age(s) of HIV/AIDS   100

4 "Now Is the Time, Now Is the Hour, Ours Is the Magick, Ours Is the Power": Casting as Coming Out in Millennial Media   139

5 "Hold Me, Thrill Me, Kiss Me, Kill Me": The Ambivalent Queer of Occult Cable TV   160

Epilogue   198

Index   201

ACKNOWLEDGMENTS

When does writing a book begin? For me, this book began in my hometown of Bethlehem, Pennsylvania, at the public library, when I was seven years old. In one of my most distinct memories from childhood, I remember approaching one of the librarians and asking to rent a film: *Dracula*. When asked, rather incredulously, if I knew which version I was looking for, I responded without hesitation: "The 1931 Universal version with Bela Lugosi, please." If a picture is worth a thousand words, the look exchanged between the librarian and my mother said it all about me as a child: a precocious kid who absolutely loved horror film and television. Now, almost three decades later, it's a rare pleasure to have the opportunity to thank those who have kept that childhood affection and fascination alive.

Desire After Dark began as a doctoral dissertation in Northwestern University's Department of Radio/TV/Film, and my first thanks go to my committee, who helped this project blossom from its earliest incarnations. Jeff Sconce has been a model of intellectual generosity, good humor, and enthusiasm since we met more than ten years ago. Never once did Jeff think I should complete this project on anyone else's terms but my own, and his acute commentary and encyclopedic knowledge have been invaluable. Lynn Spigel is as insightful about the nuances of media historiography as she is about our mutual love for *Dark Shadows*, and her eagerness to train media historians who are as passionate about the field as she is has inspired me to never accept less than my best work. And Chuck Kleinhans took me and this project on sight unseen, a gesture for which I will always fondly remember him.

Many appreciations are also due to other Northwestern faculty both within and outside RTVF. Whether through courses taken with them, feedback given at various talks, or a passing smile, Nick Davis, Hamid Naficy, Miriam Petty, Ariel Rogers, Jake Smith, Neil Verma, and Mimi White continue to make Screen Cultures at Northwestern one of the premier media studies graduate programs in the world.

This book was completed while I taught at three different institutions, all of which introduced me to amazingly supportive colleagues and mentors. At Boston College: Ashley Duggan, Don Fishman, Lindsay Hogan, Brett Ingram, Michael Keith, Marilyn Malteski, Rita Rosenthal, Mike Serazio, Matt Sienkiewicz, Anjali Vats, and Celeste Wells. At DePaul University: Paul Booth, Michael DeAngelis, Kelly Kessler, Kelli Marshall, and Allison McCracken. And here at the University of Iowa: Paula Amad, Kate Magsamen Conrad, Corey Creekmur, Brian Ekdale, Anahita Ghazvinizadeh, Chris Goetz, Chris Harris, Tim Havens, Nellie Kluz, Anna Morrison, Kathleen Newman, Kevin Ripka, Dan Singleton, Melissa Tully, Steve Ungar, and Travis Vogan.

If networking is one of the requisite features of academic life, then I have been fortunate enough to cultivate an unparalleled support team of colleagues and friends from around the world. Over conversations, meals, and much-needed laughter, these folks are a constant reminder of why I do what I do: Peter Alilunas, Ben Aslinger, Chris Becker, Ron Becker, Harry Benshoff, Caetlin Benson-Allott, Kevin Bozelka, Courtney Brannon Donoghue, Becca Burnett, Colin Burnett, Matt Connolly, Katie Day Good, Sean Griffin, Julia Himberg, Daniel Humphrey, Mary Kearney, Cáel Keegan, Patrick Keilty, Amanda Ann Klein, Derek Kompare, Kayti Lausch, Suzanne Leonard, Elana Levine, Alfred Martin, Chelsea McCracken, Paul McEwan, Taylor Miller, Brandy Monk-Payton, Candace Moore, Jen Moorman, Austin Morris, Michael Newman, Dana Och, Nora Patterson, Jen Porst, Ryan Powell, Mike Rennett, Nick Salvato, Andy Scahill, Molly Schneider, John Stadler, Kyle Stevens, Alyx Vesey, Amy Villarejo, Kristen Warner, and Patricia White.

Close friends and family outside my academic life have also provided support without which I would have never finished this book. Many thanks go to Scott Kenemore, Michael Huber, Diane Huber, Mike Huber, Jess Huber, Caroline Simon, Stanley Smith, Jody Smith, Joel Smith, Therese Smith Marquez, and Shawn Smith.

Finally, all my love and thanks to my parents, Bob and Kathy, who raised an intellectually curious son who was never satisfied with an easy answer. My parents have given me every opportunity to follow the trails I've wanted to blaze and taught me how to be compassionate, understanding, and unapologetically motivated when I saw something that I wanted. The lessons and support they continue to give are things I'll always cherish and can never adequately repay.

DESIRE AFTER DARK

INTRODUCTION
Blood, Sulfur, Sex, Magick

"There are more things in heaven and earth, Horatio, than are dreamt of in your philosophy."[1] This oft-quoted aide-mémoire from the Prince of Denmark to his friend and confidant at the conclusion of *Hamlet*'s first act is one of Shakespeare's most indelible bon mots . . . and also one of the most occultly queer. Recounting the circumstances surrounding his death to his son as a ghost from beyond the grave, Hamlet's father details a devilish twist on the archetypal Oedipal scenario: a murder at the hands of his own brother, Claudius, so that he might marry his sister-in-law, Gertrude. According to the ghost, Claudius diabolically engaged the "witchcraft of his wit, with traitorous gifts . . . wicked wit and gifts, that have the power so to seduce" in order to usurp both queen and country.[2]

Hamlet's invocation of both metaphorical and material magick are nothing out of the ordinary across the Shakespearean canon, sitting alongside other notable examples such as *Macbeth*, *A Midsummer Night's Dream*, *The Tempest*, and *The Winter's Tale*. Even still, what makes Hamlet's father's revelation unique is the distinctly queer way in which witchcraft is described. Using hebona, a questionably fictitious poisonous herb often likened to the more familiar witch's weapon of henbane, Claudius seduces not only his sister-in-law but also his own brother in order to get close enough to kill him. While Horatio can do little else but remark at the "wondrous strange" nature of the ghost's appearance and confession, Hamlet staunchly encourages him to "as a stranger give it welcome."[3] It is neither heaven nor earth that most concerns Hamlet at this moment but rather the in-between, the interstitial, the unnamable, the ephemeral, the supernatural, and the strange. Things may or may not be rotten in Denmark, but they are most assuredly queer.

While Harold Bloom's bold assertion that Shakespeare singlehandedly established the Western epistemic conditions for understanding human nature is certainly open to debate, the Bard's prose and poetry do constitute an illuminating archive to read alongside both the etymological development of the term "queer" (e.g., the "strange" conditions of *Hamlet*'s Denmark or the Weird Sisters of *Macbeth*) and the development of modern occultism.[4] Indeed, since the turn of the 1990s, much ink and blood (mostly metaphorical, some literal) has been spilt within the pages of industry trade journals, entertainment blogs and vlogs, fan websites, and popular press outlets variously appraising, admonishing, and acclaiming what appears to be a newly flourishing phenomenon across Euro-American media culture: fascinations with the sociocultural and sexual relationships between queerness and the occult.

On television, nearly every major industrial player over the past twenty-five years has tried its hand at this sensation, from *Buffy the Vampire Slayer* (The WB, 1997–2001; UPN, 2001–3), *Being Human* (BBC Three, 2008–13), and *True Blood* (HBO, 2008–14) to *The Magicians* (SyFy, 2015–20), *Shadowhunters* (Freeform, 2016–19), *Lucifer* (FOX, 2016–18; Netflix, 2019–present), *American Horror Story* (F/X, 2011–present), and a host of series that have combined to create one of the primary brand identities of the CW (*Supernatural* [2006–20], *The Vampire Diaries* [2009–17], *The Originals* [2013–18], *The Secret Circle* [2011–12], *Charmed* [2018–present], and *Legacies* [2018–present]). Garnering mostly modest critical recognition, these series, scattered across a variety of networks and platforms, have more meaningfully generated fiercely loyal fan cultures from both international and intersectional spectrums of sexuality, gender, race, ethnicity, ability, and so forth.

In film, witches, vampires, shapeshifters, and other queer things that go bump in the night have steadily amassed both box office and art house successes, demonstrated through Hollywood fare like *Interview with the Vampire* (1994), *The Craft* (1996), *The Covenant* (2006), and the *Harry Potter* (2001–11) and spinoff *Fantastic Beasts* (2016–18) franchises and *Twilight* (2008–12) franchise, as well as festival favorites such as *Only Lovers Left Alive* (2013), *The Witch* (2015), and *The Love Witch* (2016). Irrespective of screen size or medium, the support these and other productions have received and continue to receive from an eclectic array of writers, producers, directors, actors, and other industry professionals captures a dynamic cultural zeitgeist, one that has ostensibly wrenched both nonnormative sexualities and spiritual beliefs from the margins to the mainstreams of Euro-American screen cultures. Yet this instinctive reaction to read teleologically, to consider a platform, a medium, or a genre as "always already new," is an especially misleading one considering the coupling between queerness and occultism.⁵ Indeed, the strangeness, oddity, irrationality, and outré of the occult has always been essential to its enduring appeal.

Pulling back the veil on this lengthier history, *Desire After Dark: Contemporary Queer Cultures and Occultly Marvelous Media* offers a sociocultural and industrial history of occult film and television from the sexual revolutions of the 1960s to the present. Specifically, the book traces how evolving notions of queerness within the realms of gender and sexuality have been integral to the development of occult media and its popularity as both a subcultural and mainstream screen presence over the past sixty years. While many academic studies focusing on the broad significance of gender and sexuality to the horror genre have zeroed in on subcategories such as the classical and postclassical Hollywood "creature feature," the American slasher/European *giallo* film, and recurrent cycles of apocalyptic zombification, *Desire After Dark* takes two occult phenomena, witchcraft and vampirism, as its primary nexus of attention. Through an eclectic methodological mix including media historiography, audience, reception, and fan studies, industrial production studies, and original archival research, this book advances a history of the paranormal present, maintaining that occult film and television have witnessed particular patterns of prominence within the ever-cyclical realm of screen genres as a means of both exposing and working through cultural anxieties surrounding gender and sexuality. Such moments considered include the global sexual revolutions of the 1960s and 1970s, the American penchant for both "Euro-sleaze" art house cinema and theatrical hardcore pornography during the 1970s, the devastating impact of the HIV/AIDS pandemic during and beyond the 1980s, the resurgent popularity of New Age spiritualities in the 1990s, and the increasingly explicit sexualization of American cable and postnetwork television in the new millennium.

Desire After Dark is certainly not the first academic study to consider issues of queerness in relation to horror and its manifestations at particular junctures in literary, film, and television history. Nevertheless, the majority of existing investigations have appeared in insular fits and starts, in essays of edited anthologies, journal articles, book chapters, or encyclopedia entries. With few notable exceptions, scholars have yet to fully grapple with the dynamic multiplicities of queer horror over time, perhaps because the relationship between queerness and horror has either seemed so obvious as to stifle the significance of such inquiries or, on the other hand, such an aberration at the margins of media tastes that it encroaches beyond the pale of academic analysis.⁶ Casting off these hesitations, however, I wish to be clear from the outset regarding both the scope and limitations of my own intervention.

Desire After Dark focuses on a roughly sixty-year period of screen history from the 1960s to the present, as this time frame is both broad and bounded enough to sustain the strengths of a true cultural history, tracing the evolving dynamics between "structures of feeling" and particular modes of industrial production.⁷ Furthermore, beginning this study in the 1960s avoids replicating much of the well-trodden critical ground that has already been laid in relation to earlier queer horror on screen, from the classical Hollywood horror cycles of the 1930s and 1940s produced at Universal and RKO to the Monogram and Allied Artists "creature features" screened across the United States throughout the 1950s.⁸ Finally, the infamous sexual revolutions, countercultural keenness, and general nonconformity that has become so tethered to cultural memories of the 1960s, combined with the decade's renewed enchantment with the occult, provides the book's fitting historical foundation.

As previously noted, *Desire After Dark* combines media historiography, audience, reception, and fan studies, industrial production studies, and original archival research in order to grapple with the historical constellation between occultism and Euro-American film and television cultures. As such, this book is not ethnographic in method, nor does it attempt to definitively lay claim to what audiences, viewers, spectators, and so on *do* with these texts. While acknowledging that agentive concerns often confront media historians with acute methodological dilemmas, this book is based on an orientation toward informed critical conjecture, considering why particular communities might gravitate toward particular kinds of horror at particular places and times.⁹

Far from being self-evident in meaning, "queer occultism" combines two terms that demand definitional clarity. Since its academic instantiation in the mid- to late 1980s, few terms have engendered as much debate, scrutiny, and critical handwringing as "queer." Indeed, as Annamarie Jagose observes, queer's "definitional indeterminacy, its elasticity, is one of its constituent characteristics."¹⁰ Echoing this tractability, *Desire After Dark* takes the majority of its queer cues from Alexander Doty's influential study *Making Things Perfectly Queer: Interpreting Mass Culture*. As such, in what follows, queer and queerness indicates a range of "nonstraight expression in, or in response to, mass culture. This range includes specifically gay, lesbian, and bisexual expressions; but it also includes all other potential (and potentially unclassifiable) nonstraight positions... 'queer' [marks] a flexible space for the expression of all aspects of non- (anti-, contra-) straight cultural production and reception."[11] Furthermore, especially germane to the purposes of this book, Harry Benshoff extends Doty's taxonomy in order to designate queer as an orientation that "negates the oppressive binarisms of the dominant hegemony... both within culture at large, and within texts of horror and fantasy... queer suggests death over life by focusing on non-procreative sexual behaviors, making it especially suited to a genre which takes sex and death as central thematic concerns."[12] With as much consistency as possible, "gay" or "lesbian" will be used in this book specifically to demarcate same-sex sexual practices, while "queer" broadens this horizon to bring into the fold those non- (anti-, contra-) straight positions and cultural productions that disrupt heteronormative hegemony.

In its formative stages, *Desire After Dark* set out to interrogate the queer particularities of horror film and television within a broadly defined tradition of the Gothic. As outlined by Eve Kosofsky Sedgwick, the late queer theorist who began her career writing about horror, the Gothic has included several characteristic preoccupations since its establishment as a literary mode in the late eighteenth century: "monastic institutions; sleeplike and deathlike states; subterranean spaces and live burial; doubles; the discovery of obscured family ties... possibilities of incest; unnatural echoes or silences, unintelligible writings, and the unspeakable... the poisonous effects of guilt and shame; nocturnal landscapes and dreams; apparitions from the past."[13] Given such capacious concerns, according to Robert B. Heilman, the Gothic has consistently endeavored to expand horizons beyond social patterns, rational decisions, and institutionally approved emotions—"in a word, to enlarge the sense of reality and its impact on the human being. It became then a great liberator of feeling. It acknowledged the non-rational—in the world of things and events, occasionally in the realm of the transcendental, ultimately and most persistently in the depths of the human being."[14] Yet if all Gothic roads somehow lead to unlocking horizons beyond rationality and the liberation of human emotional depths, what horror isn't somehow Gothic?

Tracking a more precise and dynamic history, *Desire After Dark* focuses specifically on occult phenomena within this broadly outlined tradition of Gothic horror, exploring worlds driven by forces of magick (as distinguished from stage illusion / sleight-of-hand magic) within which figures such as witches and vampires make use of their supernatural knowledge in order to queer what otherwise appear as normative worlds.[15] It is far from coincidental, as Hugh Urban contends, that the rise of Western esotericism has gone hand in hand with concurrent explorations of sexual freedom and nonnormative erotic expression.[16] Indeed, such alliances have been found at the heart of occult film and television's enduring cultural appeals and industrial transformations over the past sixty years.

Many traits of both occultism and queerness have been repeatedly articulated around a paradoxical set of discursive foundations, simultaneously perverse and pleasurable, explicit and inferential, natural and supernatural—based, in Sedgwick's words, on an aesthetics of "pleasurable fear."[17] However, by taking the perverse, the abject, and the deviant not only as legitimate heuristics but also as vibrant sites of pleasure and agency, queer occultism constitutes a potentially problematic subdiscipline in relation to the positivist political proclivities of some branches of queer theory and LGBTQ+ media studies. Yet as Ellis Hanson argues, inspired by perverse histories of the lesbian vampire film, one of the dogged difficulties with much queer media criticism is its "cold shower of political correctness—its preoccupation with a narrow politics of representation and its search for so-called positive or accurate images which, when they finally do appear, are often dull anyway. We moralize movies to death. We disavow fantasy in favor of social realism."[18] Such critical gestures are, according to William Hughes and Andrew Smith, ironically unqueer, for to denounce horror, and queer occult film and television in particular, for what is often perceived as their "bad taste" is to simultaneously "condemn [them] for acknowledging those very alternatives to monolithic orthodoxy."[19] But what if the fantasies of the occult do indeed have more to offer? What if, following Hanson, the recurrent appearance of queer occultism across Euro-American film and television history was motivated by a wish that we could experience our lives as "more traumatic, more anxious, more paranoid, more sexually transgressive and bizarre, more overwrought; in short, [as] more interesting than [they] generally [are]"?[20] As such, *Desire After Dark* contends that queer orientations toward occult media unearth those pleasures to be found in so-called perversity, abjection, and deviance, drawing new critical horizons for queer theory, LGBTQ+ media studies, and film and television historiography.

The Horrors of Sexuality

Eroticism, as Georges Bataille famously writes, is assenting to life up to the point of death, as objects of affection and arousal become intimately imbued with often-frightening moral and ethical imperatives.[21] Indeed, eroticism has always been a somewhat horrific human endeavor, conditioned by and mythologized within popular cultural forms. One of the apexes of supernatural horror's articulation through Euro-American literature, for example, appeared at the very moment when norms of gender and sexuality were beginning to be codified for modern Western culture: "Gothic fiction offered a testing ground for many unauthorized genders and sexualities, including sodomy, tribadism, romantic friendship (male and female), incest, pedophilia, sadism, masochism, necrophilia, cannibalism, masculinized females, feminized males, miscegenation, and so on."[22] From John Addington Symonds and Richard von Krafft-Ebing to Havelock Ellis and Sigmund Freud, early luminaries in the history of sexology habitually corralled occult conventions in the service of discursively dissecting new notions of sexual subjectivity, giving life to those shadowy passageways of our erotic interiorities. As Judith Halberstam maintains, superstitious and supernatural practices have always functioned as technologies of subjectivity, directly contributing to the formation of those deviant, aberrant, and unauthorized sexual identities against which the normal, the healthy, and the wholesome become legible.[23]

While the field of Gothic criticism is as expansive as the histories and artifacts it interrogates, most interlocutors agree that the genre is a particularly generative one, especially within the realms of gender and sexuality. Indeed, as a discursive arena, analyses of the Gothic's productive capabilities would be impossible without the work of Michel Foucault, especially the first volume of his *History of Sexuality*, which invokes canonically Gothic imagery to take up the supposed horrors of sexual nonconformity. Maintaining that a certain forthrightness was common practice in matters of sexuality at the beginning of the seventeenth century, Foucault famously argues that "twilight soon fell upon this bright day, followed by the monotonous nights of the Victorian bourgeoisie. Sexuality [became] carefully confined ... on the subject of sex, silence became the rule."[24] From illumination to darkness, from clamor to silence, from freedom to restriction; this has been the stuff of Gothic occultism since the publication of works like Horace Walpole's *The Castle of Otranto* (1764), Ann Radcliffe's *The Mysteries of Udolpho* (1794), and Matthew Lewis's *The Monk* (1796).

As Foucault's work is often celebrated for revealing, we would do well not to write histories of sexuality from the standpoints of prohibition, censorship, and/or repression. Indeed, it is a seductive yet misleading temptation,

Foucault notes, "to make prohibition into the basic and constitutive element from which one would be able to write the history of what has been said concerning sex starting from the modern epoch."²⁵ Yet what if the opposite were simultaneously true? What if, similar to this book's argument vis-à-vis queerness and the occult, repression and productivity were two sides of the same coin? From this point of view, a different orientation toward sexual historiography emerges: "The prohibition of sex is [not] a ruse ... [but] since the end of the sixteenth century, the 'putting into discourse of sex,' far from undergoing a process of restriction, on the contrary has been subjected to a mechanism of increasing incitement; that the techniques of power exercised over sex have not obeyed a principle of rigorous selection, but rather one of dissemination and implantation of polymorphous sexualities."²⁶ As histories of both film and television will reveal, occult media has been one of the richest sites through which processes of sexually discursive cultural production have taken place over the past sixty years.

Such modes of productivity have not, however, been characterized by a de facto hedonistic libertinism. As Foucault elaborates, most modern societies have been founded on complex paradoxes of dedicating themselves to speaking of sexuality ad infinitum while continuing to exploit sex as the singular secret that might somehow unlock the interstices of the human condition.²⁷ What such paradoxes have given rise to, then, is a *scientia sexualis*, proliferating classificatory schemas that speak endlessly of sexual aberrations, deviance, and abnormalities.

Beginning with the nineteenth-century systematization of both sexology and psychoanalysis, the pathologizing of polymorphously perverse and peripheral human sexualities entailed an "incorporation of perversions and a new specification of individuals."²⁸ The Victorian homosexual, for instance, became "a personage, a past, a case history, and a childhood, in addition to being a type of life, a life form, and a morphology, with an indiscreet anatomy and possibly a mysterious physiology. Nothing that went into his total composition was unaffected by his sexuality. It was everywhere present in him: at the root of all his actions because it was their insidious and indefinitely active principle."²⁹ Indeed, to the extent that occult media has participated in and continues to participate in the discursive productivity of polymorphously perverse sexualities, it often does so in direct contradistinction to heteronormativity's own reproductive imperatives. As Michael Bronski maintains in *The Pleasure Principle: Sex, Backlash, and the Struggle for Gay Freedom*, "the idea that pleasure might exist unrationed in its own right, without apology and without justification, is considered radical, almost unnatural. . . . In the popular imagination there has long been a strong connection between nonreproductive, uninhibited sexuality and the decline of the social order" for which queer people have been partially blamed for centuries.[30] Taking this argument one step further, Lee Edelman famously argues that queer theory's own "death drive" presents a radical rethinking of ethics against heteronormativity's brandishing of children as the wardens of "reproductive futurism."[31] Yet while occult film and television may often replicate conventionally paranoid structures of homophobia and other sexual moral panics, they also offer a "richly historical and political language for valorizing those disreputable sexualities that the Gothic has traditionally rendered monstrous, not so much to purge them as to invest them with a sublime narrative energy."[32] To be sure, the supposed horrors of sexuality have dynamically informed our collective cultural fascination with the sexualities of horror, and they continue to do so.

The Sexualities of Horror

When serious critical attention first turned to the academic study of screen horror in the 1980s, much of this work started with a simple question: Why horror? As Noël Carroll inquires, the question is this: "Why would anyone be interested in the genre to begin with? Why does the genre persist . . . how can we explain its very existence, for why would anyone want to be horrified, or even art-horrified?"[33] Expanding these queries, Andrew Tudor notes that both critics and audiences otherwise benignly disposed toward popular culture often view horror as the "lowest of the low, and even liberal gentlefolk are suspicious about the motives and character failings of its consumers. Are they sick? Are they disturbed people indulging in nasty, perverse desires? Or have they merely become so jaded as to be addicted to ever-increasing doses of violent excess?"[34] There is indeed something quite paradoxical about horror, a genre that has always given every indication of being a source of pleasure for its audiences, but via trafficking in the very sorts of things that simultaneously provoke disquiet, distress, and displeasure.[35]

This critical fixation on "Why horror?" has been approached from a number of different avenues, but perhaps none more influential than Robin Wood's contention that the genre represents a "return of the repressed." In Wood's analysis, what returns in horror to wreak havoc across our collective screens and cultural fantasies in the guise of the monster is sexuality itself, "together with its possible successful sublimation into non-sexual creativity—sexuality being the source of creative energy in general."[36] As Wood maintains, the ideal inhabitant of our culture is the individual whose sexuality is "sufficiently fulfilled by the monogamous heterosexual union necessary for the reproduction of future ideal inhabitants, and whose sublimated sexuality (creativity) is sufficiently fulfilled in the totally non-creative and non-fulfilling labor (whether in factory or office) to which our society dooms the overwhelming majority of its members."[37] Consequently, dictates of sexual conformity are precisely what horror often resists, repels, and considers alternatives to, even though the status quo is restored more often than not in the genre's classical mode.

Much of the critical credence lent to Wood's and other formative investigations of horror has been based on a seductive invocation of psychoanalytic truisms (sublimation, repression, wish fulfillment, the subconscious, etc.) that ostensibly erect a universalizing genre theory: "One might say that the true subject of the horror genre is the struggle for recognition of all that our civilization represses or oppresses, its reemergence dramatized, as in our nightmares, as an object of horror, a matter of terror, and the happy ending (when it exists) typically signifying the restoration of repression."[38] Provocative though these paradigms might be, psychoanalysis presents significant limitations when applied to horror. First, critical heuristics like psychoanalysis shore up the "basic notion that horror's pleasures stand in need of explanation . . . theoretical approaches to horror have explained (away) the genre's pleasures by invoking their own disciplinary and theoretical norms."[39] Second, psychoanalysis tends toward pathologizing typologies of nonnormative, queer sexualities that carve out little space for pleasure that is not considered misdirected in some way (to the extent that psychoanalysis even speaks of pleasure in the affirmative). Finally, psychoanalysis establishes transhistorical, universalizing notions of sexual subjectivity that struggle to adequately account for questions of spatiotemporal specificity.

None of these concerns are meant to promote a wholesale negation of the claim that horror engages with repressed fears and desires while re-enacting residual affective conflicts surrounding these feelings.[40] On the contrary, what *Desire After Dark* offers is a history of how such sexually repressed desires as animated through the occult have been historically conditioned in ways that differ across place, time, industrial practice, and sociocultural context. Enduring genres like horror are not fixed entities, nor are they simply "bodies of textual material. They are composed as much of the beliefs, commitments and social practices of their audiences as by texts, better understood as particular 'sub-cultures of taste' than as autonomous assemblies of cultural artefacts."[41] As such, analyzing the pleasures of screening queer occultism requires an acute awareness of how particular formations of themes and conventions have evolved within distinct sociocultural and industrial milieus.

While most now-canonical screen horror scholarship does not explicitly engage in the project of queer critique, the allure of gender and sexual nonnormativity remains a formidably haunting specter across this body of work. To wit, the central effect and fascination of horror in relation to the return of the repressed is its fulfillment of our "nightmare wish to smash the norms that oppress us and which our moral conditioning teaches us to revere."[42] While shattering these norms may trade in various levels of moral, ethical, and bodily disgust, as Carroll maintains, such repulsion is part of an overall address that is "not only pleasurable, but whose potential pleasure depends on the confirmation of the existence of the monster as a being that violates, defies, or problematizes standing cultural classifications."[43] This process of monstrous confirmation is, moreover, often articulated in ways that mirror the queer dichotomy between being closeted and coming out: "Horror stories are often protracted series of discoveries: first the reader learns of the monster's existence, then some characters do, then some more characters do, and so on; the drama of iterated disclosure—albeit to different parties—underwrites much horror fiction."[44] Specifically addressing this progression of recapitulated revelation in relation to gender and sexuality, Carol Clover argues in *Men, Women, and Chain Saws: Gender in the Modern Horror Film* that the world of horror is one that knows very well that men and women are "profoundly different . . . but one that at the same time repeatedly contemplates mutations and slidings whereby women begin to look a lot like men . . . men are pressured to become like women . . . and some people are impossible to tell apart."[45] Such scholarship published in the 1980s and early 1990s laid a provocatively productive foundation on which critics addressing the explicit queerness of screen horror would go on to build.

Historically, notions of both queerness and monstrosity have shared many of the same semantic charges and anxieties surrounding sexuality and death.[46] In one of the most influential studies of queer horror across contemporary media culture, Harry Benshoff expands on this convergence:

> For the better part of the twentieth century, homosexuals, like vampires, have rarely cast a reflection in the social looking-glass of popular culture. When they are seen, they are often filtered through the iconography of the horror film: ominous sound cues, shocked reaction shots, or even thunder and lightning. Both movie monsters and homosexuals have existed chiefly in shadowy closets, and when they do emerge from these proscribed places into the sunlit world, they cause panic and fear. Their closets uphold and reinforce culturally constructed binaries of gender and sexuality that structure Western thought. To create a broad analogy, monster is to 'normality' as homosexual is to heterosexual.[47]

From the nineteenth-century queer imaginings of John Polidori's *The Vampyre* (1819), J. Sheridan Le Fanu's *Carmilla* (1871), and Bram Stoker's *Dracula* (1897) through to contemporary iterations in Anne Rice's *Interview with the Vampire* (1976), *Buffy the Vampire Slayer*, *The Vampire Diaries*, *True Blood*, and beyond, what has often been imagined through occult horror, Richard Dyer argues, is "of a piece with how people have thought and felt about lesbians and gay men—how others have thought and felt about us, and how we have thought and felt about ourselves."[48]

If monstrosity is clearly delineated as the epicenter of both narrative and spectatorial investment in horror, often juxtaposed with one-dimensional caricatures of human normativity, then the seductive queerness that vampirism, witchcraft, and other occult phenomena invoke is largely that of antiassimilation. Set against the restrictive dictates of both hetero- and homonormativity, occult film and television of the past sixty years has creatively considered the agency, freedom, and pleasure to be found in cultural, theological, political, and especially gender and sexual heterodoxies.[49] For as much as Hanson's claim endures that LGBTQ+ media criticism has struggled with and continues to struggle with cold showers of political correctness in search of affirming images, the field cannot continue to deny the familiar voices that occult horror brings so vividly to life. These are, according to Dyer, those strands of queer life that have always set themselves against respectability and fitting in, against monogamy and passing for straight, where "depravity and degradation are validated; it is the voice that prizes [queerness] as outlawry and living on the edge."[50] Being a witch or a vampire may not be fundamentally revolutionary, liberatory, or even politically progressive, but this book nevertheless maintains that such occult phenomena present formidable challenges to the cultural conservatism and reactionary orientations that are often assumed to lie at the heart of horror.

Reading, watching, and interpreting queerly, as Doty crucially reminds us, aren't reducible to "'alternative' readings, wishful or willful misreadings, or 'reading too much into things' readings. [Queer readings] result from the recognition and articulation of the complex range of queerness that has been in popular culture texts and their audiences all along."[51] As such, *Desire After Dark* contributes to a historical model of LGBTQ+ media studies that offers an alternative to those well-worn excavations of queerness from the depths of an ephemeral textual subconscious. In its place, this book maintains that occult film and television of the past sixty years presents a critical view into the ways in which texts, audiences, and industrial formations have always been well aware of the ways in which nonnormative genders and sexualities constitute the heart of some of screen culture's most enduring generic appeals.

Notes

1. William Shakespeare, *Hamlet*. *The Complete Works of Shakespeare*, ed. David Bevington (London: Pearson, 2003), 670–713.
2. Ibid.
3. Ibid.
4. See Harold Bloom, *Shakespeare: The Invention of the Human* (New York: Riverhead, 1998).
5. See Lisa Gitelman, *Always Already New: Media, History, and the Data of Culture* (Cambridge: MIT Press, 2008).
6. Such notable exceptions include Barbara Creed, *The Monstrous-Feminine: Film, Feminism, Psychoanalysis* (London: Routledge, 1993); Judith Halberstam, *Skin Shows: Gothic Horror and the Technology of Monsters* (Durham: Duke University Press, 1995); Harry M. Benshoff, *Monsters in the Closet: Homosexuality and the Horror Film* (Manchester: Manchester University Press, 1997); Paulina Palmer, *Lesbian Gothic: Transgressive Fictions* (London: Cassell, 1999); and George Haggerty, *Queer Gothic* (Urbana: University of Illinois Press, 2006).
7. See Raymond Williams, *The Long Revolution* (New York: Columbia University Press, 1961).
8. See, for example, Benshoff.
9. Andrew Tudor, "Why Horror?: The Peculiar Pleasures of a Popular Genre," in *Horror, The Film Reader*, ed. Mark Jancovich (London: Routledge, 2002), 53.
10. Annamarie Jagose, *Queer Theory: An Introduction* (New York: New York University Press, 1996), 1.
11. Alexander Doty, *Making Things Perfectly Queer: Interpreting Mass Culture* (Minneapolis: University of Minnesota Press, 1993), xvi–3.

12. Benshoff, 4–5.
13. Eve Kosofsky Sedgwick, *The Coherence of Gothic Conventions* (New York: Methuen, 1980), 9–10.
14. Robert B. Heilman, "Charlotte Brontë's 'New' Gothic," in *From Jane Austen to Joseph Conrad: Essays Collected in Memory of James T. Hillhouse*, ed. Robert C. Rathburn and Martin Steinmann Jr. (Minneapolis: University of Minnesota Press, 1958), 131.
15. The *Oxford English Dictionary* defines magick as "the use of ritual activities or observances which are intended to influence the course of events or to manipulate the natural world, usually involving the use of an occult or secret body of knowledge."
16. Hugh B. Urban, *Magia Sexualis: Sex, Magic, and Liberation in Modern Western Esotericism* (Berkeley: University of California Press, 2006), 4.
17. Sedgwick, 11.
18. Ellis Hanson, "Lesbians Who Bite," in *Out Takes: Essays on Queer Theory and Film*, ed. Ellis Hanson (Durham: Duke University Press, 1999), 191.
19. William Hughes and Andrew Smith, "Introduction: Queering the Gothic," in *Queering the Gothic*, ed. William Hughes and Andrew Smith (Manchester: Manchester University Press, 2009), 2.
20. Ellis Hanson, "Queer Gothic," in *The Routledge Companion to Gothic*, ed. Catherine Spooner and Emma McEvoy (London: Routledge, 2007), 180.
21. Georges Bataille, *Erotism: Death & Sensuality*, trans. Mary Dalwood (San Francisco: City Lights, 1986), 11.
22. Haggerty, 2.
23. Halberstam, 2.
24. Michel Foucault, *The History of Sexuality, Vol. 1: An Introduction*, trans. Robert Hurley (New York: Vintage, 1990), 3.
25. Ibid., 12.
26. Ibid., 12–13.
27. Ibid., 35.
28. Ibid., 43.
29. Ibid.
30. Michael Bronski, *The Pleasure Principle: Sex, Backlash, and the Struggle for Gay Freedom* (New York: St. Martin's, 1998), 15–16.
31. See Lee Edelman, *No Future: Queer Theory and the Death Drive* (Durham: Duke University Press, 2004).
32. Hanson, "Queer Gothic," 176.
33. Noël Carroll, "Why Horror?," in *Horror, The Film Reader*, ed. Mark Jancovich (London: Routledge, 2002), 33.
34. Tudor, 47.
35. Carroll, 33.
36. Robin Wood, "The American Nightmare: Horror in the 70s," in *Horror, The Film Reader*, ed. Mark Jancovich (London: Routledge, 2002), 26.
37. Ibid.
38. Ibid., 28.
39. Matt Hills, *The Pleasures of Horror* (New York: Continuum, 2005), 2.
40. Carol J. Clover, *Men, Women, and Chain Saws: Gender in the Modern Horror Film* (Princeton: Princeton University Press, 1992), 11.

41. Tudor, 49.
42. Wood, 32.
43. Carroll, 37.
44. Ibid., 35.
45. Clover, 15.
46. Benshoff, 3.
47. Ibid., 1–2.
48. Richard Dyer, "Children of the Night: Vampirism as Homosexuality, Homosexuality as Vampirism," in *Sweet Dreams: Sexuality, Gender and Popular Fiction*, ed. Susannah Radstone (London: Lawrence & Wishart, 1988), 51.
49. Hughes and Smith, 2.
50. Dyer, 69.
51. Doty, 16.

1

AQUARIAN ALTERNATIVES

Midcentury Media and the Quest for Occultly Queer Histories

PARIS, 1960. AFTER MORE THAN HALF A CENTURY that witnessed the publication of some of the most influential works in modern Continental thought, including Sigmund Freud's *The Interpretation of Dreams* (1900), Carl Jung's *Psychology of the Unconscious* (1912), and Georges Bataille's *The Accursed Share* (1949), two Frenchmen declared that human civilization was approaching the dawn of a new age, one that would have nothing in common with the present realm of "laborious transition in which we have to live for just a little while longer."[1] Trained respectively in journalism and chemical engineering before embarking on more esoteric endeavors, Louis Pauwels and Jacques Bergier had become increasingly disaffected with life in the modern world. The utopian promises of scientific modernity, they lamented, had been crushed in the aftermath of two cataclysmic world wars. All signs now seemed to point to the necessity for radical change and the reenchantment of a world increasingly secularized and demystified. By turning away from the philosophical lens of structuralism, through which the world could be known, rationalized, and tamed via linguistic analysis, Pauwels and Bergier advocated an alternative route to transcendence: a return to the occult.

Originally published in 1960 and translated into English in 1963, Pauwels and Bergier's *The Morning of the Magicians* (*Le Matin des magiciens*) quickly became a best seller on both sides of the Atlantic, sold over one million copies worldwide by the end of the decade, and became a primer for countless individual and collective journeys into a budding midcentury fascination with all things supernatural. Human beings were endowed with powers "at least equal, if not superior, to any technically realizable machinery, and intended to achieve the same results as any other technique," the authors believed, "namely the ability to understand and control Universal forces."[2] A belief in the dualistic synergy of body and mind, and of the latter's ability to similarly conquer the rigidities of matter, was no longer rejected as the stuff of fairy tales. On the contrary, both ancient and modern magickal literature was dedicated to "unique and fantastic moments in the life of the mind, thousands and thousands of fragmentary descriptions which ought to be brought together and compared, and which perhaps point to a method that has been lost, or possibly to one that has still to be found."[3] For Pauwels, Bergier, and their devoted readers, human control of occult energies was not anathema to nature, but rather a demonstrative revival of historically neglected natural laws that were produced in close contact with reality "perceived directly and not through a filter of habit, prejudice, conformism. Modern science has shown us that behind the visible there is an extremely complicated invisible," yet one that is nevertheless intelligible via more esoteric means.[4]

It is on this point, the verifiable legacies of the occult, that *The Morning of the Magicians* is quite clear. Anticipating poststructuralism's own project of destabilizing the dichotomy between the real and the phantasmatic, Pauwels and Bergier caution that the supernatural is by no means reducible to the imaginary. However, a "powerful imagination working on reality will discover that the frontier between the marvelous and the actual—between the visible and the invisible Universe, if you wish—is a very fine one."[5] Indeed, according to Gary Valentine Lachman, one of the founding members of the New Wave rock band Blondie, who has since transitioned from his musical career to writing popular histories of Western occultism, *The Morning of the Magicians* brought together "the future and the past, science and mysticism, philosophy and the occult, with a powerful, inspiring optimism and a new vision of human society—just about everything the sixties were about."[6] While the image of a swaying flower child wreathed in incense while grooving to the far-out sounds of a sitar might now seem cliché, there's no question that all things "occultly marvelous," as Theodore Roszak puts it, were en vogue during this period.[7] In turn, the popular resurrection of occult figures like the vampire and the witch became laden with the hopes, dreams, anxieties, and fears of a new generation.

Throughout the 1960s and early 1970s, Euro-American popular culture became swept up in a revival of esoteric occultism the likes of which hadn't been witnessed in the West since the fin-de-siècle days of Russian mystic Helena Petrovna Blavatsky's Theosophical Society and Aleister Crowley's Hermetic Order of the Golden Dawn.[8] From Los Angeles to Baltimore, nearly every national news outlet marveled at the resurgence of this phenomenon. "It is one of the stranger facts about the contemporary U.S.," *Time* reported in March 1969, that unorthodox conceptions of the universe are being taken up "seriously and semiseriously by the most scientifically sophisticated generation of young adults in history. Even the more occult arts of palmistry, numerology, fortunetelling and witchcraft—traditionally the twilight zone of the undereducated and overanxious—are catching on with youngsters."[9] As Paul Steiger of the *Los Angeles Times* observed, "around the nation, the practitioners of the occult, the mysterious and the mystical are enjoying a heyday unmatched since the Salem witch trials."[10] And as Penny Kolsrud of the *Baltimore Sun* detailed within what she termed a flourishing trend of "Aquarian Alternatives," "the new lifestyle of the young is not merely a matter of marijuana versus martini . . . it's an unconventional way of looking at the self, the world and the universe. Part of this different way of life is a burgeoning interest in ESP, Eastern religions and the occult—astrology, witchcraft, numerology, [and] tarot."[11]

More than individual searches for spiritual transcendence, however, this revived interest in all things occult translated into big collective business, particularly in the entertainment industries. On bookstore shelves, Ray Bradbury's *Something Wicked This Way Comes* (1962), Shirley Jackson's *We Have Always Lived in the Castle* (1962), Robert Bloch's *The Skull of the Marquis de Sade* (1965), and Ira Levin's *Rosemary's Baby* (1967) promised to enthrall horror-seeking readers. On television, series like *The Twilight Zone* (CBS, 1959–64), *Thriller* (NBC, 1960–62), *The Outer Limits* (ABC, 1963–65), *The Addams Family* (ABC, 1964–66), *The Munsters* (CBS, 1964–66), and *Dark Shadows* (ABC, 1966–71) turned supernatural screen narratives into staples of network programming. And in film, *Black Sunday* (1960), *Black Sabbath* (1963), *The Crimson Cult* (1968), Roman Polanski's adaptation of *Rosemary's Baby* (1968), Roger Corman's cycle of Edgar Allan Poe adaptations at American International Pictures (AIP), and the Gothic revival at England's Hammer Studios made occult storylines some of the most successful offerings in 1960s screen horror.

Indeed, this pop culture revitalization of interest in witchcraft, vampirism, and other occultly marvelous phenomena quickly ascended to the heights of 1960s counterculture, a movement composed of young people around the globe who became "deeply critical of and disengaged from the values of white middle-class suburban family life" vis-à-vis experimentation with mysticism and mind-altering drugs.[12] In the United States, such antiassimilationist and antiestablishment beliefs were both dissected and disseminated in best-selling works like Timothy Leary's *The Politics of Ecstasy* (1968), Theodore Roszak's *The Making of a Counter Culture* (1969), Jerry Rubin's *DO IT!: Scenarios of the Revolution* (1970), and Abbie Hoffman's *Steal This Book* (1971). This countercultural epoch ushered in by the peacefully innocuous hopes of Pauwels and Bergier would eventually turn, however, to what Lachman terms the "dark side of the Age of Aquarius," epitomized by Anton LaVey's Church of Satan, the rise of Charles Manson's (oc)cult of personality, and the Helter Skelter murders of August 1969.

Yet, as demonstrated throughout this book, the very fact that certain value-laden binaries (e.g., light vs. dark, good vs. evil, sin vs. sanctity, normal vs. queer, etc.) have been historically mapped onto supposedly self-evident hierarchies of spiritual belief is itself a manifestation of intermingling normative regimes working in tandem to curtail the influences of alterity. And nowhere have such efforts to restrain the unorthodox, the dissident, and the queer forces of the occult proved more contentious than in the arenas of gender and sexuality, wherein magickal practitioners have embraced "morally deviant and socially transgressive acts such as homosexual intercourse, masturbation, sadomasochism, and bestiality" as the most powerful means of unleashing supernatural powers that might dismantle the machinations of heteronormativity.[13]

Queer Hauntings of the Sexual Revolution

While the postwar period in both the United States and beyond ushered in a new age of unprecedented economic, social, and political change, the decade following such landmark events as the rise of mass suburbanization, Senator Joseph McCarthy's political witch hunts, and the widespread domestic installation of television is often remembered not only for the rise of far-reaching countercultural energies but also for those shifts in medicine, media, and cultural mores known collectively as the sexual revolution. First used by the Austrian psychoanalyst Wilhelm Reich during the 1920s, the term "sexual revolution" has come to stand in for a constellation of watershed moments whose influence reached their peak during the 1960s, among them the release of the Kinsey Reports in 1948 and 1953, the inaugural publication of *Playboy* magazine (1953), the Food and Drug Administration's approval of oral contraception ("the pill") in 1960, the publication of Helen Gurley Brown's *Sex and the Single Girl* (1962), the release of Masters and Johnson's *Human Sexual Response* (1966), and the Stonewall riots of June 1969. Yet popular mythology surrounding the sexual revolution has tended to blur the lines between fact and embellished fiction. As a corrective, many cultural studies scholars have recently refrained from focusing solely on the events of the sexual revolution and have instead turned their attention to questioning just how revolutionary the sexual revolution really was and exactly whose interests were served by it.[14]

Existing historical records leave little doubt that the 1960s and early 1970s brought both material and discursive changes, aptly described by Linda Williams as a societal transition from obscenity to "on/scenity," the progression through which a culture "brings on to its public arena the very organs, acts, bodies, and pleasures that have heretofore been designated ob/scene and kept literally off-scene."[15] By and large, such shifts feature both controversy and scandal surrounding the "increasingly public representations of diverse forms of sexuality *and* the fact that they have become increasingly available to the public at large."[16] Such on/scene transformations became manifest during the 1960s and 1970s not only by *Playboy*, the arrival of the pill, and Stonewall but also by the popularization of open, nonmonogamous relationships, the prospect of an enthusiastically awaited age of polymorphous sexualities, and the increasing visibility and viability of nudity and explicit sex in popular culture.[17] Indeed, as Eric Schaefer has demonstrated, mass media served as the "most important and visible battleground on which the sexual revolution took place. The media's artifacts linger as the primary means of accessing this unique moment in history."[18]

However, through attempts to parse what changes the sexual revolution wrought and the consequent interests that were served or ignored, the term becomes something of a nebulous misnomer. As suggested by Aniko Bodroghkozy and others, 1960s counterculture on both sides of the Atlantic was composed predominantly of overindulged baby boomers who dropped out of mainstream mass culture in order to experiment with psychedelia, sex, and the supernatural. This inclination was typified on screen in films such as *The Trip* (1967), *Psych-Out* (1968), and *Wild in the Streets* (1968) and on television programs like *The Mod Squad* (ABC, 1968–73), *Rowan and Martin's Laugh-In* (NBC, 1968–73), and *The Smothers Brothers Comedy Hour* (CBS, 1967–69) and was examined in a rich body of sociological literature.[19] Significantly, behind the "flower child" façades were most often white, heterosexual, and decidedly middle-class young people, demonstrating the kind of racial, sexual, and class privilege through which experimentation with cultural alterity became a passing fad and acquiescence to bourgeois norms was typically waiting on the other side of rebellion. Yet for those whose sociocultural mobility was not as unfettered as that of white, straight baby boomers, the rise of countercultural interests in the occult became even more significant, producing their own distinct narratives of sexual revolution.

Like so many pioneering queer people around the globe, witchcraft, magick, and other occult practices were concurrently, in a fitting turn of phrase by the *Washington Post*'s Marilyn Goldstein in 1971, "coming out of the closet" during this period.[20] In 1963, for instance, twenty-one-year-old Arthur Evans dropped out of Brown University to immerse himself in the mounting excitement of queer life in New York City's Greenwich Village. For the remainder of the decade, Evans would become involved in some of the greatest countercultural demonstrations in American history, including the student riots at Columbia University and the protests at the Democratic National Convention in Chicago in 1968. Evans even appeared with other members of the newly formed Gay Activists Alliance (GAA) on ABC's *Dick Cavett Show* in November 1970 to publicize the causes of LGBTQ+ liberation. It was also during his time in New York that Evans first became galvanized by what he saw as a historically abandoned coalition between nonnormative genders, sexualities, and powers of the occult.

If queer people were ever to break free of the oppressive reign of heterohegemony, Evans argued, then measures must be taken to "tap into deeper energies, energies that the ruling classes of Christianity and industrialism have always desperately tried to deny and repress. These are the energies of magic."[21] Lamenting that Western civilization had gradually turned away from esoteric teachings by encouraging individuals to "repress, deny, hide, and kill our natural abilities to communicate with nature spirits and our own inner spiritual energies (just as we have been told to deny and repress our sexuality)," Evans recommended that by tapping into magickal practices, queer people could return to alliances with "our own forgotten faery selves. . . . Let us invoke our friends, the banished and forbidden spirits of nature and self, as well as the ghosts of Indian, wise-woman, faggot, Black sorcerer, and witch. They will hear our deepest call and come. Through us the spirits will speak again."[22] Promoting occult practices that were decidedly antiheteronormative, antiracist, and antipatriarchal, Evans was inspired most obviously by the beliefs of Wicca, the duotheistic pagan religion first introduced to the general public in 1954 by retired British civil servant Gerald Gardner.

Witchcraft and the Gay Counterculture, Evans's magickal memoir published in 1978, presents a sexually suffused extension of Pauwels and Bergier's work, within which queer people are specifically encouraged to search for their own magickal heredity, a lineage of occult practices that faded away in the wake of the violent ascent of Judeo-Christian heteronormativity in the West. Queer people look forward, Evans claims, to reestablishing "women's mysteries and men's mysteries . . . we look forward to regaining our ancient historical roles as medicine people, healers, prophets, shamans, and sorcerers."[23] Nevertheless, short of purchasing forty acres of farmland in upstate Washington and establishing a queer magickal commune—which Evans did in 1972 with a group named the Weird Sisters Partnership—how might the curious midcentury citizen reclaim such an occultly queer heritage?

Paradoxically, this à la mode cohort of countercultural enthusiasts who endeavored to explore new horizons of sexuality through the occult was a generation seductively haunted by specters of the past.[24] As such, occult television and film of the 1960s and 1970s delved into sexualities of the supernatural in order to shepherd what I nominate as quests for queer history, linking those demonized perversities of the past with the potentially empowering, polymorphous practices of the magickal present. Indeed, significant shifts in both audiences and industries allowed midcentury occult media to marshal what Scott Bravmann terms "queer fictions of the past," a historicized approach to queer theory that takes "individual, collective, and popular memory practices seriously as cultural and political interventions into everyday life and that recognizes representations of the past as powerful social/cultural texts in their own right."[25] The specific case studies presented in this chapter became and remain queer (oc)cult objects precisely because each demonstrated the often cryptic but always palpable presence of characters, themes, and motifs that were, in surroundings both present and past, hostile to sociocultural norms and status quo sexual mores.[26]

Describing the historically agentive link between sexuality and popular media, Patricia Juliana Smith notes that for the "isolated or semi-isolated gay or lesbian individual who is bereft, for the most part, of a larger and viable queer community—as most were in the 1960s and many still are today—texts or films that represent a relatively unambiguous representation of queerness provide, for better or worse, paradigms for identity."[27] This emphasis on the importance of subjectivation to counterhegemonic communities in relation to visual media is a valuable catalyst for thinking through how such texts served not only as subcultural conduct guides for those whose own sexual revolutions were set in motion by the resurrection of occult histories on screen, but also for taking seriously the importance of antiassimilationist and nonpositivist queer paradigms during this period.[28]

Coming Out of the Coffin: *Dark Shadows* and US Countercultural TV

An orphaned young woman journeys north in search of a new life by answering an employment advertisement for a governess. A stately, haunted manor awaits her arrival and the consequent revelation of its untold secrets from the past. Such are the narrative conventions, notably explored by Sandra Gilbert and Susan Gubar in *The Madwoman in the Attic: The Woman Writer and the Nineteenth-Century Literary Imagination,* that were transposed from Victorian fiction and readapted in the Gothic literary revival of the postwar period through the work of novelists such as Phyllis A. Whitney, Joan Aiken, and Dorothy Eden and in the pages of pulp magazines like *Weird Tales*. Moreover, Gothic mysteries distributed by publishers like Harlequin and Mills & Boon became some of the best-selling romance fiction of the 1960s: powerful, if somewhat paradoxical, symbols of sexual revolution embraced by eager, primarily female readers.[29] Yet damsels in distress, reticent bachelors, shadow-filled manors, and sensual shocks would also find their way into one man's ethereal vision of a young woman named Victoria Winters, her journey to the town of Collinsport, Maine, and her interactions with the supernatural residents of an estate called Collinwood.

By the early 1960s, Dan Curtis was one of the top-ranked sales executives at NBC and MCA. Eventually deciding to pursue a career as an independent television producer, Curtis's first venture, *The CBS Golf Classic,* won an Emmy for Program Achievements in Sports in 1965. It was also that year that Curtis had a dream that spearheaded the promotional discourse for a new series that would become a landmark in television horror for so much of what followed in terms of "character, narrative and thematic tropes, as well as fan involvement."[30] In a March 1970 interview with *16* magazine, Curtis recollected, "I saw a girl with long, dark hair. She was about 19, and she was on a train that stopped in the dark, isolated town.

She got off the train and started walking and walking. Finally, she came to a huge, forbidding house. At the door, she lifted a huge brass knocker and gently tapped it three times. I heard a dog howl, and then—just as the door creaked open—I woke up!"[31]

With the encouragement of his wife, Norma, who thought the dream sounded like excellent groundwork for a television show, Curtis successfully pitched America's first supernatural soap opera to ABC. With the added help of Art Wallace, a well-established figure in the industry with previous writing credits including CBS's *Studio One* (1948–58) and murder-mystery anthology series *The Web* (1950–54), the pilot episode of *Dark Shadows* was taped on June 13, 1966, at ABC-TV-16 studios at 433 West 53rd Street in New York and aired June 27, sandwiched in the late afternoon schedule between a medical soap, *The Nurses*, and a teen variety show, *Where the Action Is*.[32]

For its first two hundred and nine episodes, between June 27, 1966, and April 14, 1967, the narrative world of *Dark Shadows* unfolded much like other contemporary suspense dramas such as *The Edge of Night* (CBS, 1956–75; ABC, 1975–84) and *The Secret Storm* (CBS, 1954–74).[33] The matriarch of the wealthy Collins family, Elizabeth Collins Stoddard (played by esteemed Hollywood star Joan Bennett), oversees the affairs at the ancestral estate in which the body of her estranged husband may or may not be buried in the basement. Her brother Roger (Louis Edmonds), estranged from his own wife, also lives at Collinwood and serves as a feeble father figure to Elizabeth's daughter Carolyn (Nancy Barrett) as well his own son David (David Henesy). Along with governess Victoria Winters (Alexandra Moltke), Collinsport was initially populated by conniving blackmailer Jason McGuire (Dennis Patrick), aloof drifter and petty thief Willie Loomis (John Karlen), the Mrs. Danvers-esque housekeeper Mrs. Johnson (Clarice Blackburn), and ingénue waitress Maggie Evans (Kathryn Leigh Scott).[34] In its transition from dream to screen, however, the potentially titillating allures of Curtis's ethereal vision were initially lost in translation.

In the June 29, 1966, issue of *Variety*, one reviewer opined that Art Wallace took "so much time in getting into his story that the first episode of this neo Gothic soaper added up to one big contemporary yawn."[35] If ratings were any indication, viewers agreed. By early 1967, *Dark Shadows* was viewed only in 2.75 million American households, translating to a twelfth-place finish and a 4.3 Nielsen rating among all network soaps.[36] With cancellation orders from ABC all but imminent, Curtis decided to take some risks with an already sinking ship. It was, in fact, the producer's own daughters

Fig. 1.1. Promotional photo of Jonathan Frid in *Dark Shadows*

who encouraged their father to exploit *Dark Shadows*' existing Gothic atmosphere and turn more dramatically in the direction of the occult's countercultural resurgence. "We were really bombing," Curtis told George Fox of the *Saturday Evening Post* in November 1968, "so I figured, to hell with it. If I'm going to fail, I'll at least have a good time. I went wild, tossed in witches and ghosts, you name it. But that vampire made the difference. Two weeks after he came on, the ratings began to climb."[37] Indeed, it was the introduction of the handsomely tragic 175-year-old vampire Barnabas Collins (Jonathan Frid, fig. 1.1), along with the arrival of vengeful witch Angelique Bouchard (Lara Parker) and cursed werewolf Quentin Collins (David Selby), that pulled Curtis's vision back from the precipice of its own grave and quickly made *Dark Shadows* an American countercultural phenomenon. In fact, when ABC affiliate WBRC-TV in Birmingham, Alabama, decided to move *Dark Shadows* to a one-week delay pickup in a morning slot in July 1968, the station received "'thousands of letters and calls' in the two weeks since from housewives and teenagers protesting the switch" and eventually bowed to their demands for a regular broadcast schedule.[38]

Indeed, the industrial landscape of 1960s American television provided ample latitude for vampires, witches, and other occultly marvelous figures to populate domestic screens. Closely following a similar trend in prime time ratings, the industrial trajectory of midcentury daytime TV in the United States was one of perennial favorite CBS continuing its march toward ratings dominance with hit programming like *As the World Turns*

(1956–2010), *Guiding Light* (1952–2009), and *Search for Tomorrow* (CBS, 1951–82; NBC, 1982–86), while NBC and ABC attempted to keep pace. As Jane Feuer, Paul Kerr, and Tise Vahimagi note, the crucial change that began to occur across industry boardrooms at the end of the decade was a sudden "de-emphasis on numbers and a greater emphasis on 'demographics,' i.e., directing television shows toward specific audience groups, [whereas previously] . . . the emphasis in ratings was on numbers alone."[39] As Mark Alvey concurs, explicit concern on the part of network executives for "composition and indeed 'quality' of audience rather than sheer size had been developing throughout the 1960s."[40] Significantly, during the height of 1960s counterculture, US television's fictional programming caught up with the topicality of its news reporting, dramatizing the various social revolutions of the decade, including the civil rights movement, black radicalism, youth unrest, women's and gay liberation, and opposition to the Vietnam War.[41] This shift in fictional programming was intended to catalyze an attendant realignment in audience demographics, with the increasingly solidified youth market seen as the most lucrative of all. And nowhere was the targeting of youth counterculture more emphatic than at ABC.

As Elana Levine details in *Wallowing in Sex: The New Sexual Culture of 1970s American Television*, the industrial image of ABC during this period was one of "an impetuous adolescent, quick to jump into bed with whatever attractive offer came by, unconcerned with how it looked to the others. . . . ABC not only trailed in ratings but also in respectability, at least in the eyes of its fellow networks."[42] While vampires, witches, werewolves, and other occultly marvelous figures seemed poised only to underscore Newton Minow's vast wasteland of escapist television during the 1960s, Dan Curtis's mounting penchant for countercultural risk-taking in the "P. B." *Dark Shadows*, a term used affectionately by fans meaning "post-Barnabas," found an opportune match with the kind of "wild-ass programming" that was being promoted by then-Vice President of ABC Daytime Programming Harve Bennett.[43] In an attempt to move out of its longtime locale in the basement of the Big Three, ABC quickly realized that corralling the interests of a youth-oriented audience steeped in the sexy, supernatural fascinations of 1960s counterculture was absolutely essential to the network's survival, a trend *Television Age* referred to in 1965 as the increasingly "sensual appetite" of young American viewers.[44] Among other alterations, *Dark Shadows*' transition from black and white to color on August 14, 1967, built a foundation for the series's recurrent experimentation with psychedelic visual palettes that made dream sequences, hypnotic trances, and time travel progressively akin to psychotropic trips. According to one student at the University of Chicago, *Dark Shadows*' "supernatural, ugly vibes are just right for when you're strung out on scag [heroin]."[45] But perhaps the show's own sorceress, Lara Parker, put it best: "It was a hot show and everybody that watched it either got scared, or they could be sexually aroused ... it was just something they could get off on."[46]

ABC's leadership in shepherding 1960s counterculture onto American domestic screens via occult programming importantly contributes to a body of critical counternarratives that argue against the assumption that nonnormative genders, sexualities, and sexual practices first began appearing on US television only at the end of the 1970s.[47] As Kevin Heffernan points out in *Ghouls, Gimmicks, and Gold: Horror Films and the American Movie Business, 1953–1968*, distributors of low-budget American films and European imports had been syndicating for television since at least the early 1950s and, by mid-decade, major studios had released "huge numbers of pre-1948 features to network affiliates and independent stations, which usually broadcast these features in the afternoon and late at night."[48] Among the most lucrative of these properties were Universal horror staples such as *Dracula* (1931), *Frankenstein* (1931), *The Bride of Frankenstein* (1935), and *The Wolf Man* (1941), films whose queer contributions to classical Hollywood cinema have been explored at length by critics like Harry Benshoff and David Hogan.[49] Indeed, supernatural horror films were a "crucial part of the TV syndication of features from the very beginning. In 1957, Screen Gems contracted with Universal-International for a $20 million, ten-year lease on 550 pre-1948 Universal features ... one of the first groups of these features that Screen Gems released was the Shock! package of fifty-two horror films from Universal's 'golden age' of horror."[50] Screen Gems' Shock! package was quickly followed by Son of Shock!, another syndication bundle that included sequels and spin-offs such as *The Invisible Man Returns* (1940) and *House of Dracula* (1945).

The popularity of both the Shock! and Son of Shock! packages, as well as other syndicated horror films, paved the way for US television networks to experiment with original programming that was built around queerly occult storylines. For example, on September 17, 1964, ABC premiered a new sitcom following the life of an ordinary American man who just happens to be married to a witch, a real "broom-riding, house-haunting, cauldron-stirring witch." With its own cast of occultly marvelous figures, including a prankster warlock uncle (soon-to-be-queer-icon Paul Lynde as Uncle Arthur), a delightfully senile aunt (Marion Lorne as Aunt Clara), and a boisterous matriarch who would match Paul Lynde as a queer icon in her own right (Agnes Moorehead as Endora), *Bewitched* quickly became the top-rated show on ABC and finished second in national ratings during its inaugural season, the best finish for an ABC series during the entire decade. Along with supernatural tales adapted into two other prime time comedies, *The Addams Family* (ABC, 1964–66) and *The Munsters* (CBS, 1964–66), *Bewitched* catalyzed the emergence of what Lynn Spigel terms the fantastic family sitcom, in which a "highly irrational, supernatural discourse" advanced formidable critiques of gender and sexual norms.[51]

Despite Samantha Stevens's (Elizabeth Montgomery) best intentions, magick on *Bewitched* routinely "recast the narrative situation so that the conventional becomes strange. Warlocks, witch doctors, and evil witches populate the traditionally decorated rooms of the Stephens's home, while powerful spells bring Ben Franklin, Mother Goose, and tooth fairies alive."[52] While Samantha's marriage to her advertising executive husband Darrin (Dick York [1964–69], Dick Sargent [1969–72]) was a mostly contented one, her station as the unruly woman waiting to wreak supernatural havoc offered a queer prism through which *Bewitched* refracted American television's conventional picture of heteronormative bliss. As Susan Douglas observes, whenever female characters like Samantha Stevens engaged their powers, the rules of patriarchal sexual difference were turned "completely upside down. Business simply could not be conducted as usual, and logic and rationality were often overthrown and rendered useless. Men were made impotent by these powers, and the husbands (or husband figures) of such women were stripped of their male authority."[53] Darrin's characterization as a stand-in for postwar masculinity was, in fact, always played for laughs, as his feeble insistence on the dignity of the natural and the normal vis-à-vis gender and sexuality was habitually squashed with the twitch of a witch's nose.

But perhaps *Bewitched*'s flouting of postwar sexual and gender conventions was pushed to its greatest extreme in Agnes Moorehead's portrayal of Samantha's meddling mother, Endora. With no need for or even interest in men, Endora served as the queer foil to her daughter's earnest attempts at normal living: "Just because you married a human, Samantha, that's no reason to overdo this grubby little household role." Continually reminded by Darrin that witchcraft would find no permanent place in the Stevens's household, Endora retorts, "What is normal to you, young man, is to us asinine." Even the normativity of heterosexual reproduction is rather queer on *Bewitched*, as siblings Tabitha and Adam Stevens both inherited the maternal magick that made neither fully human. While the counterhegemonic roles embodied by both Samantha and Endora were kept "safely in a straitjacket" through the release valve of situation comedy, the strength of their spellcasting steadily reminded viewers surrounded by the growing climate of 1960s counterculture that traditional gender and sexual norms were anything but unshakable fixtures of American life.[54]

By the time *Dark Shadows* premiered in June 1966, then, American viewers had already become accustomed to the sitcom's use of occultism as employed in the queer service of deconstructing heteronormativity. And as many of its cast members fondly recall, *Dark Shadows* echoed other contemporary programs such as *Lost in Space* (CBS, 1965–68) and *Batman* (ABC, 1966–68) via the failed seriousness that defines one of the queerest of pop culture sensibilities: camp. Popular for his portrayal of bachelor-turned-werewolf Quentin Collins, the sex symbol runner-up to Jonathan Frid's Barnabas, David Selby once called the series's style of acting "indulgent and downright hammy," alongside typical gaffes of falling Styrofoam tombstones, rubber bats suspended from visible fishing line, and botched lines of dialogue too costly to go back and retape.[55] Yet it was precisely the show's "indulgence of melodramatic identification" and the affective earnestness of its characters, however hammy, campy, or overplayed, that allowed *Dark Shadows* to successfully draw viewers into those quests for queer history encouraged by Pauwels, Bergier, Evans, and occult countercultures writ large.[56]

During the 1967–68 season, *Dark Shadows* was enjoying its highest ratings mark to date, and yet, given the demands of daytime output, Curtis and company were quickly running out of ideas. Much like the dream that inspired the series, however, the showrunner came up with a plan: "Why don't we go back into the past and find out how Barnabas became a vampire? . . . It was our most popular story."[57] Transported via séance from the present day back to a parallel universe in 1795, Victoria Winters finds herself embroiled in the goings-on of a Collinwood estate that is simultaneously strange and familiar. The sibling pair of Elizabeth and Roger Collins have become Naomi and Joshua, the married owners of Collinwood and parents to their still-human son, Barnabas. The queer resonance of this incestuous brother-sister versus husband-wife switch in the Collins family was made clear, as both Joan Bennett and Louis Edmonds were retained for their respective roles. And with the long-awaited arrival of his fiancée, Josette du Pres, in preparation for their marriage, Barnabas is also reunited with Josette's maid, Angelique Bouchard, the woman with whom he had a one-night amorous encounter several months earlier on Josette's home island of Martinique.

Yet unbeknownst to everyone at Collinwood, Angelique is quite a powerful, and quite a vindictive, witch. Spurned by Barnabas, who is unwaveringly insistent on marrying Josette, Angelique's plan for revenge is abetted by her mastery of witchcraft and other occult forces that seduce and slay any man or woman who might disrupt her intention to upset one of heterosexuality's most cherished rituals. Irrespective of their target, Angelique's magickal rites and the nondiegetic music that accompanies them routinely follow an erogenous pattern, as methodical incantations, convulsive body moments, and staccato string chords build toward emphatic climaxes qua orgasms.

After enslaving caretaker Ben Stokes (Thayer David) to do her bidding, Angelique directs her magick toward Josette, Jeremiah Collins (Barnabas's uncle), Sarah Collins (Barnabas's sister), and Victoria, all with an eye toward sabotaging Barnabas's nuptials. Concurrent with *Bewitched*'s characterization of Samantha and Endora, witchcraft as a counterproductive form of "pride, self-worth, and the promise of social change" was actively thematized and given queer historical resonance on *Dark Shadows* via Angelique.[58] Indeed, as Paulina Palmer emphasizes, the witch and the queer have shared kindred spaces for centuries through their "exclusion from mainstream society" and the threat the witch's magick poses to "heteropatriarchal values" and conventional modes of gender expression.[59] Hoping to rid himself and Collinwood of this queer force once and for all, Barnabas shoots Angelique one evening but not before she places a curse on him: "You will never rest, Barnabas. And you will never be able to love anyone. For whoever loves you will die!" As Angelique collapses to the ground, a bat bursts in through the sitting room window, bites Barnabas on the neck, and fulfills the witch's curse.

For the remainder of *Dark Shadows*' original broadcast run, Barnabas is haunted not only by the ghost of Angelique, reincarnated in present day as Roger's new wife Cassandra, but most obviously by his own vampiric condition, which proves both a great strength and a devastating affliction. Remaining in the 1795 arc, Joshua Collins discovers that the coffin of his son, who is presumed dead following the bat attack, has been moved to the basement of Collinwood. Venturing down a flight of stone stairs, Joshua arrives precisely at the moment that Barnabas rises from his candle-encircled coffin. Beyond Barnabas's actual moment of transformation via Angelique's curse and his later release into present-day Collinsport by Willie Loomis, this critically overlooked coming out of the coffin encounter between father and son on the March 11, 1968, episode may have been especially resonant with countercultural viewers in forming historical identifications with the vampire's predicament as a queer outcast trying to reclaim a place in the world. "What kind of a monster have you become?" Joshua asks his son. "Have I never known anything about you?"

During the course of their conversation, Barnabas admits to compelled acts of violence in and around Collinsport that were fueled by his newfound lust for blood. Currently housed in the Special Collections of the Charles E. Young Research Library at the University of California, Los Angeles, the original shooting script for this and other *Dark Shadows* episodes in the Dan Curtis Production Records provides a revealing look at what did and did not make it to screen. In the dialogue reproduced below, the italicized text was eliminated from the script's final version:

> BARNABAS: Go back to your own life! Forget you saw me *here*.
>
> JOSHUA: *How can I?*
>
> BARNABAS: *There have been many things you have not understood.*
>
> JOSHUA: *This will not be one of them. Why were you in that coffin?*
>
> BARNABAS: *I will not answer you.* I never wanted you to find me.
>
> JOSHUA: Have I never known anything about you?
>
> BARNABAS: Father—
>
> JOSHUA: I thought, despite our differences there was some—some feeling between us . . . some honesty at least—
>
> BARNABAS: There was.
>
> JOSHUA: You didn't care about the shame, the scandal?
>
> BARNABAS: Yes, yes I did—
>
> JOSHUA: How perverted you are. You admit the killings, yet you refuse to admit a lie!
>
> BARNABAS: I admit the killings because—because I was compelled to do them.
>
> JOSHUA: Compelled? *I do not know what that word means.*
>
> BARNABAS: *I had no choice.* I could not stop myself—I am under a curse.

> JOSHUA: A curse. You expect me to believe that?
> BARNABAS: It is true.
> JOSHUA: A curse. Who believes in curses? Who?
> BARNABAS: Anyone who has to—anyone who is under them.[60]

While this intimate encounter serves as a requisite invocation of several narrative preoccupations of the Gothic, especially the dichotomy between the rational and the supernatural and "homes and families which are haunted, tortured, or troubled in some way . . . attempting to cover up hidden secrets from the past," the antagonism between Joshua and his son regarding Barnabas's newfound perversions can also be read quite explicitly (and even more so in light of the eliminated dialogue) as the heterohegemonic policing of nonnormative desires.[61] As such, viewers struggling to write their own histories within the escalating climate of 1960s countercultures were presented with this and many other opportunities to cathect to Barnabas's supernatural condition vis-à-vis his isolation and inability to conform to the dictates of a heteronormative world. Indeed, as Lorna Jowett and Stacey Abbott argue, *Dark Shadows* enabled its gallery of monsters to develop "beyond their monstrous conditions into morally complex and attractive characters with which audiences could identify. Rather than fear the outsider, readers (and audiences), in an era that saw the rise of civil and gay rights alongside the feminist movement, increasingly identify with and/or romanticize the outsider who represents an independent spirit and a refusal to conform."[62]

The stereotypically ruthless heart of a predatory vampire does not, in fact, beat within Barnabas Collins.[63] Indeed, in a recent interview, series writer Joseph Caldwell fondly recalls the "emotional possibilities of playing on [the reluctant vampire] . . . that he really did not want to do this to people . . . he didn't want to be who he was."[64] Instead, *Dark Shadows* constructs the majority of its narrative pleasure in following the vampire's transhistoric search for identity and belonging in both the past and present worlds.[65] Jonathan Frid once remarked of his character, "I think what made the part work for me was that Barnabas was also a very nervous character if you accept the premise. He comes out of his coffin, having been in it for a hundred and fifty years or whatever, and he comes out into this new world and has to tell a lie instantly."[66] As George Fox reported in November 1968, "Frid's vampire is restrained almost to the point of rigidity, as if fighting to hold himself back from some dark, nameless act."[67]

Like innumerable other moments on *Dark Shadows* that incorporate discordant string crescendos, tight two-shots, exaggerated facial expressions, and a classically Gothic mise-en-scène, Barnabas's coming out of the coffin is played for high melodrama. And while the series's reliance on the occult shocks of vampirism, lycanthropy, and witchcraft may seem more historically suited to the drive-in theater or midnight movie house, *Dark Shadows* was first and foremost a soap opera, a genre that paradoxically made its quests for queer history especially affecting for countercultural viewers.[68] As Robert Allen maintains in *Speaking of Soap Operas*, one of the formal characteristics that has contributed to the longevity of the soap opera as a popular form of both radio and television entertainment is its "'overflow of possibilities' . . . the soap opera represents an 'over-coded' narrative form: characters, events, situations, and relationships are invested with signifying possibilities greatly in excess of those necessary to their narrative functions."[69] Invoking Umberto Eco's dichotomy between open and closed texts, the "'structural maze' of possible readings" versus the "straightforward, linear pathway of stimulus and anticipated response," Allen notes that the soap opera operates within a qualified openness, what Stuart Hall might call a negotiated semiotic position, through which some norms are reinforced while others are just as readily rejected.[70] In light of the fact that soap operas have been traditionally broadcast on mass media, whose undergirding industrial logics demand corralling a maximum number of listeners/viewers, Allen and others have argued that the ideologic flexibility of soaps is somewhat limited, perhaps even conservative. Yet while some may interpret this hedged openness as evidence that the soap opera can never truly be an oppositional or nonhegemonic format, *Dark Shadows* offers strong retorts within a generic field that has been historically coded as almost exclusively heterosexual and female identified.

In quite a literal sense, the "narrative elasticity"[71] of serial television as manifest in what Tania Modleski calls the soap opera's constant processes of "narrative deferral"[72] is perfectly suited to narrating queer tales of occult history, employing extended continuity to "enable these monsters to expand beyond their monstrosity and the fans to recognize within these creatures their own feelings of isolation."[73] For instance, when Barnabas uses the magickal powers of the I Ching, a favorite practice of 1960s esotericism, in *Dark Shadows*' 700th episode to save the life of his cousin David, the wands provide a convenient vehicle for the inauguration of another parallel world story arc in 1897. If the lore of vampires, witches, and other occultly marvelous figures has much to do with their immortality, so too can their on-screen lives projected through serial television extend almost indefinitely in countless directions. And so too, then, can the textual openness of a soap opera like *Dark Shadows* extend the resonances of its historically queer inquiries over a 1,225-episode run: Should the counterhegemonic Other be condemned as evil or rather be considered the victim of circumstance? Should queer creatures like Barnabas and Angelique simply be destroyed or somehow be incorporated into mainstream society? Are vampirism and witchcraft akin to other forms of sociocultural alterity that were beginning to make advances toward visibility during this period? And what broader changes in gender and sexual mores were occasioned by the fact that the "jaded ladies out there in detergent land are at the edge of their ennui with all the erotic goings-on in the standard soap?"[74] If, as Modleski contends, the soap opera represents one form of popular culture that enacts "loving with a vengeance," then one of the most obvious targets of *Dark Shadows*' retribution is heteronormativity itself.

By eliminating the limitations of narrative closure endemic to other formats, *Dark Shadows*' soapy, serial, supernatural storylines rarely affirm "stability or 'normality' as an ongoing or desirable state,"[75] presenting instead a queer challenge to the "reproductive futurism" that Lee Edelman maintains as constitutive of heteronormativity's own self-replicating life cycle.[76] As scholar and self-professed fan Harry Benshoff argues, the various counterhegemonic impulses of the Gothic novel and supernatural horror film are in fact exacerbated within the format of a Gothic soap opera like *Dark Shadows*, which more often "celebrates rather than rebukes the perversity of its gothic characters."[77] While figures like Barnabas and Angelique may not be fully human and may harm others, the series's decentered ideologic perspective, broadcast not once but five times per week during its original run, transformed what might have been conventional villains into celebrated antiheroes—tragic, romantic figures acting through motivations that, however perverse, are legible and even inspiring of spectatorial empathy. Indeed, precisely because Collinwood was populated with such identifiably and even pleasurably queer forces that upset the normal workings of heteronormative patriarchy, *Dark Shadows* was much more about its supernatural characters' histories of struggle with their own desires and identities than "any attempt to vanquish [them] in the name of the traditional moral order."[78] As one sexy, suggestive tagline for the first of three feature films based on the soap simply stated: "Come see how the vampires do it."[79]

Fig. 1.2. *Dark Shadows* promotional syndication ad (*TV Guide*, 1982)

After its final episode was broadcast on April 2, 1971, *Dark Shadows* spent only four years off the air before becoming the first US daytime soap opera to go into national syndication. A 1982 *TV Guide* advertisement (fig. 1.2) for the show's re-airing on WNBC-TV in New York is just one revealing example of how the occult sexualities woven throughout the series kept its popularity alive, the double entendre of necking significantly juxtaposed with the homoerotic scene from Episode 210 in which Barnabas is freed from the Collins mausoleum by Willie Loomis. In fact, *Dark Shadows* would eventually go on to become one of the flagship properties that helped launch the Sci-Fi Channel, a then-satellite offering that purchased exclusive rights to air the series between 1992 and 1997.[80] And while decisively established during its original broadcast run through both the series itself and extensive merchandising campaigns, the syndication of *Dark Shadows* doubtlessly aided in constructing one of the most vibrant, dynamic, and participatory fan cultures ever to be inspired by an (oc)cult media text.

As Lara Parker has reminisced, "*Dark Shadows* was not an ordinary show. Because of this, its fans were not just ordinary fans. They were, and are, a unique group of people. They have kept the show alive long after it ceased production. They chose to follow us and immortalize us . . . [many fans] were even experts on horror and the occult. Some wrote their own versions of the romantic saga in prose or poetry. They collected, and treasured, souvenirs such as photos and old scripts. Because of the fans, *Dark Shadows* became far more important than just another daytime soap opera."[81]

The enduring fascination of *Dark Shadows*, Parker continues, "lay in the ability of those in the audience to identify with the characters. You may ask how one can possibly identify with a witch, or a ghost, or a vampire? We have nothing in common with these appalling creatures . . . or do we?"[82] "I wish he'd [Barnabas] bite me in the neck," one avid watcher wrote to the show's producers, "I get so excited, I could smoke a whole pack of cigarettes just watching him."[83] As another anonymous viewer from Hattiesburg, Mississippi, simply stated, "If it takes blood to keep him alive, he can have some of mine."[84]

Indeed, perhaps the fusion of occultism and nonnormative sexualities that *Dark Shadows* abetted both during and after its original broadcast run is most evident in the series's multigenerational network of devoted fans. Echoing Henry Jenkins's demarcation of pop culture fandom, those cultural practices that allow "marginalized subcultural groups (women, the young, gays, and so on) to pry open space for their cultural concerns within dominant representations . . . a way of appropriating media texts and rereading them in a fashion that serves different interests,"[85] countless viewers understood vampirism, witchcraft, and other occultly marvelous phenomena on *Dark Shadows* as historical conditions that explicitly paralleled their own feelings as sociocultural outsiders: "Collinwood was my home," "Life seemed less complex when we were able to visit there," "I longed for supernatural powers," "Probably one of the most important programs of my formative years."[86] Collinwood and its residents provided an affective rapport for viewers not only in the guise of a "place of comfort and/or a fantasy of power," but especially in the series's transhistoric quest for an accepting community of queer associates with whom fans could identify.[87] Through creative forms such as slash fiction, homemade songbooks, fan zines, love letters to favorite characters, and national conventions that continue to endure, *Dark Shadows* and its fans merged 1960s counterculture and the queer appeal of the occult to form an archetypal text of cult television, in which seriality, textual density, and the nonlinearity of multiple historical time frames "create the space for fans to revel in the development of characters and long complex narrative arcs both within the commercial texts and their own, noncommercial spin-offs."[88]

Yet while *Dark Shadows* may have effectively captured the countercultural imaginations of occult enthusiasts during the 1960s and beyond, its quests for queer history were articulated most often through allegory, metaphor, and/or narrative double entendre. In an era when the National Association of Broadcasters (NAB) still retained a firm grip on the censorship standards and restrictions of the medium's content, the industrial conditions of American broadcasting made options for televising queerness limited. Indeed, both oral and written network archives from this period indicate that the queer potential embedded within the occult horror genre was knowingly corralled even within the "wild-ass programming" on ABC. As writer Joseph Caldwell recalls, "Dan was so nervous about homoeroticism that a woman got bit on the neck. A man got bit on the wrist."[89] In an April 19, 1967, memo from ABC's Department of Broadcast Standards and Practices, editor Bernardine McKenna cautioned the following: "Episode #224, page 28, 30—Please ensure that Jason's wisecracks about 'light housekeeping' and 'the lady of the house,' as addressed to Willie are delivered so that there is no insinuation that Jason suspects a sexual relationship between Willie and Barnabas."[90] If *Dark Shadows*' reimagination of the queer master-servant relationship between Bram Stoker's Count Dracula and R. M. Renfield via Barnabas and Willie were not already obvious enough, McKenna's script review makes this specter explicit. While viewers might have to make the leap of reading the "*symbolic* homosexual in the supernatural," *Dark Shadows* is far from closeted.[91] Indeed, even if the occult isn't explicitly homosexual at Collinwood, following Doty's call to recognize and critically articulate the "complex range of [nonnormativity] that has been in popular culture texts and their audiences all along," vampirism, witchcraft, and other occultly marvelous phenomena are decidedly queer.

The House that Horror Rebuilt: Queer Occultism at Hammer

On November 2, 1960, London's Old Bailey was crowded by throngs of citizens hoping for a glimpse at history in the making. Since October 20 of that year, a judge and jury had been hearing testimony in the case of *R v. Penguin Books Ltd.*, in which the British government filed suit against Penguin

Books demanding the immediate cessation of publication of the newly unexpurgated version of D. H. Lawrence's erotic masterwork *Lady Chatterley's Lover* (1928). Closely following *Roth v. United States* (1957), a watershed legal case discussed more fully in the next chapter, *R v. Penguin Books Ltd.* was intended to serve as a battleground litmus test for enforcement of the British Obscene Publications Act, under whose auspices any charge of obscenity in the UK could be refuted if the text(s) in question demonstrated sufficient measures of literary and/or artistic merit. Exhibiting a last-ditch effort on the part of a dwindling stiff-lipped British establishment to curb the inevitable tide of shifting cultural mores, chief prosecutor Mervyn Griffin-Jones famously asked the jury to consider whether *Lady Chatterley's Lover* was a book they would wish their wives and/or servants to read. Taking the stand on behalf of Penguin, such high-profile witnesses as E. M. Forster, Raymond Williams, and Richard Hoggart convincingly argued that the novel's unflinching use of sexual vocabulary to which the government objected, namely "fuck" and "cunt," was not gratuitous but rather essential to the narrative motivations and psychological complexities of Lawrence's characters. What was clearly taking place throughout the *Chatterley* trial, according to Jeffrey Weeks, was a "displacement of the anxieties aroused by the nature of the social changes . . . on to the terrain of sexuality, where hidden fears and social anxieties could most easily be stirred."[92] When a verdict of not guilty was eventually handed down on November 2, 1960, Lawrence's stepdaughter Barbara Barr offered the British press a memorable bon mot: "I feel as if a window has been opened and fresh air has blown right through England."[93]

Like the sexual revolutions concurrently taking place across the Atlantic, the 1960s and early 1970s witnessed a similar age of permissiveness that began to pervade British popular culture. Indeed, as Weeks maintains, permissiveness was discursively employed throughout the UK during this era as both political and juridical shorthand to describe a "particular legislative moment, producing a complex body of legislation . . . including reforms of the laws governing gambling, suicide, obscenity and censorship, Sunday entertainment, the abolition of capital punishment for murder, as well as liberalization of various statutes governing sexual behavior."[94] While New York, San Francisco, and Los Angeles were becoming epicenters of America's new polymorphous sexual and supernatural activities, such legal reformations allowed London and other British metropolitan areas to establish themselves as similar beacons of global permissiveness. Out of the

London Soho neighborhood, for example, where most shops had a "back room specializing in hardcore [pornographic] materials" and "Olympia Press editions of classic erotica such as *Fanny Hill*, *The Story of O*, and *The English Governess*," grew Britain's own subcultural interests in psychedelia, hallucinogenic drugs, alternative sexualities, and the occult.[95]

Yet as Catharine Arnold suggests in *The Sexual History of London: From Roman Londinium to the Swinging City—Lust, Vice, and Desire Across the Ages*, the "mod"-ness of midcentury British popular culture was paradoxically tempered by the backward historical glances of many of its participants, especially queer individuals who were rediscovering their own likenesses in the work of nineteenth-century artists like Oscar Wilde, Percy Shelly, and Lord Byron. The rise of antiquing as a leisure pursuit, for instance, was principally attributed to gay men and their provocation of a nostalgia boom that resonated throughout both the UK and United States. Many of these period artifacts associated most explicitly with queer culture attempted to preserve some form of historical expression of sexual alterity from the past—periods that, not coincidentally, have strong ties to histories of the occult.[96] As Alex Owen maintains, traditions of European occultism rejuvenated during the 1960s played to a "Victorian fondness for archaic origins, secret societies, and the Gothic that was perhaps best exemplified by the success of fiction like Rider Haggard's *She* (1887) and Bram Stoker's *Dracula* (1897)."[97] Indeed, the resurrected convergence between queer sexualities, historical nostalgia, and the occult during this age of British permissiveness was manifest nowhere more clearly than through the reemergence of one infamous Englishman's magickal teachings.

Born in 1875 to a devout Christian family of Warwickshire, Edward Alexander Crowley grew up as a rambunctious child who never shared his parents' orthodox faith. Whatever the reasons, "in a boyhood suffused with biblical imagery, Crowley seems to have made an early identification with Satan and a further connection between Satan and sexuality. This was ultimately to be worked out in the Magick of his adult years."[98] Inheriting the family fortune when his father passed away in 1887, Crowley entered Cambridge University in 1895 to study philosophy and literature, quickly changing his name to Aleister in order to "satisfy my romantic ideals."[99] In addition to developing a strong attraction toward the occult at university, Crowley also became immersed in a hedonistic lifestyle that included recreational drug use and amorous activities with members of both sexes. "In my third year at Cambridge," Crowley writes in *Magick in Theory and Practice*

Fig. 1.3. Portrait of Aleister Crowley

(1929), "I devoted myself consciously to the Great Work, understanding thereby the Work of becoming a Spiritual Being, free from the constraints, accidents, and deceptions of material existence."[100] In 1898, Crowley was initiated into one of Britain's foremost esoteric societies, the Hermetic Order of the Golden Dawn. During the early 1900s, the mage would go on to establish his own cadre of occult teachings known as Thelema and eventually become the leader of the prominent Ordo Templi Orientis (O.T.O.), an active magickal organization whose members even now continue to follow the teachings of a man known variously throughout his life as "the Great Beast 666" and "the wickedest man in the world" (fig. 1.3).

Considered by many to be Crowley's most accessible writing, *Magick in Theory and Practice* was recirculated in a new edition in 1960 and, like *The Morning of the Magicians*, became a best-selling gateway for countless countercultural journeys into occult cosmology. Neatly defined in Crowley's text, magick is "the Science and Art of causing Change to occur in conformity with Will" through the use of rituals, spells, and incantations.[101] Anyone acting on his or her true will has the "inertia of the Universe to assist him," since man is "capable of being, and using, anything which he perceives, for everything that he perceives is in a certain sense a part of his being. He may thus subjugate the whole Universe of which he is conscious to his individual Will."[102] Significantly, Crowley's emphasis on the magickal might of individual will found resonance not only with Pauwels and Bergier's own occult teachings but also with broader countercultural attitudes circulating throughout this Euro-American age of permissiveness. As Hilary Radner maintains, the various transformations in 1960s sexual mores can be seen as a "logical extension of social transformations in the twentieth century that posit the individual as the location of identity and fulfillment . . . we can discuss the public discourse surrounding sexuality as part of the formulation of an ethical system . . . that defines the relations of the self to the self and that focuses on pleasure as the source of self-fulfillment."[103] "Do what thou wilt shall be the whole of the Law," Crowley famously decreed, for man carries an ethical responsibility to "behold his soul in all its awful nakedness, he must not fear to look on that appalling actuality. He must discard the gaudy garments with which his shame has screened him; he must accept the fact that nothing can make him anything but what he is."[104] Through magickal practice, Crowley endeavored to reach back into history, as Arthur Evans later would, and revive a queer occult culture within which the arbitrary moral codes of modernity were dispensed with and ethically charged categories like good, evil, sin, and shame were all relative.

It is little surprise that a magickal practitioner who promoted the sanctity of the individual, moral relativism, and a "born this way" ethos was resurrected as a distinctly queer icon in the context of 1960s and 1970s Euro-American occultism. As Hugh Urban notes, one of the primary explanations for the talk and titillation that surrounded Crowley throughout his own life and beyond was his devotion to practices of sexual magick: "Rejecting the prudish hypocrisy of the Victorian world in which he was raised, Crowley identified sex as the most powerful force in life and the supreme source of magical power. . . . Crowley made explicit use of the most 'deviant' sexual acts, such as masturbation and homosexuality, as central components in his magical practice."[105] Reveling in rituals described as symposia of obscenity, blasphemy, and indecency, Crowley's magick presented limitless potential for discursive adoption into 1960s and 1970s pop culture permissiveness, due in large part to its emphasis on sexual transgression.[106] As Owen concurs, "a *poseur extraordinaire* in the style of Wilde, a man who set out to replicate in life the dark, wicked, luxurious world of the fictional Dorian Gray, Crowley consistently experimented with the inversion of dominant categories. This was as much the case with his magic as with his own sexuality and gender identity; in each case, and in different but related ways, he played on the [. . .] theme of perverse delinquency."[107] Against the backdrop of candlelit altars, black tapestries, and inverted crucifixes, Crowley and his disciples used sexual magick to arouse spiritual frenzies that called on irreverent deities to fuel their perversely queer activities. Sex magick, especially in its queer, transgressive, and nonreproductive forms, was anointed to the highest echelon of the Thelemic order and was believed to unleash the ultimate in spiritual powers for practitioners. These and other of Crowley's transgressive beliefs circulated so widely throughout British counterculture, in fact, that the mage was famously featured as a member of the celebrity montage that composes the album cover of the Beatles' *Sgt. Pepper's Lonely Hearts Club Band*. Moreover, Crowley was once allegorized as a "bloated, lisping queen" in a 1968 film adaptation of Dennis Wheatley's occult novel *The Devil Rides Out*, and in other occultly marvelous on-screen counterparts that British occultism inspired at one particular studio that became equally and infamously queer.[108]

Founded in 1934 by businessman and London stage performer William Hinds, Hammer Productions Ltd. produced only five films before liquidating and filing for bankruptcy due to a slump in the British film industry in 1937. Even still, Hammer's associate distribution company, Exclusive Films, was able to survive the depression and officially resurrected the company as Hammer Film Productions in 1949 under the joint direction of Hinds and his son Tony, in partnership with Exclusive's own father-son team of Enrique and James Carreras. After dabbling in mysteries and thrillers during the early 1950s, Hammer's first hit in the horror genre came in 1955 with an adaptation of the BBC's 1953 television serial *The Quatermass Xperiment*. Soon after, this success was followed by critically and financially successful screen versions of two canonical Gothic classics, *The Curse of Frankenstein* (1957) and *Horror of Dracula* (1958), the latter canonizing Christopher Lee as one of cinema's most iconic Carpathian counts and beginning a cycle of increasingly erotic occult films for which Hammer would become notorious during the next two decades.

Analogous to the industrial conditions of American network television that brought the countercultural sexualities of the occult to *Dark Shadows* and ABC, the new market of possibility for combining supernatural horror and sexuality that Hammer emphatically exploited during the late 1960s and early 1970s was abetted by broader institutional forces.[109] While the queerness of *Dark Shadows* was limited mostly to allegory, innuendo, and narrative misdirection in light of NAB censorship standards, the changing parameters of film regulation and exhibition practices in both the UK and United States allowed Hammer to represent its own quests for queer history more explicitly through sex itself. At a time when the Motion Picture Association of America (MPAA) was reconsidering its ratings structure after then-president Jack Valenti declared the official death of the Hollywood Production Code (a.k.a. the Hays Code) in 1968 with the introduction of a new voluntary system, the British Board of Film Classification (BBFC) felt similarly compelled to reassess its extensive history of often-puritanical censorship. Significantly, echoing the term that reverberated throughout so much countercultural discourse in the UK, president John Trevelyan noted that in an "increasingly permissive age," the BBFC would do well to "modify our attitude to the introduction of sex."[110] The official instantiation of this amended outlook came on July 1, 1970, when the BBFC revised the qualifications for its X rating certificate, paving the way for new heights of explicit sexuality and violence on screen by raising the age of entry for such films from sixteen to eighteen.

While the BBFC was in the midst of this ratings reassessment, Hammer was searching for a new direction of its own. With the success of *The Curse of Frankenstein* and *Horror of Dracula* in the late 1950s, Hammer had decisively established a visual house style, largely attributed to the first use of the Technicolor process in mainstream horror, which connoted a newly recognizable quality in supernatural cinema. But as 1960s countercultures developed across the UK and United States both as cultural phenomena and market demographics, Hammer's brand identity and formulaic spinoffs were increasingly criticized by reviewers and audiences as derivative, banal, and out of touch with audience interests, unable to capitalize on the countercultural cache that *Dark Shadows* was concurrently cashing in on. "Count Dracula's been dug up for another run over the course," *Variety*'s review of *Dracula Has Risen from the Grave* (1968) began, "but this is a tired episode, which may be okay with a strong codualler but will not stir the addicts much. The story's slight, the horror and bloodcurdling essential to these pix is minimal and even Dracula himself appears bored at being resurrected yet again."[111] In the space of just eight years, Hammer churned out sequels (e.g., *The Brides of Dracula* [1960], *The Kiss of the Vampire* [1963], *The Evil of Frankenstein* [1964], *Dracula: Prince of Darkness* [1966], *Frankenstein Created Woman* [1967], *Dracula Has Risen From the Grave* [1968], and *Frankenstein Must Be Destroyed* [1969]) that were only minor modifications on the same central conceits. So when James Carreras, who had since become the studio's chairman and managing director, was approached in late 1969 with a proposal to adapt a Victorian novella centering on the same-sex desires of a female vampire, Hammer hoped that the fresh air blown through England after the *Chatterley* trial could similarly revitalize occult cinema for a new age of permissive moviegoers.

As reported in a 1971 issue of *The Ladder*, the magazine of the Daughters of Bilitis, the first official lesbian organization in the United States, J. Sheridan Le Fanu's *Carmilla* (1872)[112] was rediscovered during the 1960s and quickly became a "sub-basement Lesbian classic" for countercultural readers around the world.[113] Detailing the queer desires of vampire Carmilla Karnstein as narrated from the perspective of one of her female lovers/victims, Le Fanu's novella inspired a trilogy of films from Hammer, the first of which, *The Vampire Lovers*, began filming on January 19, 1970, and was released in the UK on October 4, just three months after the BBFC's amendment of the X certificate.[114] Adapting *Carmilla* for the screen was neither groundbreaking nor unprecedented at the time of *The Vampire Lovers'* release, as the story had provided inspiration across American and European film culture at least as far back as Carl Dreyer's *Vampyr* (1932) and Lambert Hillyer's *Dracula's Daughter* (1936) and more recently in Roger Vadim's *Blood and Roses* (1960). What was unique on Hammer's part, however, was the explicitly sexualized representation of *Carmilla*'s occultly queer storyline, the agentive qualities of its female characters, and its narration through a tripartite chronicle detailing the queer histories of the Karnstein family.

Starring Polish-born beauty Ingrid Pitt in the role that would launch her to international stardom, *The Vampire Lovers'* largely faithful adaptation of Le Fanu's novella paints Carmilla Karnstein, like Barnabas Collins, through complex, multifaceted strokes. She is both the chameleonic marauder who sucks her way between young ingénues of aristocratic Bavarian nobility in the late 1700s and a tragic antihero who, as one of the few surviving members of her family, seeks an ideal partner with whom to share the erotic pleasures of eternal life. Quickly seducing and dispatching Laura (Pippa Steele), the niece of one General von Spielsdorf (consummate conquering Hammer hero Peter Cushing), Carmilla moves on to the wealthy Morton family and turns her attentions to the youthful Emma (Madeline Smith). As the two women quickly form a close-knit bond, their shared affections become more than innocent flirtation. "Don't you wish some handsome young man would come into your life?" Emma inquires, to which Carmilla replies with stunted delivery, "No . . . neither do you I hope." Later, what begins as a prosaic nude bathing scene concludes with both women chasing each other playfully around Emma's bedroom before falling onto the bed and making love while Carmilla anxiously sinks her teeth into one of Emma's bared breasts.

As Emma is swiftly taken ill by fatigue, anemia, and night terrors of an oversized cat that stalks her, the same ailment that afflicted Laura before her death, the film's confluence between vampirism and same-sex desire becomes explicit:

> EMMA: It [the cat] lies across me. Warm and heavy with its fur in my mouth... and then...
>
> CARMILLA: ... and then...
>
> EMMA: It turns into you, Carmilla.
>
> [...]
>
> CARMILLA: I love you. And I don't want anyone taking you away from me... I want you to love me for all your life.

While the introduction of the 18-X certificate in the UK allowed for more explicit explorations of on-screen sexuality by moving away from subtextual camouflaging, such envelope-pushing scenes in *The Vampire Lovers* were not accepted without considerable concern and resistance on the part of John Trevelyan and his peers. As reviewer Audrey Field, a long-time antagonist of horror in general and Hammer in particular, wrote in the BBFC's memo file on the film,

> The very overt emphasis on lesbianism here goes far beyond anything we have allowed, except the uncut version of [*The Killing of*] *Sister George*. We are very concerned with the combination of nudity into horror. There are some very sick things here—Carmilla bares Emma's breasts, lowers her face, breast and her head towards and down her body (off/screen). We see a close up of Emma's face with a very strange sensual expression. We do not think we can possibly accept this sequence. We do feel that this film without considerable cuts will set a very bad precedent. It has a very horrible atmosphere in parts.[115]

The BBFC may have amended its attitude toward the representation of on-screen sex by 1970, but this changing of the guard came with certain caveats regarding the particular kinds of sexuality the board was willing to accept and through which generic modes. What's particularly remarkable about Field's memo is not only its blatant homophobic tone but also the tacit incredulity that Emma Morton could possibly find her queer encounter with Carmilla pleasurable. How could such a loathsome creature as a vampire initiate the "very strange sensual expression" qua orgasm Emma experiences at the climax of this scene? Although the queer female vampire film may allow "nudity, blood, and sexual titillation in a 'safe' fantasy structure" vis-à-vis occult Gothic conventions, as Bonnie Zimmerman, Andrea Weiss, and others have noted, some members of the BBFC were obviously not convinced by the genre's supposedly innocuous representation of non-normative sexual pleasures.[116] Indeed, as David Hogan writes in an apt turn of phrase, effective supernatural fantasy, "because it speaks so pointedly to our subconscious, is infinitely more affecting than a *'straight'* narrative [emphasis mine]."[117]

After much hand-wringing on the part of the BBFC and persuasion on the part of Hammer, *The Vampire Lovers* was eventually released in both the UK and United States practically uncut aside from two brief scenes that have since been restored to home video releases. Indeed, the film and its two sequels (*Lust for a Vampire* [1971] and *Twins of Evil* [1971]) have become something of critical ur-texts for both academic and popular press commentators regarding the representation of same-sex desire through occult media, where lines drawn in the critical sands are striking. As Weiss contends, the Karnstein trilogy shores up a narrative formula that, with minimal deviation, helped to define a new subgenre of occult horror during the early 1970s by fully exploiting the pornographic potential of the relationship between the female-desiring female vampire, her victim, and their titillated, presumably heterosexual, male audience.[118] Echoing this sentiment, acts like the nude bathing/dressing/lovemaking/biting scene between Carmilla and Emma are, according to David Pirie, patently voyeuristic and obviously engineered to offer as much "mild sexual titillation as possible," demonstrating that the "overall problem with the Karnstein films is that they pose little positive alternative to the all-engulfing figure of the female vampire, and consequently tend to denigrate into overwrought exercises in sensuality."[119] By characterizing such engrossing figures as ultimate literalizations of the monstrous vagina dentata, the "vampire-rapist who violates and destroys her victims,"[120] the Karnstein trilogy has been consequently vilified within many feminist and queer circles as more indicative of heterosexual men's fascination with the pleasures and dangers of female sexuality than representative of any authentic expression of same-sex desire.[121]

Yet do these films truly cater only to a position that posits heteromasculinity as the sole locus of spectatorial pleasure in occult horror? Although we certainly shouldn't discount the fact that Hammer was attempting to capitalize on the market for heterosexual male-targeted pornography that was expanding exponentially in both the UK and United States during this age of permissiveness, critiques of the Karnstein trilogy tend to deviate little outside the previously cited range of critical artillery. Such assessments may, in fact, be symptomatic of one of media studies' own enduring vampires: the tenacity of classical psychoanalytic theory within which the cinematic apparatus and those working behind it typify a heterosexual male point of view that functions only to fetishize, contain, and constrain female sexuality. Indeed, as Ellis Hanson maintains of queer media studies' reluctance to engage with queer horror on its own terms, "We are loath to enjoy ourselves, as long as there is a straight man somewhere who delights over the same images."[122] While the bodies of Ingrid Pitt in *The Vampire Lovers*, Yutte Stensgaard in *Lust for a Vampire*, and Mary and Madeleine Collinson in *Twins of Evil* are doubtlessly eroticized through tight framing, barebreasted close-ups, and lushly exotic mise-en-scènes, these women actually do their own fair share of active looking. Contrary to what commentators have noted regarding the slaying of the queer female vampire and the reestablishment of heterohegemony by the films' finales, the queer ghosts of the Karnstein family survive surreptitiously beyond these final frames as historical specters that can never be fully dispatched. Indeed, *The Vampire Lovers*, *Lust for a Vampire*, and *Twins of Evil* are not only narratively invested in sustaining the queer occult history of the Karnstein family, manifest especially in the trilogy's penchant for rituals of magickal resurrection, but they also simultaneously explore a new horizon of countercultural possibility in the occult horror genre: the tenability of an agentive gaze that may be both female and queer.

In the dream to which Emma Morton earlier referred in the excerpted dialogue from *The Vampire Lovers*, the corresponding shot-reverse shot pattern and flexible point of view places both women in a sexualized spectatorial relationship unmediated by any masculine presence, especially in light of the not-so-subtle euphemistic association between the feline and female sexual anatomy. This and other scenes might endeavor to replicate a classically fetishistic male point of view, but the Karnstein trilogy simultaneously presents an adjacent problematization of that gaze, thematizing it as a central dilemma aptly articulated by Hanson: "The gaze is forever in danger of appropriation and reconfiguration by the very lesbian vampire it seems to have dreamed into existence."[123] The true challenge throughout the Karnstein trilogy is one that has little to do with men, becoming instead a gynocentric battle between the culturally repressed sexuality typified by the latent same-sex desires of Laura and Emma and the "libidinous irrationality" of the occult so obviously associated with Carmilla.[124] Consonant with the countercultural resurgence of Crowley's sexual magick as a potent source of supernatural power, many of Hammer's queer female vampires possess agentive sexualities that they depend on "more heavily than any cunning or unnatural strength to acquire blood and guard the secret of [their] affliction."[125] Given new industrial latitude by the BBFC to probe more explicitly into the often violent and perversely sexual aspects of occult mythology, the Karnstein trilogy utilizes agentive female vampires to restore the psychological depths of Le Fanu's source work, creating Hammer's own quest to reclaim queer history.[126]

Like *Dark Shadows*' own exploration of ancestral story worlds, Hammer's decision to set *The Vampire Lovers*, *Lust for a Vampire*, and *Twins of Evil* in distant pasts allowed both Karnstein antiheros and their antagonists to revive the family's queer occult history, a cue taken explicitly from the source material itself. After Carmilla and Laura, the ingénue of Le Fanu's novella, become acquainted, the two women confess that each has been haunted by dream visions of the other for the past twelve years. Carmilla affirms to her confidant, "I saw you—most assuredly you—as I see you now; a beautiful young lady, with golden hair and large blue eyes, and lips—your lips—you as you are here. Your looks won me; I climbed on the bed and put my arms about you, and I think we both fell asleep."[127] As their relationship becomes more intimate, Laura (re)discovers hidden feelings through the same internalized struggle between repression and occultly queer liberation previously referenced: "I did feel . . . 'drawn towards her,' but there was also something of repulsion. In this ambiguous feeling, however, the sense of attraction immensely prevailed. She interested and won me . . . I was delighted with my companion; that is to say, in many respects."[128] As Laura articulates in her own words, her feelings toward Carmilla represent the acceptance of historically repressed queer instincts and desires.[129]

In a significant plot twist omitted from the Hammer films, it is revealed that Laura's deceased mother was also a Karnstein, queering the relationship between Carmilla and Laura not only through same-sex attraction but also through the additional element of hereditary incest. Laura's search for queer familial belonging is not only metaphorical in Le Fanu's story but also literal. "Why you must die," Carmilla assures her lover. "Everyone must die; and all are happier when they do. Come home . . . But to die as lovers may—to die together, so that they may live together."¹³⁰ Resurrecting the occult heritage of the Karnstein clan is not contingent on the heteronormative Law of the Father but rather reflects a history based on what Paulina Palmer calls the "direct exchange of body fluids. It resembles queer relationships and groups in furnishing a transgressive alternative to the patriarchal familial formation and the values which it encodes."¹³¹ Simply put, by finding Carmilla, Laura finds herself, her past, and her queer sexuality, even as her dispatched lover's spirit continues to linger after death: "To this hour the image of Carmilla returns to memory with ambiguous alternations—sometimes the playful, languid, beautiful girl; sometimes the writhing fiend I saw in the ruined church; and often from a reverie I have started, fancying I heard the light step of Carmilla at the drawing-room door."¹³² As Gina Wisker notes, the queer history that Carmilla animates never ceases to fill both her lover's dreams and our readerly imaginations with unending traces of excitement.¹³³

The pleasure Laura derives from shedding the oppressive weight of heteronormativity and "coming home" at the conclusion of *Carmilla* is one that carries over into the Karnstein trilogy as a type of identificatory viewing practice for occult enthusiasts comparably searching for their own queer histories. Through their chameleonic abilities to change shape and form at will, their refusal of traditionally normative sexual and gender roles, and their ability to laugh at, snub, and even hypnotically ensnare those who would see their perverse pleasures destroyed, Hammer's Karnstein family becomes a queer historical signifier of an "alternative economy of sexual pleasure which is more emotionally intense and fulfilling than its heterosexual counterpart."¹³⁴ This is especially true of the agency afforded the female vampire in the trilogy's second film, *Lust for a Vampire*.

Resurrected through a black magick ritual in the opening moments of the film, Carmilla Karnstein masquerades in *Lust for a Vampire* as Mircalla, a new student arriving at an all-female finishing school in 1830. As supernatural occurrences, same-sex trysts, and disappearing students become more frequent, Giles Barton (Ralph Bates), one of the school's instructors, decides to investigate. Cornering Mircalla in a local graveyard one evening, Barton emphatically asserts that the past has returned to haunt the present: "I went back. I checked my histories. I knew what I was looking for. The portrait of Carmilla Karnstein, died 1710. One hundred twenty years ago. And do you know who the portrait was of, Mircalla? The portrait of Carmilla Karnstein? It was you!" Imploring her to stay with him so that he might learn black magick as a servant of the devil, Mircalla feeds on Barton but does not turn him into a vampire, leaving him for dead while she retreats back to the school to continue her queer bloodlust.

According to Hayden White, a "specifically historical inquiry is born less of the necessity to establish that certain events occurred than what certain events might mean for a given group, society, or culture's conceptions of its present tasks and future prospects."[135] As such, one of the most meaningful attractions of occult film and television in the context of 1960s and 1970s countercultures was its thematic and diegetic constructions of queer history: cross-generational journeys that presented opportunities for identification with the vampire and/or the witch's power, her/his supernatural appeals, and how she/he uses them against patriarchal and/or heterosexist institutions, even if her/his physical body is dispatched by the series's/film's conclusion.[136] The bite of the vampire, inaugurating an incestuously queer relationship as simultaneous lover and parent, "pierces platonic metaphysics and subject/object positions; and her fanged kiss brings her the chosen one, trembling with ontological, orgasmic shifts, into the state of the undead. What the dominant discourse represents as an emptying out, a draining away, in contrast to the impregnating kiss of the heterosexual" rather becomes an exercise in queer ancestral formation.[137] These occult figures are thus not the product of heteronormative reproduction vis-à-vis "a single maker's potency," but rather represent the genealogy of a queer family who may simultaneously be each other's makers, confederates, and lovers.[138]

While the "full-throttle performances, cheap sets, and outlandish narrative events"[139] of both *Dark Shadows* and Hammer's Karnstein trilogy may invite interpretations as laughable camp, more specifically as the kind of naïve camp described by Susan Sontag as "'seriousness that fails,'" these texts and their respective industries also engaged in the more serious project of resurrecting queer fictions of the past.[140] Indeed, as Bravmann argues, even popular culture at its seemingly cheapest, basest, and most derivative "deserve[s] and need[s] to be taken seriously as social/cultural texts that produce, contest, and destabilize historically contingent fictive identities," encouraging us to expand what counts as history for LGBTQ+ media studies.[141] Considering individual, collective, and popular memory practices as politically charged sites for the construction, maintenance, and contestation of meaning, these queer fictions of the past afford nonnormative historical subjects one avenue to begin making sense of their position in the present.[142]

Notes

1. Louis Pauwels and Jacques Bergier, *The Morning of the Magicians*, trans. Rollo Myers (New York: Stein and Day, 1964), vii.
2. Ibid., 236.
3. Ibid., 244.
4. Ibid., ix.
5. Ibid., xi.
6. Gary Lachman, *Turn Off Your Mind: The Mystic Sixties and the Dark Side of the Age of Aquarius* (London: Sidgwick & Jackson, 2001), 17.
7. Cited in ibid., 6.
8. For a history of turn-of-the century supernatural thought and its influence across sociocultural and political life, see Alex Owen, *The Place of Enchantment: British Occultism and the Culture of the Modern* (Chicago: University of Chicago Press, 2004).
9. "Astrology: Fad and Phenomenon," *Time*, March 21, 1969.
10. Paul E. Steiger, "Big Business: Practitioners of Occult Enjoy a Rich Heyday," *Los Angeles Times*, May 28, 1969.
11. Penny Kolsrud, "Aquarian Alternatives: Search for the Self Leads Youth to Witchcraft, the Occult," *Baltimore Sun*, February 25, 1971.
12. Aniko Bodroghkozy, *Groove Tube: Sixties Television and the Youth Rebellion* (Durham: Duke University Press, 2001), 61.
13. Hugh B. Urban, *Magia Sexualis: Sex, Magic, and Liberation in Modern Western Esotericism* (Berkeley: University of California Press, 2006), 4.
14. See, for instance, David Allyn, *Make Love, Not War: The Sexual Revolution, An Unfettered History* (New York: Little, Brown and Company, 2000); Aniko Bodroghkozy, *Groove Tube: Sixties Television and the Youth Rebellion*; Lessie Jo Frazier and Deborah Cohen, eds., *Gender and Sexuality in 1968: Transformative Politics in the Cultural Imagination* (New York: Palgrave Macmillan, 2009); Hilary Radner and Moya Luckett, eds., *Swinging Single: Representing Sexuality in the 1960s* (Minneapolis: University of Minnesota Press, 1999); Patricia Juliana Smith, ed., *The Queer Sixties* (New York: Routledge, 1999); and Lynn Spigel and Michael Curtin, eds., *The Revolution Wasn't Televised: Sixties Television and Social Conflict* (New York: Routledge, 1997).
15. Linda Williams, "Porn Studies: Proliferating Pornographies On/Scene: An Introduction," in *Porn Studies*, ed. Linda Williams (Durham: Duke University Press, 2004), 3.
16. Ibid.
17. David Allyn, *Make Love, Not War: The Sexual Revolution, An Unfettered History* (Boston: Little, Brown and Company, 2000), 5.
18. Eric Schaefer, "Introduction: Sex Seen: 1968 and Rise of 'Public' Sex," in *Sex Scene: Media and the Sexual Revolution*, ed. Eric Schaefer (Durham: Duke University Press, 2014), 2.
19. See, for instance, Terry H. Anderson, *The Movement and the Sixties* (New York: Oxford University Press, 1995), David Farber, *The Age of Great Dreams: America in the 1960s* (New York: Hill and Wang, 1994), Martin A. Lee and Bruce Shlain, *Acid Dreams: The CIA, LSD, and the Sixties Rebellion* (New York: Grove, 1985), and Todd Gitlin, *The Sixties: Years of Hope, Days of Rage* (New York: Bantam, 1987).
20. Marilyn Goldstein, "Strange Things Are Happening in the Occult," *Washington Post*, July 25, 1971.

21. Arthur Evans, *Witchcraft and the Gay Counterculture* (Boston: Fag Rag, 1978), 148.
22. Ibid., 148–49.
23. Ibid., 154–55.
24. Todd Gitlin, *The Sixties: Years of Hope, Days of Rage* (New York: Bantam, 1987), 84.
25. Scott Bravmann, *Queer Fictions of the Past: History, Culture, and Difference* (Cambridge: Cambridge University Press, 1997), 24.
26. Patricia Juliana Smith, "Introduction: Icons and Iconoclasts: Figments of Sixties Queer Culture," in *The Queer Sixties*, ed. Patricia Juliana Smith (New York: Routledge, 1999), xv.
27. Ibid., xx.
28. Ibid.
29. The paradox here being the fact that such romance fiction operated around a fairly conservative decency code, rarely extending sexual explicitness beyond kissing. It was, however, the elliptical implicitness of sexual acts embedded in these novels that allowed imaginations to run wild and contributed to their success. In the adjacent televisual genre of the soap opera, a similar sort of sexual suggestiveness was one of the driving forces behind the popularity of *Dark Shadows*. For an influential discussion that reads changes in gender and sexual mores through romance fiction and its audiences, see Janice A. Radway, *Reading the Romance: Women, Patriarchy, and Popular Literature* (Chapel Hill: University of North Carolina Press, 1984).
30. Lorna Jowett and Stacey Abbott, *TV Horror: Investigating the Dark Side of the Small Screen* (London: I. B. Tauris, 2013), 204–5.
31. Cited in Craig Hamrick and R. J. Jamison, *Barnabas & Company: The Cast of the TV Classic* Dark Shadows (New York: iUniverse, 2003), 3.
32. *Dark Shadows* originally aired at 4:00 p.m. EST and PST and 3:00 p.m. CST. On April 2, 1967, the show was moved to 3:30 EST and PST, led in by ABC soap staple *General Hospital*.
33. Jeff Thompson, *The Television Horrors of Dan Curtis: Dark Shadows, The Night Stalker and Other Productions, 1966–2006* (Jefferson: McFarland, 2009), 56–57.
34. Mrs. Danvers, the scheming housekeeper portrayed by Judith Anderson in Alfred Hitchcock's *Rebecca* (1940), has extended throughout screen history as an archetype for the duplicitous warden of family secrets, often with her own ulterior motives.
35. "Television Reviews: Dark Shadows," *Variety*, June 29, 1966.
36. George Fox, "Can a 172-Year-Old Vampire Find Love and Happiness in a Typical New England Town?," *Saturday Evening Post*, November 30, 1968.
37. Cited in ibid.
38. "'Dark Shadows' Reprieve a WBRC-TV Horror Tale; Five Segs in One Sitting," *Variety*, July 31, 1968.
39. Jane Feuer, Paul Kerr, and Tise Vahimagi, *MTM: "Quality Television"* (London: British Film Institute, 1984), 3.
40. Mark Alvey, "'Too Many Kids and Old Ladies': Quality Demographics and 1960s U.S. Television," *Screen* 45, no. 1 (Spring 2004): 44.
41. Ibid., 43–44.
42. Elana Levine, *Wallowing in Sex: The New Sexual Culture of 1970s American Television* (Durham: Duke University Press, 2007), 20.
43. Cited in Helen Wheatley, *Gothic Television* (Manchester: Manchester University Press, 2006), 128.
44. "Younger and Older," *Television Age*, January 18, 1965.
45. "Turned-on Vampire," *Newsweek*, April 20, 1970.

46. Cited in Hamrick and Jamison, xviii.

47. See, for example, Quinlan Miller, *Camp TV: Trans Gender Queer Sitcom History* (Durham: Duke University Press, 2019), and Amy Villarejo, *Ethereal Queer: Television, Historicity, Desire* (Durham: Duke University Press, 2014).

48. Kevin Heffernan, *Ghouls, Gimmicks, and Gold: Horror Films and the American Movie Business, 1953–1968* (Durham: Duke University Press, 2004), 155–56.

49. See Harry M. Benshoff, *Monsters in the Closet: Homosexuality and the Horror Film* (Manchester: Manchester University Press, 1997); and David Hogan, *Dark Romance: Sexuality in the Horror Film* (Jefferson: McFarland, 1986).

50. Heffernan, 156.

51. Lynn Spigel, "From Domestic Space to Outer Space: The 1960s Fantastic Family Sitcom," in *Welcome to the Dreamhouse: Popular Media and Postwar Suburbs* (Durham: Duke University Press, 2001), 117.

52. Ibid., 120.

53. Susan J. Douglas, *Where the Girls Are: Growing Up Female with the Mass Media* (New York: Times Books, 1994), 126–27.

54. Ibid., 126.

55. David Selby, "Foreword," in *Dark Shadows Almanac: 30th Anniversary Tribute*, ed. Kathryn Leigh Scott and Jim Pierson (Los Angeles: Pomegranate, 1995), viii.

56. Wheatley, 155.

57. David Gregory, *Master of Dark Shadows: The Gothic World of Dan Curtis*, DVD, 2019.

58. Benshoff, 174.

59. Paulina Palmer, *Lesbian Gothic: Transgressive Fictions* (London: Cassell, 1999), 29.

60. *Dark Shadows* Shooting Script [Episode 446], Dan Curtis Productions Records (Collection PASC 1). UCLA Library Special Collections, Charles E. Young Research Library, UCLA.

61. Wheatley, 3.

62. Jowett and Abbott, 205–6.

63. Tim Kane, *The Changing Vampire of Film and Television: A Critical Study of the Growth of a Genre* (Jefferson: McFarland, 2006), 54.

64. Gregory.

65. Thompson, 80.

66. Gregory.

67. Fox.

68. The paradox here being that the soap opera has traditionally been analyzed as a conservative, realist, and heterosexual form of domestic entertainment marketed to and enjoyed almost exclusively by middle-aged women.

69. Robert C. Allen, *Speaking of Soap Operas* (Chapel Hill: University of North Carolina Press, 1985), 84.

70. Ibid., 82.

71. See Jeffrey Sconce, "Dickens, Selznick, and *South Park*," in *Dickens on Screen*, ed. John Glavin (Cambridge: Cambridge University Press, 2003): 171–87.

72. See Tania Modleski, *Loving with a Vengeance: Mass-Produced Fantasies for Women* (New York: Methuen, 1984).

73. Jowett and Abbott, 209.

74. Joan Barthel, "Out in Detergent Land: A Hard Day's Fright," *New York Times*, July 30, 1967.

75. Harry M. Benshoff, *Dark Shadows* (Detroit: Wayne State University Press, 2011), 26.
76. See Lee Edelman, *No Future: Queer Theory and the Death Drive* (Durham: Duke University Press, 2004).
77. Benshoff, *Dark Shadows*, 26.
78. Ibid., 31–32.
79. *House of Dark Shadows* was released in the United States by MGM in October 1970, followed by *Night of Dark Shadows* in August 1971, and Tim Burton's more recent adaptation in May 2012.
80. Wheatley, 146–47.
81. Lara Parker, "Fans," in *Dark Shadows Almanac: 30th Anniversary Tribute*, ed. Kathryn Leigh Scott and Jim Pierson (Los Angeles: Pomegranate, 1995), 39.
82. Lara Parker, "Out of Angélique's Shadow," in *The Dark Shadows Companion: 25th Anniversary Collection*, ed. Kathryn Leigh Scott (Los Angeles: Pomegranate, 1990), 17.
83. Cited in Barthel.
84. Cited in ibid.
85. Henry Jenkins, "*Star Trek* Rerun, Reread, Rewritten: Fan Writing as Textual Poaching," in *Close Encounters: Film, Feminism, and Science Fiction*, ed. Constance Penley et al. (Minneapolis: University of Minnesota Press, 1991), 174.
86. Harry M. Benshoff, "Resurrection of the Vampire and the Creation of Alternative Life: An Introduction to *Dark Shadows* Fan Culture," *Spectator* 13, no. 3 (Summer 1993): 53.
87. Ibid.
88. Sara Gwenllian-Jones and Roberta E. Pearson, "Introduction," in *Cult Television*, ed. Sara Gwenllian-Jones and Roberta E. Pearson (Minneapolis: University of Minnesota Press, 2004), xvii.
89. Gregory.
90. ABC Department of Broadcast Standards and Practices memo [April 19, 1967], Dan Curtis Productions Records (Collection PASC 1). UCLA Library Special Collections, Charles E. Young Research Library, UCLA.
91. Darren Elliott-Smith, "'Blood, Sugar, Sex, Magik': Unearthing Gay Male Anxieties in Queer Gothic Soaps *Dante's Cove* (2005–2007) and *The Lair* (2007–2009)," in *Melodrama in Contemporary Film and Television*, ed. Michael Stewart (New York: Palgrave Macmillan, 2014), 96.
92. Jeffrey Weeks, *Sex, Politics, and Society: The Regulation of Sexuality Since 1800* (London: Longman, 1981), 254.
93. Cited in Alan Travis, "The War on Obscenity: Alan Travis on the Lady Chatterley Trial," *Guardian*, October 28, 2010, http://www.theguardian.com/books/2010/oct/28/lady-chatterley-trial-war-on-obscenity.
94. Weeks, 249.
95. Catharine Arnold, *The Sexual History of London: From Roman Londinium to the Swinging City—Lust, Vice, and Desire Across the Ages* (New York: St. Martin's, 2011), 311–12.
96. Benshoff, *Monsters in the Closet: Homosexuality and the Horror Film*, 209.
97. Owen, 28.
98. Ibid., 189.
99. Aleister Crowley, *The Confessions of Aleister Crowley: An Autohagiography* (London: Arkana, 1989), 139.
100. Aleister Crowley, *Magick in Theory and Practice* (New York: Castle, 1960), xii.
101. Ibid.

102. Ibid., xv–xvii.
103. Hilary Radner, "Introduction: Queering the Girl," in *Swinging Single: Representing Sexuality in the 1960s*, ed. Hilary Radner and Moya Luckett (Minneapolis: University of Minnesota Press, 1999), 4.
104. Crowley, *Magick in Theory and Practice*, xxiv.
105. Urban, 109–10.
106. Leon Hunt, "Necromancy in the UK: Witchcraft and the Occult in British Horror," in *British Horror Cinema*, ed. Steve Chibnall and Julian Petley (London: Routledge, 2002), 84.
107. Owen, 213.
108. Hunt, 87.
109. Denis Meikle, *A History of Horrors: The Rise and Fall of the House of Hammer* (Lanham: Scarecrow, 1996), 231.
110. Cited in ibid.
111. "Pictures: *Dracula Has Risen from the Grave*," *Variety*, November 20, 1968.
112. *Carmilla* was originally published in the British magazine *The Dark Blue* in 1872 and was reprinted in Le Fanu's collection *In A Glass Darkly* the same year.
113. See Gene Damon, *The Ladder*, February/March 1971.
114. *The Vampire Lovers* was financed as a coproduction between Hammer and well-established horror/B-movie house American International Pictures (AIP), earning distribution on both sides of the Atlantic. *The Vampire Lovers* was released in the United States on October 22, 1970, with an R rating from the MPAA.
115. Cited in Sian Barber, *Censoring the 1970s: The BBFC and the Decade That Taste Forgot* (Newcastle upon Tyne: Cambridge Scholars, 2011), 34.
116. Bonnie Zimmerman, "Daughters of Darkness: Lesbian Vampires," *Jump Cut*, no. 24–25 (March 1981): 23.
117. Hogan, 156.
118. Andrea Weiss, *Vampires & Violets: Lesbians in Film* (New York: Penguin, 1993), 88.
119. David Pirie, *A New Heritage of Horror: The English Gothic Cinema* (London: I. B. Tauris, 2008), 183.
120. Zimmerman, 24.
121. Benshoff, *Monsters in the Closet: Homosexuality and the Horror Film*, 195.
122. Ellis Hanson, "Lesbians Who Bite," in *Out Takes: Essays on Queer Theory and Film*, ed. Ellis Hanson (Durham: Duke University Press, 1999), 191.
123. Ibid., 185.
124. Alain Silver and James Ursini, *The Vampire Film: From* Nosferatu *to* Interview with the Vampire (New York: Limelight Editions, 1997), 126.
125. Ibid., 111.
126. Ibid., 123.
127. J. Sheridan Le Fanu, *Carmilla* (Smashbooks, 2013) Nook file, 23.
128. Ibid., 23–24.
129. Ibid., 28.
130. Ibid., 29–34.
131. Palmer, 104.
132. Le Fanu, 90.
133. Gina Wisker, "Devouring Desires: Lesbian Gothic Horror," in *Queering the Gothic*, ed. William Hughes and Andrew Smith (Manchester: Manchester University Press, 2009), 126.
134. Palmer, 101–2.

135. Hayden White, "Historical Pluralism," *Critical Inquiry* 12, no. 3 (Spring 1986): 487.
136. Benshoff, *Monsters in the Closet: Homosexuality and the Horror Film*, 200.
137. Sue-Ellen Case, "Tracking the Vampire," *Differences* 3, no. 2 (1991): 15.
138. Nina Auerbach, *Our Vampires, Ourselves* (Chicago: University of Chicago Press, 1995), 39–40.
139. Benshoff, *Dark Shadows*, 74.
140. Ibid.
141. Bravmann, ix.
142. Ibid., 24–30.

2

LE SEXE QUI PARLE DU SURNATUREL

Supernatural Sexualities and Satanic Subcultures in the 1970s

MARCH 12, 1964. NINE DAYS AFTER HIS ARREST for organizing a screening of Jack Smith's *Flaming Creatures* (1963) at the New Bowery Theatre in New York City's East Village, avant-garde filmmaker Jonas Mekas took to his regular "Movie Journal" column in the *Village Voice* to issue a statement regarding the current climate of sexuality in the cinema. "There is nothing surprising," Mekas remarked, "about the fact that suddenly this wave of 'obscenity' has flooded the arts. It's just that artists have become a little bit more frank. At least they are trying to be more frank."[1] A queer horror featurette that debuted on April 29, 1963, at New York's Bleecker Street Cinema, *Flaming Creatures* was deemed obscene by a state criminal court almost immediately after its premiere and was just one of a host of films that had been censored in the wake of a landmark legal decision six years earlier. In *Roth v. United States* (1957), the US Supreme Court affirmed that obscenity was not protected under the constitutional guarantees of the First Amendment and that the issue should henceforth be judged as "whether to the average person, applying contemporary community standards, the dominant theme of the material taken as a whole appeals to the prurient interest."[2] It was the ambiguous leeway granted within the "contemporary community standards" caveat of what became known as "the *Roth* test" that paradoxically fostered the revival of an erotic literary avant-garde (e.g., the work of James Joyce, D. H. Lawrence, and others) in both the United States and UK, yet simultaneously allowed legal officials to seize prints and outlaw screenings of so-called smutty films like Smith's *Flaming Creatures*, Jean Genet's *Un Chant d'Amour* (1950), and the erotic shorts of Kenneth

Anger. But let's not fool ourselves, Mekas prompted his readers: "All men, including the judges and the police and the District Attorney, are naked under their clothes, and they make love in at least two dozen different ways... this is only the beginning, the very first blabberings of frankness."[3] Mekas's statement would indeed prove prophetic.

On January 5, 1967, in an editorial nestled in the Arts section of the *New York Times*, columnist Vincent Canby took an opportunity to reflect further on the sexual influence of American Underground cinema and assess the future direction of the medium's erotic and artistic aspirations. Inspired by word that a recent hit play dealing with a gay love affair, Christopher Hampton's *When Did You Last See My Mother?* (1964), would soon go into screen production, Canby remarked that the drama was the latest in a series of anticipated films dealing with "so-called 'adult themes' that would not have been touched by filmmakers as recently as five years ago."[4] Before monikers like "adult" and "mature" became both industrial and popular shorthand for pornography by the beginning of the next decade, such terms signified a gradually expanding latitude of on-screen frankness during the late 1960s, including portrayals of drug use, explicit violence, and a wide assortment of sexual "perversions," including BDSM, polyamory, and homosexuality. If Audrey Field and the BBFC saw Hammer's candid treatment of queerness in films like *The Vampire Lovers* as a push against the acceptable boundaries of cinema content in the early 1970s, they were in good critical company among writers like Mekas and Canby, who had been making the same observation, albeit to much different ends, several years earlier. Mirroring previous discourses on the representational leeway granted within art cinema, it was clear to both critics and consumers of the late 1960s that the movies, "once the mass medium of entertainment, are going through a revolution that could remove all the old taboos concerning subject matter and treatment."[5] Like Mekas, Canby's editorial proved prophetic by highlighting a statement from the first vice president of United Artists, David Picker: "What may be a provocative theme today, may seem quite ordinary three or four years from now."[6]

As the countercultural fervor dispersed through 1960s media culture approached the dawn of a new decade, the entwined sociopolitical struggles for sexual liberation and queer rights came to a notorious head. In the early morning hours of June 28, 1969, New York City police raided the Stonewall Inn, a hub of queer nightlife located on Christopher Street in Greenwich Village. Prior to that morning, police presence in major metropolitan gay bars and nightclubs across the United States was certainly nothing new. In light of the fact that many of these establishments lacked liquor licenses and frequently violated local health, fire, and safety codes, law enforcement bribery often kept business running, even if proprietors had to occasionally endure an inconvenient arrest alongside their patrons. But something that Saturday morning in 1969 was different. Those customers dressed in drag, normally required to accompany a female police officer into bathrooms for verification of their true sex, refused to cooperate. Patrons who had been forced to line up along the walls of the bar declined to produce identification for inspection. And those who had been released from the Stonewall, estimated by most accounts at between one hundred and one hundred and fifty people, began to form a crowd outside.

By the time the first police patrol vehicle arrived on Christopher Street and those inside the bar were escorted out, one woman complaining that her handcuffs were latched too tight had been beaten by officers with billy clubs. Imploring the growing crowd for help, bystanders hurled bottles, rocks, and bricks from a nearby construction site at the approaching paddy wagons. Violence escalated quickly, and those officers who had taken shelter within the Stonewall were overcome by the mob that entered and began to set fire to the bar. When the Tactical Police Force finally arrived and forced the bedlam back outside, the horde of so-called queens, swishers, and sissies formed jubilant chorus girl kick lines, reveling in their ostensible aberration by mocking the machismo of the officers, who continued to herd them off the streets. As participant Michael Fader recalls,

> We all had a collective feeling like we'd had enough of this kind of shit. It wasn't anything tangible anybody said to anyone else, it was just kind of like everything over the years had come to a head on that one particular night in the one particular place. . . . Everyone in the crowd felt that we were never going to go back. It was like the last straw. It was time to reclaim something that had always been taken from us. . . . All kinds of people, all different reasons, but mostly it was total outrage, anger, sorrow, everything combined, and everything just kind of ran its course. It was the police who were doing most of the destruction. We were really trying to get back in and break free. And we felt that we had freedom at last, or freedom to at least show that we demanded freedom. We weren't going to be walking meekly in the night and letting them shove us around—it's like standing your ground for the first time and in a really strong way, and that's what caught the police by surprise. There was something in the air, freedom a long time overdue, and we're going to fight for it. It took different forms, but the bottom line was, we weren't going to go away. And we didn't.[7]

The Stonewall rebellion did not, in fact, dissolve quickly, lasting until the midpoint of the following week with extensive press coverage by major media outlets including the *New York Post*, the *New York Daily News*, and the *New York Times*. Reflecting on the postapocalyptic décor of the neighborhood after the smoke had finally cleared, beat poet Allen Ginsberg, a long-time resident of Christopher Street, offered the following thoughts: "Gay power! Isn't that great! . . . It's about time we did something to assert ourselves. . . . You know, the guys there were so beautiful—they've lost that wounded look that fags all had 10 years ago."[8]

In the historiographic record of LGBTQ+ liberation, the Stonewall riots are often given pride of place above all else—the celebratory moment when queers from all walks of life stood their ground, refused to yield to the discriminatory status quo, and launched a movement whose legacy continues to be felt to this day. Yet while Stonewall was undoubtedly a major milestone in queer history, the riots were hardly the beginning of queer activism or community formation among sexual subcultures in the United States. As George Chauncey demonstrates in his landmark study *Gay New York*, queer culture generated within American urban centers can be traced back well prior to the turn of the twentieth century.[9] In the immediate postwar era, organizations such as the Mattachine Society and the Daughters of Bilitis became beacons of homophile visibility fighting for the civil rights of gay and lesbian citizens. Perhaps Joan Nestle, cofounder of the Lesbian Herstory Archives, sums up the situation best: "I certainly don't see gay and lesbian history starting with Stonewall . . . and I don't see resistance starting with Stonewall. What I do see is a historical coming together of forces, and the sixties changed how human beings endured things in this society and what they refused to endure . . . it's more complex than saying that it all started with Stonewall."[10]

Such complexities are further exacerbated by the fact that not all queer groups agreed on the merits of the riots. Long known for its commitment to conservatism, propriety, and a narrow definition of respectable gay life, the Mattachine Society condemned the Stonewall kick line displays as an embarrassment, nothing more than a reification of the grotesque effeminacy that the ruling heteronormative establishment tethered to characterizations of queer deviance. Yet if, as Harry Benshoff contends, sociosexual analogies of the decade continued to equate queerness with lurking specters creeping out of the shadows of horror films ("monster is to 'normality' as homosexual is to heterosexual"), there were also those who continued the fight to reclaim their horrific eccentricities and employ them as cornerstones of their respective post-Stonewall political agendas.[11] Almost immediately after the dust had dissipated on Christopher Street, local community members founded the Gay Liberation Front (GLF), an organization that adopted a broad-based political platform with aspirations toward dismantling the hegemony of heterosexuality as well as ending injustices of sexism, militarism, and racism across the globe. For those seeking an exclusively queer-centric focus, dissident members of the GLF soon after formed the Gay Activists Alliance (GAA), the organization in which Arthur Evans played a leading role and through which he developed his work on the historical associations between queer sexualities and magick.

While still maintaining backward glances into queer fictions of the past, certain segments of Euro-American media culture at the turn of the 1970s also began looking forward to both a queer present and future—time-spaces in which nonnormative genders, sexualities, and sexual practices could finally abandon their shadowy shrouds of allegory, metaphor, and innuendo toward achieving new heights of screen visibility. As numerous cultural historians have pointed out, perhaps the biggest marker of the sexual revolution's transition from the late 1960s into the 1970s was the emergence of an unmatched sexual frankness in moving-image culture, exemplified most obviously by the phenomenal rise of hardcore pornography in both the United States and around the globe. "That we're in a presence these days of an unprecedented and steadily increasing quantity, range and intensity of public sexual expression is an observable fact," Richard Gilman wrote in the *New York Times Magazine* on September 8, 1968. "Nudity in the films and now on the stage; the employment as theme or as incidental reference in movies, plays and books of such conditions and practices as lesbianism and homosexuality ... incest, sadism and masochism, group sex, oral sex, etc."[12] As Elana Levine summarizes, "watching a porn film at the local theater, flipping through a sex advice manual in line at the grocery store ... all were markers of sexual sophistication ... American popular culture of the 1970s was rife with just this sort of commodified sexual expression ... during the 1970s sex was for sale and millions of Americans were buying."[13]

The inauguration of what Ralph Blumenthal of the *New York Times* famously termed "porno chic" in 1973 did not, however, materialize within an industrial, sociocultural, or even spiritual vacuum.[14] This chapter traces the rise of 1970s Euro-American queer sex media as it became intimately enmeshed with the history of one particular occult subculture that was also coming out of the closet immediately preceding and following Stonewall: Satanism. Specifically, the liberation, hedonism, and queer pleasures celebrated by Satanic subcultures contributed to and were reflected within a constellation of polymorphous sexual perversities woven throughout American Underground film, theatrical hardcore pornography, and "Eurosleaze" cinema imports. As Frank Trippett observed in an article for *Look* magazine in October 1970, "Our times surely must become known as the Age of the Great Disrobing. Public sex pops up everywhere. Across an ever-expanding vista we behold natural rites hitherto closed off by an ancient rule of privacy. Now we witness it all."[15] Whether intentionally or not, Trippett's observation in relation to natural rites and ancient creeds clearly resonates within the exploratory sexual atmospheres that attracted so many queer people to occultism in general and Satanism in particular. If sex began to speak explicitly on its own behalf during the 1970s, as Jamie Gillis's character discovers while watching the fictitious *Le sexe qui parle* (*The Sex that Speaks*) during the opening scene of Radley Metzger's *The Opening of Misty Beethoven* (1976), it was sex that spoke decidedly of queer supernatural pleasures.

Lucifer Rising from Underground

Historically sharing not only similarly clandestine production, distribution, and exhibition practices but also enduring critical markers of "low genre," "bad object," "smut," and so forth, both horror and sex media have often been allied as kindred spirits. Typically, these partnerships have been culled from a shared legacy vis-à-vis the exploitation film, where shock, awe, arousal, and disgust all mingled simultaneously under the roofs of "bump-and-grind houses, marketed to patrons of body genre pictures"[16] during the first half of the twentieth century.[17] Typically framed as exposés of "contemporary problems, educational tracts, or morality plays," Eric Schaefer notes, "classical exploitation films maintained their position in the market by including moments of spectacle unlike anything seen in mainstream movies: scenes set in nudist camps, shots of striptease dances, and footage of childbirth, victims of venereal disease, and people engaging in a range of vices."[18] By the end of the 1950s, the classical exploitation period's shallow veneer of "redeeming social value" documentaries gave way to more knowingly salacious offerings such as Russ Meyer's *The Immoral Mr. Teas* (1959), Doris Wishman's *Bad Girls Go to Hell* (1965), the scandalously

Satanic *I Drink Your Blood* (1970), and a new era of sexploitation films, where "nudie-cuties" gradually abandoned their didactic "square-ups" in favor of narrativized fictions that included "nudity in the context of sexual situations, and, in time, simulated sexual activity."[19] To many increasingly permissive moviegoers of the late 1960s, the subsequent production and exhibition of feature-length narrative films that would display nonsimulated sex acts seemed all but a foregone conclusion.

To the extent that moving-image pornography continues to solidify as a legitimate object of scholarly attention in media studies, histories of its industrial practices and innumerable productions have relied largely on what Schaefer calls an overly rigid chronology: "filmmakers jumping across a series of hurdles, offering greater explicitness with each leap on their way to a predetermined end—nonsimulated representations of [typically heterosexual] sexual acts on screen."[20] Porn films may have generally evolved toward greater latitude in representing explicit sex between the end of the classical exploitation era and the beginning of porno chic, but that isn't to say that sex media proceeded on one solitary course without ruptures, fissures, and divisions in the kinds of material that would ultimately become feasible, marketable, and profitable. While chronicles of both classical exploitation and the later sexploitation film are vital to a richer understanding of how increasingly explicit sex came to movie screens and climaxed with the rise of hardcore pornography, "the visual (and sometimes aural) representation of living, moving bodies engaged in explicit, [unfaked], sexual acts with a primary intent of arousing viewers," closer attention needs to be paid to those bordering genres, movements, and industrial modes that were equally interested in pushing the boundaries of cinema's sexual content.[21] As Tzvetan Todorov has argued, even the most codified of textual genres are permeable and must be defined "in relation to the genres adjacent to [them]."[22]

As such, it is the intergeneric, hybridic history of sex media's queer relationship to occultism, paralleled in various narrative modalities, filmic techniques, and industrial contexts, that this chapter investigates. While the classical exploitation film began to overlap with marginal Hollywood products during the 1950s, that decade also witnessed the full ascent of the American Underground, an experimental movement whose apex would arrive concomitant with the sexual and supernatural fervor of the 1960s. Indebted to the work of European avant-garde filmmakers of the 1930s and 1940s, while further eschewing the formulaic narratives and mainstream esteem of classical Hollywood, the American Underground was initially defined as a group of subcultural filmmakers whose pictures were made on a "shoestring budget with mainly amateur actors and shown primarily for private audiences."[23] As an avant-garde undertaking centered mainly in New York at exhibition locales such as the New Bowery Theater and the Bleecker Street Cinema, the American Underground famously included the work of multimedia artists such as Jack Smith, Stan Brakhage, Paul Morrissey, Andy Warhol, Maya Deren, and Kenneth Anger.

In his history of the Underground penned in 1969, Parker Tyler reminds readers that one of the keys to appreciating the nuances of this movement is the fact that aesthetic ingenuity is not to be equated with the material means of filmmaking: "on the contrary a great pride of the true avant-garde filmmaker is that he can produce extraordinary effects through manipulations that in themselves are not costly."[24] By rebuffing the rampant commercialism of mainstream narrative cinema, from both the technical/production and exhibition arenas, Underground media makers returned their cameras to one of film's original yet most neglected functions: "invading and recording realms which have to some degree remained taboo—too private, too shocking, too immoral for photographic reproduction."[25] Situated in its sociohistorical context, it is little surprise that the tabooed proclivities of the Underground to exhibit what was "rare, tempting, unusual, [and] thrilling" gradually took on countercultural resonance, both sexual and supernatural.[26] Indeed, if hardcore pornography would later become caught up in what Linda Williams terms a "frenzy of the visible," narrative vehicles for the "spectacular, involuntary presentation of the knowledge of pleasure as confessions of socially disruptive 'sexual truths,'" then the Underground can be historicized as a queer occult progenitor of later Euro-American sex media, forming a confessional constellation of socially disruptive sexual and spiritual truths.[27]

Akin to the emergence of camp as a reading protocol that allowed mostly gay men to find subcultural resonance among classical Hollywood grande dames like Judy Garland, Marlene Dietrich, Joan Crawford, and Bette Davis, the Underground's abstract, sexually explicit, and occult aesthetics provided a similar avenue toward the possibility of nonnormative community formation catalyzed around emergent queer media. As Janet Staiger notes, the experience of going to the Underground cinema "contradicted impressions of isolation as it also elevated images of perverts and subjects gone awry. It vaunted sexual Otherness as an avant-garde aesthetic. . . . The underground cinema of the 1960s was a space for validation, empowerment, and often ironic resistance that used sexuality, politics, popular cultural iconography, and humor to establish community among subcultures."[28] Even the term itself, as suggested by J. Hoberman and Jonathan Rosenbaum, reverberated with titillating echoes of "danger, secrecy, subversion, resistance, liberation; not to mention perversity, alienation, even madness."[29] While the very representation of nonnormative sexualities was critical to the Underground's subcultural success in major metropolitan centers across the United States, it was the movement's depiction of occult sexualities in particular that proved especially effective in celebrating queer Otherness. As Tyler succinctly notes, it is nearly impossible to separate the Underground's interest in both artistic and sexual expression from its concern with dream-fantasy and the supernatural.[30]

Born February 3, 1927, Kenneth Anger (originally Kenneth Anglemeyer) shot his first short on scraps of 16mm film stock when he was just ten years old. After the Anglemeyer family pulled up stakes and moved to Hollywood in 1944, Kenneth, a Beverly Hills High School attendee, began devoting all of his leisure time to two main passions: filmmaking and a budding interest in the occult. Often attending silent film screenings at the American Contemporary Gallery on Hollywood Boulevard, Anger soon struck up a friendship with Curtis Harrington, a fellow film director and occult enthusiast. Harrington had previously been a mentee of Maya Deren, herself a renowned Underground filmmaker and initiated priestess in Haitian vodun, and was the man who first introduced Anger to the writings of Aleister Crowley. The Great Beast 666 would henceforth serve as Anger's primary artistic and spiritual interlocutor.

After enrolling at the University of Southern California to formally study filmmaking, the twenty-year-old Anger decided to commit his increasing involvement with the queer subculture of Los Angeles to celluloid. The first result, *Fireworks* (1947), starring Anger himself, is an occultly queer classic produced while his parents were away from their Beverly Hills home for the weekend. As the film opens, a close-up of a prostrate young man (Anger) gradually zooms out to reveal a well-muscled, uniformed navy sailor carrying him toward the foreground. While several scholars have remarked on the sacrificial Pietà imagery of this establishing shot, a more queerly occult comparison to the classical horror film is also striking, especially given *Fireworks*' black and white cinematography, crashing claps of thunder on the soundtrack, and the extratextual point that James Whale, the openly gay director of Universal monster classics such as *Frankenstein* (1931), *The Invisible Man* (1933), and *The Bride of Frankenstein* (1935), was among the first to receive an invitation to view the completed film. As Hoberman and Rosenbaum observe, early Underground filmmakers like Anger cultivated a taste for the "tawdry exoticism of despised film genres," most notably "cheap horror flicks."[31]

As the camera fades out and back in, Anger is shown lying on a living room mattress covered by nothing but a bed sheet. As the perspective tilts down to a nearby end table carved with Thelemic runes, the viewer is presented with a close-up examination of a ceramic hand decorated with a diverse assortment of lines, symbols, and esoteric writings, the most popular divination tool employed in the occult art of palmistry. But something is amiss here; each of the five fingers of the hand has been severed in half (perhaps evoking castration) with only their bases remaining. Whether or not this detail is an ominous omen of future events remains to be seen. What is apparent, however, is that the Thelemic table and divination hand underscore *Fireworks* as an explicit meditation on occult eroticism, particularly as the camera tilts back from the table and hand to Anger, who is sporting what appears to be what can only be described as a tent pole erection under the bedsheet until an African tribal statue is revealed as the culprit of the bawdy joke.[32] Lingering, fetishizing close-ups of the young man dressing follow, until Anger eventually exits the room through a door simply marked "GENTS."

If one of the cinema's foundational functions was to invade and record realms that have remained taboo, "too private, too shocking, too immoral for photographic reproduction," then the medium has been an inherently voyeuristic one since its inception. In the context of both the American Underground and its later hardcore pornographic counterpart, this predilection comes to the fore as "'peephole excitement,'" showcasing what Tyler calls "fetish footage . . . the literal exposure of a private hang-up, whatever the hang-up may be."[33] As Anger emerges from the living room and appears inside a communal men's restroom framed by a painted saloon backdrop, an erotically charged juxtaposition of traditionally homosexual and heterosexual spaces of sexual signification, the voyeurism of the previous scene is exacerbated by the ritualized performance of queer fetishism. Surrounded by a group of sailors dressed exactly like the one from the film's opening, Anger is trapped by the servicemen, stripped, pinned to the ground, and whipped with links of chain metal in a frantic montage of sadomasochistic revelry. Anger's progressively blood-soaked face contorts in a horrific amalgamation of agony and orgiastic ecstasy before a broken beer bottle is used to slice open his chest, dig through the internal organs underneath his ribcage, and reveal a compass pointing north. As Richard Dyer observes, gay men are traditionally "beaten up and/or arrested in these spaces but *Fireworks* neither documents nor protests this. Rather, it turns it into a part of sexual pleasure."[34]

In the composition of the frame, north points to Anger's face, where *Fireworks* reaches its climax both literally and figuratively. Transitioning to a profile view, the camera arrives just in time for the young man to be doused from above with streams of a thick, viscous liquid. Although Williams maintains that it was not until the early 1970s, "with the rise of the hard-core feature, that the money shot assumed the narrative function of signaling the climax of a genital event," this soon-to-be infamous orgasmic trope is abstracted yet unmistakable in *Fireworks*' queer sex ritual, whether simulated or not.[35] What's more, to drive this point home, the very next shot is at medium length of one of the sailors standing back in Anger's living room with a lit Roman candle protruding from the fly of his pants. The bottle rocket erupts. The visual orgasm metaphor is repeated.

In the film's final scene, a gradual dissolve returns the viewer to the living room, where Anger and the sailor from the first shot are sleeping next to each other in front of a crackling fire. Another downward tilt concentrates on the table with the divination hand, fingers now reattached, before the final fade to black. Though ultimately indulging in the "it was all just a dream" cliché, it is clear that Anger's fourteen-minute "gay gang-rape fantasy . . . saturated in Crowleyan imagery" has much to say about occultly queer sexualities and the possibilities for their on-screen representation as exercises in magickal wish fulfillment.[36] If the castrated divination hand predicted or employed occult forces to influence the events that occur once Anger enters the "GENTS" door, the pain it foresaw in his ritualized S&M sacrifice becomes a source of extremely queer sexual pleasure. Indeed, it is only within *Fireworks*' occult world of eroticized otherness that sexual repression can be overcome and the truth of interior subjectivity can be set free.[37] As later experimental filmmaker Guy Maddin reflects, "It is because we are all lodged firmly up inside Anger's occult id" that his films are especially memorable.[38] *Fireworks*' attention to sexualities of the occult were, moreover, consciously courted by Anger during initial exhibition engagements, as not only James Whale but Dr. Alfred Kinsey, the renowned

American sexologist, were among the first to receive screening invitations. Anger and Kinsey became close friends soon after *Fireworks*' premiere, and the filmmaker actively aided in the doctor's sexuality research until Kinsey's death in 1956.

Although *Fireworks* was immediately extolled by many subcultural communities as a queer classic, the film also faced a harsh barrage of censorship during its numerous theatrical runs over the next decade. The same year as the film's release, a California appellate court upheld a statute, dating back fifty years to the US Supreme Court's decision in *Dunlop v. United States* (1897), that obscenity charges could be brought forth if the product(s) in question possessed a "substantial tendency to deprave or corrupt . . . by inciting lascivious thoughts or arousing lustful desire."[39] Following Anger's subsequent arrest in Los Angeles after local officials deemed *Fireworks* nothing but an exercise in perverse pornography, theater managers also became the subject of intense legal scrutiny. Raymond Rohauer, for example, managed LA's Coronet Theatre, an eccentric combination of "art house, film society and exploitation cinema," and was struck with a lawsuit in 1958 for screening Anger's film.[40] In what would become a lengthy obscenity trial taken all the way to the chambers of the California Supreme Court, *Fireworks* was ultimately sanctified with artistic merit, largely because of its "refined editing, and cinematic visual style."[41] This victory was a tempered one, however, as the phobic-laden legal precedents that lumped homosexuality and pornography together into categories of illicit and perverse sexual practices remained largely intact. As reported in the March 4, 1959, issue of *Variety*, it was the opinion of the court that "homosexuality is 'not to be approved but society should understand' its causes and effects."[42] Nevertheless, Rohauer's victory in California set a foundation on which Anger and other Underground filmmakers engrossed in the associations between queer sexuality and the occult were able to build, particularly as their supernatural interests turned increasingly Satanic.

As a phantasmatic enterprise operating on the margins of media making, it is fitting that many Underground filmmakers who worked into the 1960s and beyond continued to derive inspiration for the supernatural sexualities of their films from ever-emergent shadows, both literal and metaphorical. Born April 11, 1930, in Chicago, Anton Szandor LaVey (originally Howard Stanton LaVey) was a child fascinated by magick and the occult from an early age. Through conversations and time spent with his Transylvanian grandmother, Anton learned of the "superstitions that [were] still extant in that part of the world. These tales whetted his appetite for the outré leading him to become absorbed in classic dark literature such as *Dracula* and *Frankenstein*. He also became an avid reader of the classics of the horror and science fiction genres."[43] According to his personal confidant and fellow magus Peter H. Gilmore, Anton's queer eccentricities "marked him as an outsider, and he did not alleviate this by feeling any compulsion to be 'one of the boys.' He despised gym class and team sports and often cut classes to follow his own interests.... His taste for flashy apparel also served to amplify his alienation from the mainstream."[44] In fact, as soon as he could muster both the courage and financial resources, LaVey followed the stereotypical young outcast's dream and ran away to join the circus, working first as a lion tamer before putting his magickal predilections and flair for the dramatic to productive use as a carnival mentalist and hypnotist. He would later indulge his musical talents under the big top as an organist and calliope player.

At the conclusion of his carnival career, LaVey settled in San Francisco and found employment as a crime scene photographer for the city's police department. Detecting his enthusiasm for the morbid and macabre, SFPD officials encouraged LaVey to take up a position as a phone operator, and he advanced his occult education by answering "nut calls" from local Bay Area residents who swore they had made contact with incubi, succubae, ghosts, witches, vampires, and almost every other manner of supernatural entity. Expanding his income as both a local ghost buster and speakeasy organist, LaVey quickly became something of a minor San Francisco celebrity. Having purchased a large Victorian home in the city's Richmond district in 1956 that he proceeded to paint entirely in black, LaVey began holding weekly Friday evening occult lectures in the early 1960s on topics ranging from the teachings of Crowlean Thelema to contemporary incarnations of the Satanic Black Mass. Magick really works, LaVey told *McCall*'s columnist Judith Rascoe in a March 1970 issue dedicated entirely to the explosion of countercultural occultism in America: "You can call it alpha, beta, delta, or gamma wave energy or whatever scientists are dabbling in now, but I've been practicing it for years."[45] Regular attendees at LaVey's initial metaphysical get-togethers included such notable supernatural enthusiasts as Michael Harner, Forrest J. Ackerman, Fritz Leiber, Dr. Cecil E. Nixon, and Kenneth Anger.

As journalist and occult authority Gavin Baddeley observes, these and other central members of LaVey's "Magic Circle" were "an interestingly diverse bunch.... LaVey began to discern a common thread of 'productive alienation' among people who, like him, were regarded with suspicion because of their curious tastes and individuality but who were more creative and alive than the masses who sneered at them."[46] Analogous to the esoteric atmosphere that drove Aleister Crowley's reemergent popularity as a queer occult figure, LaVey knew it was no coincidence that his modern Church of Satan was founded in 1966 at the peak of the countercultural revolution, amid an individualistic generation eager to transgress the boundaries of American society through drugs, music, and sexual experience.[47] Although the High Priest of the Satanic Church hardly shied away from the seductively dark ambiance of Gothic horror, LaVey made it quite clear that his congregation didn't worship some "actual anti-deity named Satan who is the opposite of some imagined God."[48] "It's showmanship," LaVey admitted to *Los Angeles Times* reporter Dave Smith in July 1970: "Calling it a church enabled me to follow the magic formula of nine parts outrage and one part social respectability that is needed for success."[49]

Indeed, modern Satanism might best be described as indulgence in ritualistic performance practices and cultural productions that revel in "radical materialism and hedonistic individualism, [celebrating] the human body, ego, and sensual pleasure."[50] In a series of interviews captured by Ray Laurent in the rarely screened documentary *Satanis: The Devil's Mass* (1970), LaVey insistently indicts what he sees as the hypocrisy of most orthodox religions to pass judgment on both the sexual and spiritual lives of others: "We've taken all these hang-ups and turned them into useful situations. If you're going to be a sinner, be the best sinner on the block.... Sexual freedom is something we believe is very important as a necessary requisite of The Satanic Church.... I think it should be brought out that we not only condone, but we encourage all types of what would be called sexual perversities and deviations because we feel that in a few short years it'll be established that everyone is a sexual deviant, pervert, fetishist, or something or other."[51]

Further elaborated within the pages of LaVey's *Satanic Bible*, released the year before Laurent's documentary, Satanic magick endorses any type of sexual activity that "properly satisfies your individual desires—be it heterosexual, homosexual, bisexual, or even asexual, if you choose. Satanism also sanctions any fetish or deviation which will enhance your sex life, so long as it involves no one who does not wish to be involved."[52] Although the queer environment of LaVey's Satanic congregation as manifest in its members' curious tastes, nonconformity, and individuality did not necessarily extend to same-sex relationships for all, nonnormative sexual practices were embraced by many.

As members of LaVey's Satanic congregation delved deeper into esoteric teachings during the early 1960s, "[practicing] black magic, [putting] curses on their enemies, and [following] a philosophy of 'indulgence instead of abstinence,'" both their sexual and magickal rites bowed toward the darker sides of the occult.[53] As Jeffrey Sconce remarks in a fitting turn of phrase, Satanism became the "ultimate 'underground,'" presenting an aggressive hybridization of "subterranean sexuality with a fascination for increasingly 'adventurous,' thus taboo, forms of sexual behavior."[54] Although activities like human sacrifices were never officially reported at these gatherings, it was a well-publicized fact that one of the highest distinctions in the Church of Satan was to be chosen as "the altar," a naked young person on whom magickal rites were worked with knives, chalices, blood, semen, and so forth. These promiscuous practices were taken up during this period not only by LaVey and his followers but also by the Process Church of the Final Judgment, commonly known simply as the Process.

As Kenneth Anger became fond of saying during this period, "Making a movie is like casting a spell."[55] Aiming to expand on the subcultural success of *Fireworks*, Anger began work in 1961 on a new film that aimed to explore not only the captivatingly covert worlds of Satanic ritual and queer sex but also the burgeoning fetish iconography of gay leather-clad motorcycle riders made famous by Finnish artist Touko Valio Laaksonen, often known simply as Tom of Finland. The result, *Scorpio Rising*, is the short film for which the director is perhaps best known. Produced with a $10,000 grant from the Ford Foundation, whose members agreed with the California Supreme Court that Anger's work represented envelope-pushing artistic expression rather than prurient pornography, *Scorpio Rising* premiered in October 1963 at New York's Gramercy Arts Theater. Hailing it as the first crossover success of the American Underground, Elenore Lester of the *New York Times* wrote that the film offers, "in phantasmagoric color, a necromantic view of the horrors and charm of the motorcycle set, with its fetishistic leather and chains, its primitive rites and its death-sex-leather syndrome."[56]

Following one evening in the Satanic sex lives of a group of young men led by Scorpio (Bruce Byron), a leather-arrayed biker who becomes the embodiment of his namesake zodiac symbol, both the "house of death" and the "sexual sign," *Scorpio Rising*'s four-act structure differs from *Fireworks*' own magickally queer eroticism in significant ways.[57] Whereas *Fireworks* opts for a moody, melodramatic instrumental score reminiscent of a 1930s Universal horror film, *Scorpio Rising* features a medley of contemporary 1960s pop favorites. During the film's opening sequence, "Boys & Bolts," a group of young men engage in various rituals to prepare their bolts, both mechanical and genital, for a night out.[58] One young man in denim jeans and a black T-shirt uncovers his motorcycle and begins to tinker with and tweak the gears to Ricky Nelson's "Fools Rush In." Another, comparably dressed, polishes the chrome on his bike in masturbatory rhythm with the Angels' "My Boyfriend's Back." And another still, surrounded by bedroom walls plastered with images of James Dean, Marlon Brando, and one particularly prominent photograph of Bela Lugosi's Dracula, smokes a cigarette and strokes a cat to Elvis Presley's "(You're the) Devil in Disguise." All of these activities are intercut as Anger's camera consciously dwells on both the beefcake physiques of these young men, evocative of 1950s gay erotica magazines such as *Muscle Builder, Strength and Health*, and *VIM* (*Vigor Intellect Might*) that showcased "huge back muscles, tautened abdomens and hard flesh," and their fetishistic clothing: leather jackets, jeans, studs, and belts.[59]

If Anger and other Church of Satan members became absorbed in the darker sides of the occult during the 1960s, *Scorpio Rising*'s upbeat pop soundtrack paradoxically serves to both draw attention to and queer this shift. Songs that either presumptively or explicitly address relationships between men and women, staples of supposedly wholesome, mass mediated Americana, are refashioned in the film's homoerotic milieu of black magick, death, and queer desire. Fools rush in, Nelson's song tells us, "where angels fear to tread," an apt reference not only to hell itself but also to the leather-clad biker cult of Hell's Angels. For the young man whose boyfriend has returned, a black shrouded skeleton is present to oversee his masturbatory chrome polishing from a workbench on high. And while the biker enamored with Dean and Brando may attempt to usurp their staunchly heterosexual "bad boy" machismo as his own form of devilish disguise, it is also clear that the cat he gently strokes serves as an occult gender-bending device, as female witches were often thought to possess animal familiars sent by Satan to aid in their magickal workings.

Like *Fireworks*, *Scorpio Rising*'s climax is similarly centered on a genital event: a section entitled "Walpurgis Party." This queer bacchanal, a modernized form of the central and northern European witches' Sabbath known as Walpurgisnacht, features the male bikers arriving with other gay men at an abandoned warehouse turned Gothic church, removing several articles of clothing, and engaging in a bawdy Black Mass to the tunes of Claudine Clark's "Party Lights" and Kris Jensen's "Torture." As *Playboy* reported in a May 1974 exposé entitled "The Devil and the Flesh," clothing has always been discarded at the outset of the Satanic Black Mass: "nakedness is considered essential to the raising of the life forces that make magic work."[60] Yet whether or not *Scorpio Rising* expands the explicit visuality of queer occult sex already present in Anger's oeuvre is open to question.

On one hand, the film does present several shots of varying lengths displaying both flaccid and erect male genitalia. In addition to the climactic display of the money shot, the presentation of the male, especially erect, organ has often been framed as one constituent element that brackets hardcore pornography off from other "softer" forms of cinema's sexual representations. What's more, television inserts from a 1952 episode of *The Living Bible* entitled "The Last Journey to Jerusalem," wherein a blind man healed by Jesus kneels in front of the messiah, are intercut with close-ups of the bikers' erections. The queer defilement of Christian sacrament and the sacrilege of man-on-man fellatio are unmistakable. Indeed, as repressed by so-called pleasure-hating Christian orthodoxy, sexuality is naturally assumed to tend toward "many pathological forms. In such an instance, Satanism can be used to liberate oneself from this trap."[61] Yet on the other hand, the majority of *Scorpio Rising*'s queer Black Mass is choreographed as more humorous than harrowing. Although male genitalia are obviously present, pantless men mostly feign humping their companions as the erect shafts of others slap giggling faces. Whereas *Fireworks* is clear in marking the climax qua orgasm of its own occult narrative, such an obvious peak in *Scorpio Rising* is much more difficult to distinguish.

Describing the film in his own words, Anger once called *Scorpio Rising* a "death mirror held up to American culture . . . Thanatos in chrome, black leather, and bursting jeans."[62] Both *Scorpio Rising* and *Fireworks* present Satanic, subcultural fantasy worlds of phantasmagoric perversity in which practically everything is ripe for censure by heteronormative Christian orthodoxy. This is, as Dyer notes, precisely the point. The censure of metaphysical divination, Satanic worship, and queer sex is a surefire sign of their aptitude for "Magick invocation. If they were not conventionally wrong," then they could not possibly be occultly right.[63]

To be sure, such flouting of conventional norms emerged consistently across the pages of the US popular press in the late 1960s as the primary appeal of being a Satanist, bringing the sexual, spiritual, and psychedelic politics of booming hippie countercultures into sharp focus.[64] What Gavin Baddeley describes as the "sin, devil worship & rock 'n' roll" that began with *Scorpio Rising* was fully exacerbated later in the decade by performers like Jim Morrison, Jimmy Hendrix, and Arthur Brown. Brown seemed destined to become, Robb Baker of the *Chicago Tribune* wrote on September 8, 1968, "a priest of a new black cult in pop music. To them nothing is sacred. . . . Closely tied with the satanic is the erotic, stemming back to the sexy bad boy images of The Rolling Stones and The Animals. Anything that is taboo quickly becomes a *cause celebre*; lyrics are filled with allusions to homosexuality, promiscuity, prostitution, sado-masochism, etc."[65] Baker's reflections wouldn't take long to materialize in their full Satanic splendor, as the following year saw the premiere of Anger's twelve-minute short film, *Invocation of My Demon Brother*.

Set to the sounds of a Moog synthesizer played by Rolling Stones front man Mick Jagger, *Invocation of My Demon Brother* revels in a psychedelic tapestry of queer occult images, including rituals of fully nude men caressing each other on couches while fellow Satanic congregants smoke drugs out of a human skull. Within the lore of Anger's oeuvre, these twelve minutes were supposedly the opening of a first attempt at *Scorpio Rising*'s sequel, *Lucifer Rising*, whose own welcoming of a new Satanic dawn eventually did come to fruition when released in 1981. In *Invocation of My Demon Brother*'s queer bacchanal, the revelry is overseen both by His Satanic Majesty Anton LaVey (fig. 2.1) and Lucifer, played by Bobby Beausoleil.

Ironically, however, Anger's invocation of his demon brother in the person of Beausoleil would prove prophetic of tragedies to come later that year. In the same 1970 *Los Angeles Times* interview cited above, LaVey noted that Satanism was based on a foundational belief that man "cannot control his aggressions and hostilities until he faces up to them, admits they exist, then puts them to work in an unashamed pursuit of what he wants—be it emotional, sensual, or material."[66] To say that this creed was taken to an extreme late in 1969 would be a vast understatement. Indeed, as popular mythology had it, the devil was running wild in Southern California that summer.

On the evening of August 8, members of cult leader Charles Manson's "Family," an organization in which Beausoleil was purportedly a leading member, famously murdered the occupants at 10050 Cielo Drive just north of Beverly Hills, including Hollywood starlet Sharon Tate. Former "Family"

Fig. 2.1. Anton LaVey in *Invocation of My Demon Brother* (1969)

member Danny DeCarlo testified in September 1970 that the "bearded hippie leader [Manson] masqueraded as the 'devil' in the weeks preceding the murder of the blond movie star Sharon Tate and four others in August 1969. 'He said he was the devil, and that the devil was on the loose,' said Mr. DeCarlo, who ran the motorcycle gang the Straight Satans until he joined the Manson Family."[67] Satanism may have celebrated "access to any and all sensual pleasures—an invitation to lustful exploration that resonated within the postwar era's ongoing disarticulation of sex, marriage, and reproduction," but its hedonistic creeds walked a thin and often dangerous line.[68] This devilish confluence of "violence, filth, obscenities, mystery, [and] sex" would continue to be taken up by queer media on both sides of the Atlantic during the 1970s.[69]

The Devil Made Them Do It: Satanic Sexualities in 1970s Hardcore Pornography

Following the initial "blabberings of frankness" circulated by the work of Kenneth Anger and other Underground filmmakers, critics like Jonas

Mekas became keenly aware that the fusion of queer sexualities and the occult abetted by the movement was rapidly growing into a cinematic force to be reckoned with. Films like *Fireworks, Scorpio Rising,* and *Invocation of My Demon Brother* presented a world of "flowers of evil, of illuminations, of torn and tortured flesh; a poetry which is at once beautiful and terrible, good and evil, delicate and dirty. . . . These artists are without inhibitions, sexual or any other kind. . . . There is now a cinema for the few, too terrible and too 'decadent' for an 'average' man in any organized culture."[70] Although the Underground may have begun as a subcultural movement that flew in the face of most normative mores of the day, often representing queer subjects gone awry who were having an exceptionally fun time while they went there, such films should also be contextualized as part of broader developments in Euro-American cinema during this period, throughout which the introduction of "sexually explicit themes in fantasy form" quickly drove the silver screen toward the short-lived yet significant reign of the blue movie.[71]

By the latter half of the 1960s, what had originally begun as a list of "don'ts" and "be carefuls" in 1930 and gradually transformed into the fully fledged Motion Picture Production Code (a.k.a. Hays Code) in 1934 was over thirty years old. While the last bastions of the crumbling code were revised in 1966, it was obvious to MPAA president Jack Valenti that the rippling effects of 1960s counterculture on American society at large, "insurrection on the campus, riots in the streets, rise in women's liberation, protest of the young, doubts about the institution of marriage, abandonment of old guiding slogans, and the crumbling of social traditions," were simply unavoidable.[72] Consequently, on October 7, 1968, Valenti and the MPAA announced a new rating system that would take effect for all commercial films released in the United States after November 1: G (Suggested for General audiences), M (Suggested for Mature audiences), R (Restricted: Persons under 16 not admitted, unless accompanied by parent or adult guardian), and X (Persons under 16 not admitted). Although publicly couched as a response to consumer clamor for more mature and adult-oriented fare, including themes that the American Underground had dealt with for decades prior, the new rating system was first and foremost a business proposition: "The studios needed to update their product lines and the new rating system was a means toward that end. The new film classification system supported a product overhaul."[73]

The industrial endorsement of this product renovation was anticipated at least in part by the nearly unprecedented box office success of the horror genre that same year, capped off by the release of George Romero's *Night of the Living Dead* on October 1. But before then, on June 12, 1968, Paramount released a screen adaptation of Ira Levin's shocking Satanic thriller *Rosemary's Baby*, the best-selling horror novel of the 1960s. Directed by European art house auteur Roman Polanski, produced by American horror mogul William Castle, and starring Mia Farrow and John Cassavetes as a newlywed couple who become embroiled in the occult affairs of their necromantic neighbors in a New York City apartment building, *Rosemary's Baby* was nothing short of a massive commercial hit, earning over $33 million domestically on its way to becoming the eighth top-grossing film of the year. It had been eight years, since Alfred Hitchcock's *Psycho* shocked moviegoers in the summer of 1960, that a horror film had even managed to crack the American box office top ten. In one especially memorable scene throughout which occult forces arouse nonnormative sexual desires, Rosemary Woodhouse (Farrow) experiences a feverish hallucination in which she is ravished and raped by the devil during a nude Satanic orgy thrown by her neighbors after her husband has promised them their unborn child in exchange for help with his struggling acting career. The woeful irony, of course, is that Rosemary's dream turns out to be a crushing supernatural reality. And while never officially confirmed, rumors circulated among occult circles and in the popular press after the film's release that Polanski had employed Anton LaVey himself to serve as both the demonic impregnator and technical advisor for this infamous scene.

By the time the MPAA's new rating rubric took effect on November 1, 1968, then, it was clear that two of the often-overlapping product sectors that shaped and would subsequently be most affected by this new industrial shift were horror films and movies dealing with explicit sexual content. As Jon Lewis notes, the primary purpose of the rating system's inauguration was to "differentiate between product lines, to inform parents about film content and more importantly to better describe and promote in advance of release films with erotic, violent, and/or controversial content."[74] Nevertheless, while the MPAA may have encouraged a more adult-oriented revamping of motion pictures during the late 1960s, it had no intention of driving the American film industry toward a pruriently focused product line. Submission of films to the Classification & Ratings Administration (CARA), the independent agency that administered the new rating system, was voluntary but lack of submission, review, and approval meant the potential alienation not only of audiences but also of theaters that would only exhibit MPAA-sanctioned films under the auspices of the National Association of Theater Owners (NATO). Moreover, given that Valenti and his peers never planned to officially recognize those films ghettoized into the final category, copyright protection for the X rating was never sought.

Between 1968 and 1972, not all X-rated films were de facto pornographic. But the fact that the X rating could be self-imposed by independent distributors as a ballyhoo marketing tactic, a "come-on to adult audiences and a guarantee of a certain kind of entertainment," quickly equated broadly controversial content more specifically with "prurient content (which ranged from soft-core simulation to hard-core live action)."[75] Paradoxically, the self-imposition of the X rating, eventually giving way to both XX and finally XXX, actually lent such films an air of legitimacy, advertising an official MPAA designation even though CARA review never took place. Major studios shied away from the production of X-rated films for fear of alienating audiences and losing revenue, and such reluctance consequently allowed independent producers and distributors to exploit this market segment: "Within six months of the institution of the MPAA ratings system, companies such as American International, Cinerama, Cinemation, Times Films, and Trans-Lux" were all self-applying the X rating to their films.[76]

By April 1970, *Variety* staff writer Addison Verrill remarked that a significant segment of the American public had begun enthusiastically purchasing screen sex in "all its variations," especially while flocking to experience the titillating novelty of X-rated films.[77] On a screen-by-screen basis, X-rated productions were outearning a majority of major studio releases. Supported by the introduction of 16mm as a legitimate theatrical gauge, driving down the cost of production and exhibition in comparison to 35mm, what began as a series of salacious storefront exhibitors playing "beaver loops" and "straight stag loops with two or more people doing what comes naturally and not faking it" suddenly took on more sophisticated possibilities.[78] As William Paul reported on May 20, 1971, in the *Village Voice*, "First-class pornography on the order of the stag films normally shown in the privacy of one's home . . . has made its way into ordinary movie theatres in varying shapes and sizes, becoming a big money maker in New York's entertainment industry. Porn has slowly insinuated itself into the public eye and sidestepped the law . . . which managed both to satisfy and whet curiosity at the same time with the question, what could they do next?"[79]

X-rated films had finally gone all the way in terms of explicitness and transparency of sexual representation, marking the transition from softcore allusion to hardcore frankness, so the next logical step for porn producers seemed to be the inclusion of these acts within broader story arcs amassed from the narrative conventions of established film genres. "Without plot," Michael Goodwin of the *Village Voice* wrote, "believable characters are impossible; and without believable characters, all you've got are impossibly inexpressive cocks and cunts."[80]

No matter how much it was still regarded as an industrial outsider, hardcore narrative pornography was now "more a genre among other genres than it was a special case. As if to insist on this fact, hard-core narratives went about imitating other Hollywood genres with a vengeance, inflecting well-known titles and genres with an X-rated difference."[81] Americans could anxiously look forward, Paul predicted, to the introduction of gangster porn, cowboy porn, musical-comedy porn, and, of course, horror porn.[82] As the "dark overlord of a larger interest in occult sexuality," Sconce argues, Satan and his devilish minions presided over a "ludic proliferation of transgressive temptation and 'forbidden' pleasures in adult media," inaugurating a prominent occult subgenre in the era's "developing and increasingly brazen pornography industry."[83] Considering the upsurge of interest in countercultural occult practices and exposés detailing their "odd piece[s] of sexual behavior" reported across the country in publications like *Time*, *Esquire*, *McCall's*, *Look*, and *Playboy*, it was hardly surprising that hardcore pornographers began using magick, witchcraft, and Satanism as topical frameworks around which to build big-screen erotic fantasies.[84]

"Nothing is so fascinating," Anton LaVey was often fond of saying of both sex and the supernatural, "as that which is not meant to be seen."[85] While the hardcore pornographic phenomenon was beginning to cast its own spell across the globe, Satanism was still very much in vogue. By 1972, LaVey claimed that there were over twenty thousand card-carrying members of the Church of Satan dispersed throughout its congregations in the United States alone. Having already achieved massive crossover success with a comedic porn feature, the infamous *Deep Throat*, adult auteur Gerard Damiano decided to use this Satanic fervor in the service of checking another hybrid product off of William Paul's prophetic list. The result, *The Devil in Miss Jones*, premiered at New York's 57th Street Playhouse on March 28, 1973, to widespread critical acclaim and subsequently broke all box office records for a commercial adult film.

In a review for the *Chicago Sun-Times*, Roger Ebert praised Damiano's production as the "best hard-core porno film I've seen," and applauded its star, Georgina Spelvin, as "not only the best, but possibly the only, actress in the hard-core field. By that I mean when she's on the screen, her body and actions aren't the only reasons we're watching her."[86] Echoing this appraisal, *Variety* favorably compared *The Devil in Miss Jones* to Jean-Paul Sartre's existential masterwork *No Exit* and wrote that "with 'The Devil in Miss Jones,' the hardcore porno feature approaches an 'art form,' one that critics may have a tough time ignoring in future. For its genre, the pic is a sensation, marked by a technical polish that pales some recent Hollywood product and containing some of the most frenzied and erotic sex sequences in porno memory."[87]

Justine Jones (Spelvin) is a woman whose earthly existence has trudged along day to day without much in the way of actual living. Pensively peering out the window of her shoddy apartment onto a dreary, rain-soaked street, this young yet matronly woman decides that her only course of action is simply to end it all. Stripping off her silk kimono, drawing a bath, and procuring a razor blade, Justine slits her wrists and waits for death to whisk her away. Yet after a fleeting fade to black, Justine is revived, fully clothed in a black dress, white shawl, and white gloves while walking toward a large wooden table inside the drawing room of what appears to be a European chateau. Seated at the table on a high-backed wooden chair is Mr. Abaca (John Clemens, a.k.a. Gregory Pecker), who guardedly informs Miss Jones that, having committed the unpardonable sin of suicide, she is presently waiting in purgatory before being sent directly to hell. Abaca's name, of course, is an abbreviated form of the mystic *abracadabra* incantation used not just by modern stage illusionists but also by esoteric magicians dating as far back as the Gnostics, meaning "I will create as I speak."

"If you have to go to Hell," *The Devil in Miss Jones*'s tagline reads, "go for a reason." It is the satisfaction of this reason that drives the remainder of the film's narrative. "If only I'd done something, anything," Justine laments of her damned fate, "it wouldn't be so bad." Responding to her brooding grief, Abaca nudges, "How about lust?" "Yes, lust," Justine responds in an impulsive burst of enthusiasm, "If I did have my life to live over . . . I would live a life filled . . . engulfed . . . consumed by lust." As *New Yorker* drama critic Brendan Gill writes in an advertisement for the film, "Mr. Damiano is at once a moralist (suicide is the unforgiveable sin on which the plot of the movie turns)" and an unabashed hedonist, "for whom the naked human body is the beginning and end of joy."[88] Granted the brief stint of worldly lasciviousness she pines for, Justine is shown into an adjacent room after her meeting with Abaca and is dispassionately greeted by a robed man known only as the Teacher (hardcore icon Harry Reems). Commanded to undress before him, Justine's lustful journey commences when the magickal will of the Teacher overcomes Justine's initial reluctance, persuading her to bend over and receive a butt plug as the first step in her wanton initiation toward appreciating boundary-pushing pain alongside her sexual pleasure. Indeed, as Sconce notes, Satanism is a religion of "power and will. . . . Accordingly, occult sexploitation [and later hardcore pornography] most typically involved perverse scenarios of sexual domination," wherein the mind and/or body of the subject is compelled by the will of occult forces.[89] Typically tight-framed, hardcore action shots between Justine and the Teacher follow, including both vaginal and anal intercourse, while the viewer becomes increasingly aware that Reems's character, teaching Miss Jones the earthly ways of sin and lust, is a well-endowed embodiment of Satan himself. "I've waited for you so long," Justine says in a direct addresses to the Teacher's erect penis qua magick wand, "I must have your power."

In his *Film Maker's Guide to Pornography*, Stephen Ziplow recommends that in order to satisfy the desires of heterosexual male audiences, the demographic most aggressively targeted during the porno chic era, the conventions of the hardcore feature should be reduced to seven essential elements: masturbation, straight sex, lesbianism, oral sex, ménage à trois, orgies, and anal sex.[90] While *The Devil in Miss Jones* certainly fulfills these requirements, particularly a prolonged female-on-female tryst, it also adds its own queerly occult spin on them. Practices of Satanic magick in the 1970s were not simply intent on promoting "healthy, happy, pleasurable sex for a more open society," but were especially invested in exploring "sexual areas that were considered most taboo: sexual fetishes and deviant desires of all varieties."[91] Spelvin's masturbation sequences, for instance, all include the use of various animate and inanimate props. In one especially infamous scene, Justine lies nude on a bed while caressing, tantalizing, teasing, and masturbating with a live snake, both a reference to Satan in the Garden of Eden often taken up in ritual practices of LaVey's congregation and, like the cat stroked by the biker in *Scorpio Rising*, an animal familiar for Miss Jones's magickal use.

But perhaps *The Devil in Miss Jones*'s most unexpectedly queer flaunting of normative hardcore conventions comes toward the conclusion of the film, in the requisite ménage à trois/orgy sequence. Consumed by a magickal sex drive that refuses to quit and ultimately conquers the passion of her partners, Justine lies face down between two men, one penetrating her from below while the other penetrates her from behind. Miss Jones is, however, little else than a queer interlocutor between these two men, variously addressing her partners with such orgasmic exclamations as "Can you feel your prick against his?," "Does it feel good?," "Can you feel his prick?," and "Can you feel your cocks together?" As a pornographic plot device, magick poses distinct advantages: "Once under this invisible influence, otherwise 'straight' subjects could be compelled into group sex, fetishism, bestiality, and homosexuality."[92] Yet in the context of the 1970s hardcore feature, these otherwise straight subjects performing acts of perverse deviance were almost invariably assumed to be women, displayed for the titillation of a presumptively heterosexual male audience. *The Devil in Miss Jones* isn't unique for the repertoire of sexual gymnastics that Georgina Spelvin performs but rather is exceptional for using Satanic magick as a catalyst for the inclusion of both female and male homoeroticism. Even though Williams confidently claims that "in heterosexual porno . . . no male-to-male relations of any kind occur," this ménage à trois sequence in *The Devil in Miss Jones* demonstrates that this structuring absence is really not much of an absence at all.[93] As both this scene and its participants reach their respective climaxes, the "meat shot" from behind displays both men pulling out of Miss Jones's body and simultaneously orgasming not on her but rather on each other.

According to Laura Kipnis in *Bound and Gagged: Pornography and the Politics of Fantasy in America*, pornography is an infinitely revealing genre, "and what it reveals isn't just a lot of naked people sweating on each other. It exposes the culture to itself. . . . Pornography begins at the edge of the culture's decorum. Carefully tracing that edge . . . gives you a detailed blueprint of the culture's anxieties, investments, contradictions. And a culture's borders, whether geographical or psychological, are inevitably political questions."[94] As pro-sex feminists during the porno chic era and beyond have argued, critiques of pornography are too often reduced solely to the question of whether the acts, bodies, and pleasures represented provide a progressive model for female sexuality. What staunchly pro-censorship critics like Andrea Dworkin and Catharine MacKinnon have often dismissed is pornography's intimate engagement with individualized sexual fantasies. While Justine Jones is sent to a personal hell in which she can no longer achieve orgasm at the conclusion of *The Devil in Miss Jones*, her continued attempts at doing so before the final fade to black provide a similar mixture of pleasure and pain to that which the Teacher first introduced her.

One truth that hardcore pornography may tell, then, is that all people have the opportunity to conceptualize their sexualities any way they see fit, even if it involves initiation into queer occult sex rituals facilitated by Satan himself. Indeed, as Marty Klein notes of hardcore's politics of personal fantasy, "Social norms regarding age and beauty, religious norms about godly and ungodly sex, personal fears about acceptance, cultural myths about the human body—all of these are ignorable; none are inevitable. Each of us can triumph [through pornography] over the ways social institutions attempt to control our sexual experience and expression."[95] Even still, hardcore pornography was not the only 1970s screen genre that adopted fantasy as doubly articulated: as both sexual and supernatural.

Le sexe qui parle du surnaturel: Queer Occultism in the European Art House

Prior to the arrival of porno chic in the early 1970s, adventurous American filmgoers on the lookout for sexual titillation could often find the excitement they sought not only in those "bump-and-grind houses" that catered to patrons of sexploitation films but also in the halls of art house cinemas that screened such stimulating European imports as Ingmar Bergman's *Summer with Monika* (1953), Roger Vadim's *And God Created Woman* (1956), Louis Malle's *The Lovers* (1958), and Vilgot Sjöman's *I Am Curious (Yellow)* (1967). As film historians have documented at length, the popular rise of European art cinema in the postwar United States can be attributed to a variety of intertwining factors above and beyond the Paramount Decision's heralding of classical Hollywood studio decline in 1948: "The increased American interest in all things foreign; the end of political isolationism; increased travel opportunities; the increased sophistication of the viewing public," and the powerful transformation of sexual mores among certain segments of the American public.[96] Comparatively explicit representations of sexuality joined with the "pacing, the blatant disregard for the cause-effect logic of classical Hollywood cinema, the strategic use of discontinuous editing, [and] the painterly composition of certain scenes" all served to bracket off particular European imports as sophisticated art cinema for discerning American audiences.[97] Akin to the later narrative consolidation of hardcore pornography, midcentury European art cinema similarly distinguished itself through more abstracted, experimental, and sexually explicit takes on canonical film genres, with horror proving no exception.

Beginning in the early 1960s, through a whirlwind scramble for product to fill theater billings, domestic distributors such as American International Pictures, Trans American Films, and Aquarius Releasing, Inc. began importing a series of supernatural films from France, Italy, Spain, and elsewhere that celebrated the graphic, excessive, ritualistic, perverse, and queer sides of the occult; movies that often explored the boundaries between terror and eroticism in ways that were atypical of the more prudish American horror productions being released at the time.[98] These same distributors would also be among the very first to self-apply the MPAA X rating to their films after 1968. Indeed, the stateside success of films like Mario Bava's *Black Sunday* (1960) and *Black Sabbath* (1963), Roger Vadim's *Blood and Roses* (1960), and Sergio Corbucci and Antonio Margheriti's *Castle of Blood* (1964) drew attention to an aspect of art cinema generally overlooked, according to Joan Hawkins, in cultural analysis: namely, the degree to which high culture "trades on the same images, tropes, and themes that characterize low culture."[99] If horror and sexuality had been kindred spirits of low genre pedigree since at least the classical exploitation era in the United States, their thematic incorporation into European art cinema made for similarly popular, if somewhat more paradoxical, bedfellows.

As Hawkins, Ian Olney, and others have suggested while peering through a Bordieuan lens of distinction, the history of film studies' struggle to become a legitimate scholarly discipline goes a long way in explaining why popular cinematic forms like horror and pornography have been marginalized by the academic intelligentsia.[100] Such affect-laden films, characterized by their capacity to "thrill, frighten, gross out, arouse, or otherwise directly engage the spectator's body," have marked these genres as especially tainted forms of cinematic culture, incapable of maintaining the spectatorial distance assumed to be one of the key criteria for the contemplative, refined, and mature appreciation of the medium.[101] During the 1960s and 1970s, that topless witches, lesbian vampires, Satanic dungeon masters, and crumbling Gothic chateaus of iniquity, all queer hallmarks of the emergent Euro-sleaze subgenre, should be hybridized into an art house tradition pioneered by names like Bergman, Fellini, De Sica, and Bresson seemed unlikely to some, ludicrous to more, and simply blasphemous to many. Yet taking the occult films of artists like Jean Rollin seriously, as both popular and academic critics have been reluctant to do, reveals not only how European horror films have partaken in art cinema's "'high' culture project of exploring new means of formal and narrative expression," but also how art cinema's unending search for new creative horizons queered its "low" cultural associations with both sex and the supernatural.¹⁰²

Born November 3, 1938, in the Nueilly-sur-Seine region of France, Jean Rollin was a member of a theatrically inclined family that actively encouraged his blossoming attraction to motion pictures and popular culture from an early age. During this formative period, the young Jean not only fell in love with the magic of movies but also with American serial comics such as *Jungle Jim*, *The Shadow*, and *The Mysterious Dr. Satan*, all stories of the occultly marvelous that would productively haunt the aspiring filmmaker throughout his career. At sixteen, Rollin landed his first job at Les Films de Saturne, a French production company specializing in industrial shorts and documentaries. Later, during his required stint in the French armed services, Rollin worked as an editor in the military cinema department alongside Claude Lelouch, whose 1966 film *A Man and a Woman* would go on to win the Palme d'Or at the Cannes Film Festival.

After producing several of his own shorts, Rollin's first feature, the expressionistic *Le Viol du Vampire* (*The Rape of the Vampire*), was only one of two new films to arrive on the screens of Parisian movie houses the week of its premiere in May 1968, the same month that student protests and union strikes brought both the DeGaulle government and the French nation to the brink of collapse. As Cathal Tohill and Pete Tombs emphasize of France's very first vampire film, "The spirit of insurrection was in the air. People were looking for something new and startling. They certainly found it in *Le Viol du Vampire*."¹⁰³ A self-proclaimed "melodrama in two parts," the latter following the meandering narrative of a Sapphic, pagan-worshipping, topless vampire queen in her queer quest for a new bride and blood, *Le Viol du Vampire*'s "bizarre concoction of Surrealism, Dadaism, and poetry" became the subject of vehement criticism from Rollin's critics, colleagues, and audiences in and around Paris.¹⁰⁴

By all accounts, even his own, Rollin's first feature was a failure. After *Le Viol du Vampire*'s release and subsequent critical defamation, Rollin was cast as an indelible *enfant terrible* of the French filmmaking scene. The film's efforts toward representing the pensive, abject nuances of nonnormative sexualities were deemed artificial, and its attempts at aestheticizing conventions of occult horror were condemned as laughably incompetent. Nevertheless, in spite of this supposedly botched attempt at rearticulating the supernatural charms of the cinema, it was precisely the *success de scandale* of *Le Viol du Vampire* that earned Rollin his reputation as an auteur of queer occult erotica, one that would make his name an increasingly popular one among permissive moviegoers on both sides of the Atlantic.

By the turn of the 1970s, the expectation that European imports would include more explicit displays of sexuality than was feasible in a domestic American production led to a causal industrial logic in which European film, art film, adult film, and sex film became practically synonymous.[105] For example, the American press kit for Columbia's release of Just Jaeckin's *Emmanuelle* was headlined by the following statement: "X has never been known for its elegance. Or for its beautiful people. Or for its intelligent story line. X has been known for other things. At Columbia Pictures we're proud to bring you a movie that will change the meaning of X. A movie that begins with the sensual and takes it places X has never been before."[106] This assumption of a more explicit sexual repertoire became a maxim not only for audiences across major metropolitan centers in the United States but also for European audiences as well, particularly in blue-collar and immigrant communities like Marseilles, who expected certain segments of their domestic film industries to live up to a budding international reputation for unbridled eroticism and perverse titillation.

During early-stage filming for *Le Viol du Vampire*, Jean Rollin befriended American expatriate producer Samuel Selsky (later credited as $amuel $elsky), who agreed to both produce his first feature and back it financially. Foreseeing the swelling tides of cine-erotic change across the Atlantic, Selsky anticipated that Rollin's penchant for refracting the queer sexualities of the occult through the prism of art cinema could be successfully exported to ride the wave of both racy European imports and explicitly pornographic fare that was appearing at exponential rates across the United States. Yet after the domestic scandal that surrounded *Le Viol du Vampire* as a pretentious, obtuse, and impenetrable navel-gazing exercise, the film never made it across French borders until its home video incarnation in the early 1990s. In an effort to garner at least some measure of financial return on later productions, Rollin began bowing to Selsky's demands for more straightforwardly supernatural, Satanic, and sexually driven fare, creating continental companions to Hammer's own refashioning of the lesbian vampire film. Remaining committed to his conviction that the horrors of sexuality could still be expressed through the poetic characteristics of the cinema, however, Rollin aspired to introduce "fantastic elements into the everyday world, to push the normal until it becomes super-normal . . . the creation of an atmosphere in which anything could happen—and frequently does."[107]

Both *Le Frisson des Vampires* (*The Shiver of the Vampires*) and its follow-up, *Requiem pour un Vampire* (*Requiem for a Vampire*), fuse queer sexualities and the occult in ways best understood through Tzvetan Todorov's notion of "the fantastic." Originally published in 1970, Todorov's *Introduction à la littérature fantastique* (*The Fantastic: A Structural Approach to a Literary Genre*) describes situations in which individuals are confronted with supernatural events that cannot be explained by natural laws: "In a world which is indeed our world, the one we know, a world without devils, sylphides, or vampires, there occurs an event which cannot be explained by the laws of this same familiar world. The person who experiences the event must opt for one of two possible solutions: either he is the victim of an illusion of the senses ... or else the event has indeed taken place; it is an integral part of reality."[108] The fantastic, then, is composed of those moments of hesitation and indecision experienced by a person who knows "only the laws of nature, confronting an apparently supernatural event."[109] In Hammer films like the Karnstein trilogy, truly fantastic moments are rare, as vampirism, witchcraft, and other occultly marvelous occurrences are always already naturalized as part of the folkloric milieu of a distant past. In both *Le Frisson des Vampires* and *Requiem pour un Vampire*, however, both queer sexualities and Satanic magick are presented as fantastic phenomena that must be accepted, learned, and incorporated into new horizons of occult reality.

In *Le Frisson des Vampires*, what begins as a pastoral love story between two newlyweds quickly develops into a queer necromantic nightmare. En route to a honeymoon holiday following their marriage, Antoine (Jean-Marie Durand) and Isle (Sandra Julien) agree to take a detour in order to visit the country chateau of Isle's cousins, estranged family members whom she has not seen since early childhood. On arriving at the cousins' village, however, the couple is informed by a local widow that the two men died the previous day and have already been buried in the chateau's graveyard. Compelled to pay their last respects, Isle and Antoine arrive at the chateau and find an interior decor far from anticipated, as a measured 360° pan reveals an austere master dining room where emblematic occult paraphernalia (decaying skulls, burning torches, lit candles, etc.) are set against stone walls that abound with overly saturated colors.

Rather than consummating their marriage that evening, Isle implores Antoine to be left alone with her grief for just one night. As the young bride later strips nude at the stroke of midnight, a grandfather clock in the corner of her bedchamber creaks open to reveal Isolde (Dominique), a female

Fig. 2.2. Isolde (Dominique) in *Le Frisson des Vampires* (1971)

vampire clad in purple tunic and hippie jewelry, emerging from within (fig. 2.2). This image, one of the most iconic in Rollin's oeuvre, poses a suggestive juxtaposition of the Old World superstition of a vampire emerging from her coffin with the look of an à la mode young woman expressing herself through countercultural fashion. As Danny Shipka notes, crumbling castles populated by the souls of undead Satanic servants may be archetypal features in *Le Frisson des Vampires* and other Rollin productions, but "mining the rebellious nature of France's youth in the early 1970s is where Rollin takes his inspiration . . . scenes of semi-nude female vampires (with extraordinarily large teeth) rising out of grandfather clocks was a clear signal that Rollin believed the youth of France was waking up."[110] Indeed, such newfound awareness comes to the fore most often in Rollin's films vis-à-vis which side of the hesitation to accept the fantastic and supernatural characters ultimately land on. For Isle, her incredulous facial reactions to a female vampire emerging from a grandfather clock and gently caressing her hair and bare breasts quickly give way not only to occult acquiescence but also to its queer sexual pleasures. As Isolde ushers Isle out of the chateau and into the night with the assurance that there are many things she has yet to learn, a Satanic mass complete with pentagrams and black candles awaits in the graveyard for the two nude women to consummate their magickal union.

Noticing a distinct change in his bride the following evening, Antoine is shocked when Isle's presumed-dead cousins (Jacques Robiolles and

Michel Delahaye) suddenly appear to greet the couple over dinner. Chalking their deaths up to innocuous rumormongering among the village locals, the cousins embark on a lengthy exposition of their reclusive lives and occult research. Both men, dressed similarly in crushed velvet blazers, white ruffled shirts, and rainbow-tinted velvet pants, and adorned with gold necklaces, rings, and bangles, are visually coded as an incestuously queer twosome. As both men explain in tandem, Isle's family has been responsible for maintaining the worship of an ancient pagan god after its prohibition as witchcraft in the Middle Ages, including the continued practice of certain esoteric rites deemed blasphemous by the Catholic Church. Significantly, almost every shot of the cousins' espousals on metaphysics and magick abandons an equitable shot-reverse-shot pattern and is framed by low-angle close-ups from Antoine's point of view, indicating that his status as the lone arbiter of heterosexual masculinity is under assault within the walls of this queer Gothic chateau. While Antoine writes her cousins off as nothing but a couple of superstitious buffoons, Isle feels that she has finally come home to her rightful family.

For the remainder of *Le Frisson des Vampires*, Antoine fights to save Isle from the tightening queer grips of both her cousins and Isolde. Having been heterosexually coupled vampire hunters in their previous lives, the cousins are revealed as Isolde's victims who now serve her and an unidentified "Master of the World," a clear reference to Satan given the film's penchant for repeated stagings of the Black Mass. Despite his best efforts, however, Antoine cannot stop Isle from falling farther under the spell of Isolde's queer magick. "I belong to the world of darkness," Isolde tells her lover, "whose eternal joys will be yours. Your cousins and I are messengers down here . . . you will become one of us and others like us." Though Isolde is eventually dispatched when locked in a mausoleum and poisoned by the necessity of drinking her own blood, Antoine's heterosexual prowess does not win the day, as both Isle and her cousins flee to a beach at dawn and are suddenly evaporated by the rays of the rising sun, leaving the bridegroom frantically flailing down the shoreline while calling out for his bride.

Released in 1970, *Le Frisson des Vampires* was produced on the "very cusp of change in French erotic cinema," when full frontal nudity and hardcore sex were still forbidden, at least officially, by national censorship guidelines.[111] It wasn't until October 1976, with the passage of France's "X Law," that hardcore pornography was formally sanctioned as a legitimate option for screening among movie house fare. Yet as Dominique's image on the cover of the Autumn 1970 issue of *Midi Minuit Fantastique*, a French film quarterly specializing in horror and science fiction, reveals, *Le Frisson des Vampires* consciously drew on the allures of the female centerfold and other pornographic tropes to narrate its occultly queer tale. What's more, magazines like *Midi Minuit Fantastique* built on a storied tradition of American publications that had exploited occult sex rituals and Satanism since at least the 1950s, including such titles as *Satan, Satana, Black Magic, Naked, Satan Sex Ceremonies, Bitchcraft, Sexual Witchcraft*, and *Witches & Bitches*.

To make the pornographic potential of Euro-sleaze art cinema even more enticing during the early 1970s, films like *Le Frisson des Vampires* were often packaged by distributors with optional "hardcore inserts" that proved especially popular among permissive audiences in France, Italy, Spain, and the United States: faceless, generic sex acts having nothing to do with the film's plot or characters but ones that could easily be spliced into appropriate scenes should exhibitors deem it lucrative for business. Indeed, as Olney argues, one of the most distinctive features of European occult cinema of this period is the way in which such films tended to fuse "sex with violence to tell stories that could be described as both horrific and pornographic."[112] In *Le Frisson des Vampires*' follow-up, *Requiem pour un Vampire*, this pornographic impulse was pushed to even greater extremes, earning Rollin his most critically and financially successful American import during the 1970s.

Released in France in 1971 and stateside in 1973, Rollin wrote *Requiem pour un Vampire* at the behest of producer Lionel Wallmann, who was looking for a "sex-horror project that could be shot inexpensively on a four-week schedule."[113] The resulting film tells the story of Michelle (Mireille Dargent) and Marie (Marie-Pierre Castel), two young women who, on the run from an unknown crime, find themselves in a country graveyard at dusk and are bitten by two lingering bats. Reflecting their consequent trancelike voyage with visible bite marks on their necks, extreme canted angle shots bring the two women to the gates of a Gothic chateau similar to the one that served as the setting of *Le Frisson des Vampires*. Once inside, Marie and Michelle discover a fur-lined bed on which they sit, strip, and begin to caress each other lovingly. Like Isle's first encounter with Isolde, this occultly motivated sex scene seems entirely natural and pleasurable for both parties. Within Rollin's oeuvre, queer sex and acquiescence to the fantastic's supernatural laws become two sides of the same coin.

After their trance-induced tryst is interrupted by clashing sounds coming from outside the bedchamber, Marie and Michelle quickly dress to explore the chateau, only to happen on a dilapidated chapel where a Satanic Black Mass appears to be in progress. As the robed figures present are shown one by one, each is revealed to be a cloaked skeleton except the one playing the organ, who slowly turns around to expose herself as the vampire Erica (Dominique), sporting massively protruding fangs. Fleeing to avoid an impending demise, the women eventually find themselves back at the same graveyard from which they began their journey. They are cornered by Erica, an older female vampire named Louise (Louise Dhour), and their gang of Neanderthal henchmen, but the entire group is silenced when an ancient male vampire known only as the Master (Michel Delesalle), possibly the unseen "Master of the World" from *Le Frisson des Vampires*, emerges from a mausoleum. Two bats fly out from under the Master's cape and once again attach themselves to Marie and Michelle's necks as the entire entourage slowly descends into the mausoleum's dungeon.

In discussing generic conventions of pornography, Williams argues that the hardcore feature closely resembles the structure of the classical Hollywood musical vis-à-vis its predilection to give particular "numbers" the "conflict-resolving function or expression of ultimate satisfaction of the musical's love song."[114] In *Requiem pour un Vampire*, this episodic combination of number and narrative becomes apparent as Erica and Louise's henchmen abandon the group at the entryway of the mausoleum's dungeon to enact a brutal, lascivious bacchanal on other imprisoned young women who are already nude and chained to stone pillars. Bathed in a Satanically surreal red light, the sexual number that follows doesn't include hardcore meat or money shots, but the narrative is unquestionably interrupted in the service of drawing extended attention to the spectacle of fully nude female bodies being sexually ravished. The final shot of the sequence, a slow tilt from bared breasts down to a close-up of a bat performing cunnilingus on one of the women, becomes a fitting aide-mémoire of the ways in which Rollin's films consciously associate the occult with pleasurable sexual perversities.

Enlisted to serve the Master after receiving his "blessed malediction," both Marie and Michelle are tasked with drawing local villagers to the chateau so that its resident vampires might feed. One of these targets, a young man named Frédéric (Philippe Gasté), befriends Marie and learns of her and Michelle's plight. As Frédéric begins snooping around the chateau, however, Louise and Erica demand that Michelle and Marie tell them where Frédéric has suddenly gone into hiding so that he may be silenced. Before the latter two women escape the castle together by the film's conclusion, Michelle implores Marie to give the vampires the information they seek. When Marie refuses, Michelle, who has just confessed her undying love for her friend, is forced by Erica to take Marie into the chateau's dungeon, strip her naked, and whip her until Frédéric's location is disclosed.

Perhaps the most infamous section of *Requiem pour un Vampire*, this intensely homoerotic whipping scene between Michelle and Marie represents a significant sexual number that replicates the "sadie-max" (sadomasochism) tradition of the hardcore feature. What marks the sadie-max number as especially transgressive and particularly perverse is not necessarily the "extremity of violence enacted or endured . . . but rather the way in which violence, aggression, and pain become vehicles for other things—for staging dramas of suspense, supplication, abandon, and relief that enhance or substitute for sexual acts."[115] Akin to Anger's ritualistic sacrifice in *Fireworks* or Justine Jones's acquiescence to limit-pushing sexual acts in *The Devil in Miss Jones*, Marie's facial expressions reflect a similarly gruesome combination of pleasure and pain as she and Michelle work through dominant versus submissive, top versus bottom, and other dichotomous fantasies of queer power exchange previously latent in their relationship.

Significantly, however, the queer resonances of this scene are not limited to the surface of a ritualized female-on-female S&M act. As Williams remarks of hardcore's sadie-max practices, particularly its female-on-female forms, "It certainly seems possible that male viewers can [also] identify with the active woman. . . . But perhaps we should not rule out less active forms of identification—that is, identification with the passive woman who is given pleasure and abandons herself to the control of the other. Spectatorial pleasure in such scenes may very well involve the ability to identify both ways."[116] This gender-bending sexual flexibility of identificatory viewing positions is achieved in *Requiem pour un Vampire*'s own sadie-max number not only through the sexual fantasy structures of the Satanic diegesis but also formally through a shot-reverse-shot pattern that, like Carmilla's feline attack on Emma in *The Vampire Lovers*, places the spectator in a revolving-door relationship between Marie and Michelle: between activity and passivity, dominance and submission, predator and prey. Recalling Carol Clover's formative analysis of the serial killer versus Final Girl relationship in the modern slasher film,[117] the mixture of queer sexuality and occultism that characterizes Rollin's and other European horror films of the 1970s affords viewers the potential to do what Olney terms "'play dead'—to approach film spectatorship as a form of performance in which they are free to adopt multiple viewing positions and to experiment with different subjectivities in a fashion generally proscribed by mainstream cinema and the dominant social order."[118]

Indeed, it was precisely such hardcore-reminiscent sequences that were responsible for earning *Requiem pour un Vampire* an American theatrical release through Boxoffice International, the powerhouse exploitation distributor headed by mogul Harry Novak that was famous for releases which "always carried what was then known as a 'soft X' rating."[119] As Tohill and Tombs note, it is hardly surprising that many European directors and producers in the early 1970s were casting "envious glances over the waters to the U.S., where films like *Deep Throat* were creating a porno boom that was making fortunes from very low investments."[120] Dubbed into English and released under the title *Caged Virgins* in January 1973, *Boxoffice*'s original review of *Requiem pour un Vampire* noted that Rollin's film was "replete with blood-seeking, groans, gestures, and gesticulations calculated to endear the goings-on to the horror buff. There's some nudity as the girls are worked over by the weird sect."[121] Although *Caged Virgins* seemed to herald the materialization of a permissive media marketplace "relatively wide open as far as sheer vampire horror, per se, is concerned," the occult zenith of both porno chic and the Euro-sleaze phenomena was short-lived.[122]

On June 21, 1973, the US Supreme Court handed down its ruling in what has become one of the most influential obscenity trials in American history: *Miller v. California*. In 1971, Marvin Miller, operator of a modest mail-order business specializing in pornographic books and films, was arrested in his home state of California for distributing brochures that advertised sexually explicit materials. Under the local community standards statute of the *Roth* test, the Superior Court of Orange County found Miller guilty of all charges. However, since the high court of the nation had been interested in revisiting obscenity jurisprudence for several years prior, Miller was granted a writ of certiorari and his appeal was taken to Washington.

Miller's case was argued before the US Supreme Court on January 18 and 19, 1972, and was overseen by Chief Justice Warren Burger. Appointed in 1969 by Richard Nixon, Burger was a staunch conservative who believed that government should be granted a more far-reaching hand in banning obscene materials. He was joined in his majority decision by justices Byron

White, Harry Blackmun, Lewis F. Powell Jr., and William Rehnquist, and *Miller v. California* broadened the definition of what constituted legal obscenity in the United States. In Burger's written opinion, obscenity was still subject to regulation on a state-by-state basis but could now be prosecuted under a new three-pronged statute that superseded the *Roth* test and soon after became known as "the *Miller* test": "(a) whether 'the average person, applying contemporary community standards' would find that the work, taken as a whole, appeals to the prurient interest, (b) whether the work depicts or describes, in a patently offensive way, sexual conduct specifically defined by the applicable state law; and (c) whether the work, taken as a whole, lacks serious literary, artistic, political, or scientific value."[123] For the first time at the national level, the Supreme Court's decision specifically defined what constituted hardcore pornography in the eyes of the law and how it could be legally driven out of public spaces: "It is possible . . . to give a few plain examples of what a state statute could define for regulation: (a) patently offensive representations or descriptions of ultimate sexual acts, normal or perverted, actual or simulated; and (b) patently offensive representation or descriptions of masturbation, excretory functions, and lewd exhibition of the genitals."[124] We've already seen, in the case brought against Raymond Rohauer in 1958 for screening Anger's *Fireworks* in Los Angeles, how legal statutes referring to "lewd," "perverted," and/or "patently offensive" sexual conduct have often served as thin veneers to disguise, among other things, broader queerphobic agendas.

Most criticisms of sex media in 1970s America, both popular and academic, reference the impact of *Miller v. California*, but fewer refer to its equally significant companion case, *Paris Adult Theatre I v. Slaton*. Handed down the same day as the *Miller* decision, the Supreme Court's ruling in *Paris Adult Theatre I v. Slaton* granted all states the authority to ban the exhibition of pornography in public theaters even if all patrons present at screenings were consenting adults. Referring to a prior precedent set in *Stanley v. Georgia* (1969), Burger's majority maintained that the personal privacy of domestic space upheld in that case did not apply to public commercial venues exhibiting hardcore sex features. Not surprisingly, then, arrests at and prosecutions of adult theaters across the United States skyrocketed after June 1973 and sent many portions of the industry into gradual decline, although its fascination with sex, Satanism, and the occult continued sporadically throughout the remainder of the decade in films such as *High Priestess of Sexual Witchcraft* (starring *The Devil in Miss Jones*'s

Georgina Spelvin, 1973), *Sexorcist Devil* (1974), *Night of Submission* (1976), and *Lust at First Bite/Dracula Sucks* (1979).

Cinema of the fantastic, Jean Rollin once noted, is "always a good vehicle for discussing certain political ideas in the form of symbols and metaphors ... the fantastic cinema is always political, because it is always in opposition. It is subversive and it is popular, which means it is dangerous. I made films with sex and violence at a time when censorship was very strong, so that was certainly a political statement as well."[125] What began with the American Underground's penchant for "invading and recording realms which have to some degree remained taboo—too private, too shocking, too immoral for photographic reproduction" created a seductive synergy between queer sexuality and the occult, specifically Satanism, that would be taken up by both hardcore pornography and Euro-sleaze art cinema of the 1970s as thematized political questions of sexual and spiritual identity, definitions of the explicit, and struggles over cinematic censorship.

Notes

1. Jonas Mekas, "Movie Journal," *Village Voice*, March 12, 1964.
2. *Roth v. United States*, No. 354 U.S. 476 (Supreme Court of the United States, June 24, 1957).
3. Mekas.
4. Vincent Canby, "'Adult Themes' Head for Screen," *New York Times*, January 5, 1967.
5. Ibid.
6. Cited in ibid.
7. Cited in David Carter, *Stonewall: The Riots That Sparked the Gay Revolution* (New York: St. Martin's, 2004), 160.
8. Cited in Donn Teal, *The Gay Militants* (New York: Stein & Day, 1971), 7.
9. See George Chauncey, *Gay New York: Gender, Urban Culture, and the Making of the Gay Male World, 1890–1940* (New York: Basic, 1994).
10. Cited in David Deitcher, *The Question of Equality: Lesbian and Gay Politics in America Since Stonewall* (New York: Scribner, 1995), 74.
11. Harry M. Benshoff, *Monsters in the Closet: Homosexuality and the Horror Film* (Manchester: Manchester University Press, 1997), 2.
12. Richard Gilman, "There's a Wave of Pornography, Obscenity, Sexual Expression," *New York Times Magazine*, September 8, 1968.
13. Elana Levine, *Wallowing in Sex: The New Sexual Culture of 1970s American Television* (Durham: Duke University Press, 2007), 1–2.
14. Ralph Blumenthal, "Pornochic; 'Hard-Core' Grows Fashionable—and Very Profitable," *New York Times*, January 21, 1973.
15. Frank Trippett, "What's Happening to Sexual Privacy," *Look*, October 20, 1970.

16. Joan Hawkins, *Cutting Edge: Art-Horror and the Horrific Avant-Garde* (Minneapolis: University of Minnesota Press, 2000), 7.

17. The body genre designation comes from an influential essay by Linda Williams, in which the "low" genres of horror, pornography, and melodrama are connected by the fact that the "body of the spectator is caught up in an almost involuntary mimicry of the emotion or sensation of the body on screen.... What seems to bracket these particular genres from others is an apparent lack of proper esthetic distance, a sense of over-involvement in sensation and emotion." See Williams, "Film Bodies: Gender, Genre, and Excess," *Film Quarterly* 44.4 (Summer 1991): 2–12.

18. Eric Schaefer, "Gauging a Revolution: 16 mm Film and the Rise of the Pornographic Feature," in *Porn Studies*, ed. Linda Williams (Durham: Duke University Press, 2004), 372–73.

19. Ibid., 373.

20. Ibid., 371.

21. Linda Williams, *Hard Core: Power, Pleasure, and the "Frenzy of the Visible"* (Berkeley, University of California Press, 1999), 30.

22. Tzvetan Todorov, *The Fantastic: A Structural Approach to a Literary Genre* (Ithaca: Cornell University Press, 1975), 27.

23. Fred Lutz, "'Scorpio Rising' Film of Dark Evil," *Toledo Blade*, April 12, 1967.

24. Parker Tyler, *Underground Film: A Critical History* (New York: Grove, 1970), 4.

25. Ibid., 1.

26. Ibid.

27. Williams, 30.

28. Janet Staiger, "Finding Community in the Early 1960s: Underground Cinema and Sexual Politics," in *Swinging Single: Representing Sexuality in the 1960s*, ed. Hilary Radner and Moya Luckett (Minneapolis: University of Minnesota Press, 1999), 39.

29. J. Hoberman and Jonathan Rosenbaum, *Midnight Movies* (New York: Harper & Row, 1983), 39.

30. Tyler, 165.

31. Hoberman and Rosenbaum, 33.

32. Richard Dyer, *Now You See It: Studies on Lesbian and Gay Film* (London: Routledge, 2003), 126–27.

33. Tyler, 15. The peephole metaphor is, of course, closely linked to the history of moving-image pornography, as early stag films often used the trope as a narrative vehicle toward inciting voyeuristic on-screen action.

34. Dyer, 126.

35. Williams, 93.

36. Gary Lachman, *Turn Off Your Mind: The Mystic Sixties and the Dark Side of the Age of Aquarius* (London: Sidgwick & Jackson, 2001), 297.

37. Thomas Schatz, *Boom and Bust: American Cinema in the 1940s* (Berkeley: University of California Press, 1999), 456.

38. Guy Maddin, "Everyone Needs a Sailor Friend," *Film Comment* 43, no. 3 (June 2007): 38.

39. *Dunlop v. United States*, No. 165 U.S. 486 (Supreme Court of the United States, February 15, 1897).

40. William K. Everson, "Raymond Rohauer: King of the Film Freebooters," *Grand Street*, Summer 1994.

41. Matt Mazur, "The Films of Kenneth Anger, Vol. 1," *PopMatters* (blog), March 4, 2007.

42. "Homosexual 'Theorizing' Itself Okay—Judges," *Variety*, March 4, 1959.
43. Peter H. Gilmore, "Foreword," in *The Satanic Bible* (New York: Avon, 2005), 10.
44. Ibid., 11.
45. Judith Rascoe, "San Francisco's Church of Satan," *McCall's*, March 1970.
46. Gavin Baddeley, *Lucifer Rising: Sin, Devil Worship & Rock 'N' Roll* (London: Plexus, 1999), 70.
47. Hugh B. Urban, *Magia Sexualis: Sex, Magic, and Liberation in Modern Western Esotericism* (Berkeley, University of California Press, 2006), 191.
48. Ibid., 203.
49. Cited in Dave Smith, "Satanist Speaks to Set Record Straight," *Los Angeles Times*, July 17, 1970.
50. Urban, 204.
51. Ray Laurent, *Satanis: The Devil's Mass*, Blu-ray (AFGA, 2019).
52. Anton Szandor LaVey, *The Satanic Bible* (New York: Avon, 2005), 67.
53. Rascoe, 75.
54. Jeffrey Sconce, "Altered Sex: Satan, Acid, and the Erotic Threshold," in *Sex Scene: Media and the Sexual Revolution*, ed. Eric Schaefer (Durham: Duke University Press, 2014), 245.
55. Cited in Elenore Lester, "From Underground: Kenneth Anger Rising," *New York Times*, February 19, 1967.
56. Ibid.
57. Ibid.
58. The names of *Scorpio Rising*'s four sections are not included in the film itself in any demonstrable way but rather appear in Anger's original production notes below an introductory quotation from Crowley's *Magick in Theory and Practice*. These production notes have been reprinted in P. Adams Sitney, *Visionary Film: The American Avant-Garde, 1943–2000* (New York: Oxford University Press, 2002), 103.
59. Dyer, 129.
60. "The Devil and the Flesh," *Playboy*, May 1974.
61. Baddeley, 31.
62. Cited in Bill Landis, *Anger: The Unauthorized Biography of Kenneth Anger* (New York: HarperCollins, 1995), 112.
63. Dyer, 131.
64. Sconce, 237.
65. Robb Baker, "Revolutionary, Satanic Imagery Sweeping the Rock World," *Chicago Tribune*, September 8, 1968.
66. Cited in Smith.
67. Martin Waldron, "Witness Recalls Manson as 'Devil': He Says Murder Defendant Posed as Satan on Loose," *New York Times*, September 18, 1970.
68. Sconce, 240.
69. M. V. Kamath, "Satan Raises His Head in the U.S.," *The Times of India*, March 3, 1974.
70. Jonas Mekas, "On the Baudelairean Cinema," *Village Voice*, May 2, 1963.
71. Staiger, 42–65.
72. Jon Lewis, *Hollywood v. Hard Core: How the Struggle over Censorship Saved the Modern Film Industry* (New York: New York University Press, 2000), 136–37.
73. Ibid., 135.
74. Ibid., 153.

75. Ibid., 193, 165.

76. Justin Wyatt, "Selling 'Atrocious Sexual Behavior': Revising Sexualities in the Marketplace for Adult Film of the 1960s," in *Swinging Single: Representing Sexuality in the 1960s*, ed. Hilary Radner and Moya Luckett (Minneapolis: University of Minnesota Press, 1999), 112.

77. Cited in Lewis, 169.

78. Addison Verrill, "Skinpix Face 'New Dilemma'," *Variety*, October 21, 1970.

79. William Paul, "New York's New Porn: Holding Our Own," *Village Voice*, May 20, 1971.

80. Michael Goodwin, "What Happened to Miss Jones's Devil?," *Village Voice*, February 2, 1976.

81. Williams, 120.

82. Paul.

83. Sconce, 239–43.

84. Francis King, *Sexuality, Magic and Perversion* (London: Spearman, 1971), 167.

85. Cited in Urban, 205.

86. Roger Ebert, "Review of *The Devil in Miss Jones*," *Chicago Sun-Times*, June 13, 1973.

87. "Review of *The Devil in Miss Jones*," *Variety*, February 21, 1973.

88. Cited in the *Village Voice*, May 31, 1973.

89. Sconce, 255.

90. Steven Ziplow, *The Film Maker's Guide to Pornography* (New York: Drake, 1977), 31–32.

91. Urban, 212.

92. Sconce, 255.

93. Williams, 128–30.

94. Laura Kipnis, *Bound and Gagged: Pornography and the Politics of Fantasy in America* (Durham: Duke University Press, 1999), 161–62.

95. Marty Klein, "Pornography: What Men See When They Watch," in *Pornography: Film and Culture*, ed. Peter Lehman (New Brunswick: Rutgers University Press, 2006), 253.

96. Hawkins, 21.

97. Ibid., 25.

98. Ian Olney, *Euro Horror: Classic European Horror Cinema in Contemporary American Culture* (Bloomington: Indiana University Press, 2013), 7.

99. Hawkins, 3.

100. Olney, 4.

101. Hawkins, 4.

102. Olney, 8.

103. Cathal Tohill and Pete Tombs, *Immoral Tales: European Sex & Horror Movies, 1956–1984* (New York: St. Martin's, 1995), 135.

104. Tim Lucas, *The Rape of the Vampire* Liner Notes (Kino Lorber Films, 2012).

105. Mark Betz, "Art, Exploitation, Underground," in *Defining Cult Movies: The Cultural Politics of Oppositional Taste*, ed. Mark Jancovich, et al. (Manchester: Manchester University Press, 2003), 205.

106. Cited in Lewis, 229.

107. Tohill and Tombs, 143.

108. Todorov, 25.

109. Ibid.

110. Danny Shipka, *Perverse Titillation: The Exploitation Cinema of Italy, Spain and France, 1960–1980* (Jefferson: McFarland, 2011), 277.

111. Lucas, *The Rape of the Vampire* Liner Notes.
112. Olney, 30.
113. Tim Lucas, *Requiem for a Vampire* Liner Notes (Kino Lorber Films, 2012).
114. Williams, 133.
115. Ibid., 195.
116. Ibid., 140.
117. See Carol J. Clover, *Men, Women, and Chain Saws: Gender in the Modern Horror Film* (Princeton, Princeton University Press, 1992).
118. Olney, 42.
119. Lucas, *Requiem for a Vampire* Liner Notes.
120. Tohill and Tombs, 149.
121. "Feature Reviews: Virgins and the Vampires," *Boxoffice*, January 15, 1973.
122. Ibid.
123. *Miller v. California*, No. 413 U.S. 15 (Supreme Court of the United States, June 21, 1973).
124. Ibid.
125. Cited in Shipka, 274–75.

3

THE BLOOD IS THE LIFE/DEATH

Queer Contagion and Viral Vampirism in the Age(s) of HIV/AIDS

"THE BLOOD IS THE LIFE, MR. RENFIELD." Few lines of dialogue in the history of screen horror are as haunting as Bela Lugosi's ominous observation to Dwight Frye during the opening act of Tod Browning's *Dracula* (1931). Ask almost anyone what the primary characteristic of a vampire is and the answer will inevitably be the same: the need for blood. "Common consensus demands that real vampires drink blood," Arlene Russo points out, "and this one prerequisite denotes the existence and reality of a vampire. Whether an individual drinks blood to satisfy a physical or psychological craving, the fact remains the same: vampires need blood to survive."[1] To be sure, the life-giving properties of blood have been found at the heart of vampirism and other occult phenomena as their lore has been adapted across well more than a century's worth of iterations for print, stage, and screen. Through sanguinary ingestion, vampires can either nourish themselves and/or create others of their kind. This blood exchange, likened to sexual intercourse vis-à-vis penetration, consequently engenders a uniquely queer and decidedly supernatural style of reproduction, wherein death gives way to new horizons of everlasting life and the progenitive act is disarticulated from heterosexual norms, as the sex of the parent is no obstacle to procreation.

In the previous two chapters, I've considered the ways in which the enmeshed cultures of sexual liberation and occultism during the 1960s and 1970s created both backward glances into esoteric pasts and new magickal spaces for queer occultism to inflect popular culture in the United States, UK, and elsewhere. But by the turn of the 1980s, drifting into a rising tide of neoconservative Reaganesque and Thatcherite politics, the polymorphous sexual abandon with which so much of modern occultism was associated came, at least ostensibly, to a grinding halt. And the life that was wed both physiologically and psychologically to blood transformed into a powerful association with death, specifically with queer death.

During the summer of 1981, a smattering of reports began appearing across American national newswires concerning a mysterious set of maladies that incongruously seemed only to affect young to middle-aged, and otherwise healthy, gay men. On June 5, the Associated Press reported that a "'type of pneumonia found in five men, two of whom died, may be likened to "some aspect of a homosexual lifestyle," the national Centers for Disease Control said Friday.'"[2] On July 3, a brief article in that Friday morning's *New York Times* described the occurrence of a rare form of cancer diagnosed within a conglomerate of forty-one gay men among New York, San Francisco, and Los Angeles. The previous month, a handful of similar cases had been observed alongside the pneumonia cases reported by AP but warranted only passing mention in the CDC's *Morbidity and Mortality Weekly Report*. According to correspondent Dr. Lawrence K. Altman, one of a few medical professionals of the day to be employed full-time by a major national newspaper, the American incidence of Kaposi's sarcoma (KS), typically thought to affect only men of Mediterranean heritage during and after their fifties, had been estimated by the CDC to be "less than six-one-hundredths of a case per 100,000 people annually, or about two cases in every three million people."[3] Why this many cases of KS appeared so suddenly among young to middle-aged persons in specific geographic locations, why eight of the victims died less than two years after diagnosis, and why the cancer and its attendant immunosuppression seemed only to afflict gay men baffled local, national, and CDC medical professionals. What's more, Dr. Alvin Friedman-Kien, a dermatologist at New York University Medical Center, found it especially peculiar that not only were almost all of his KS patients gay men but also that most had had "multiple and frequent sexual encounters with different partners, as many as 10 sexual encounters each night up to four times a week."[4] Cancer, as far as the modern medical establishment knew, was neither a contagious nor infectious condition. That all forty-one of these KS cases were limited to gay men was, according to Dr. James Curran, a researcher in the CDC's Sexually Transmitted Diseases division, the best evidence against contagion at the time.[5]

The AP report of June 5, 1981, and Altman's article from July are two of the earliest national reportings on a medical phenomenon that would quickly develop a death grip on the imagination of an entire nation, not to mention on the bodies of its untold victims. These gaunt, pallid, blood-ailment sufferers were, like vampires, reappropriated in print and on screens across the United States as a new, spectacularized shorthand for the phantasmatic associations between queer identity and sexual pathology. As Deborah Lupton observes, one of the strongest threads running throughout the subtextual layer of meaning in this discourse of disease was an attempt to control, police, and demonize sexual expression in any arrangement not conforming to heterosexual monogamy.[6] On the June 17, 1982, edition of *NBC Nightly News*, for example, anchor Tom Brokaw began a headlining story by stating unequivocally that the "lifestyle of some male homosexuals has triggered an epidemic." Reporting for the same segment, correspondent Dr. Robert Bazell noted, "Researchers at the National Centers for Disease Control said they had found several cases where people who had been sex partners both had the condition. The scientists say this probably means they are dealing with some new, deadly sexually transmitted disease." The day after Bazell's NBC report, Altman, writing again for the *New York Times*, remarked that what had become colloquially known across the country as "gay cancer" was now officially recognized as such by CDC scientists, who designated the immune disorder GRID, or gay-related immunodeficiency disease.[7]

By August 1982, finally acknowledging that the condition could in fact be passed from one party to another and was also spreading among nonqueer populations, including intravenous drug users, blood transfusion patients, and impoverished communities of color, the CDC settled on a new name for this mysterious illness: AIDS (Acquired Immune Deficiency Syndrome). In May 1986, after American researchers at the CDC and National Institutes of Health, along with French scientists at the Pasteur Institute, finally managed to isolate AIDS's etiological agent, the viral malady that activated the syndrome was also officially named: HIV (Human Immunodeficiency Virus). As James Kinsella maintains in *Covering the Plague: AIDS and the American Media*, making the disease as "spooky as possible helped make AIDS a national issue, but it also fed on Americans' fears and did little to inform them."[8] As we'll see, Kinsella's use of the term "spooky" is far from coincidental.

During the 1980s, the looming threat of HIV/AIDS infection and transmission played out across the American cultural imaginary as if its worst epidemiological anxieties culled from the frames of Don Siegel's *Invasion of the Body Snatchers* (1956) or Ubaldo Ragona's *Last Man on Earth* (1964) had finally been realized as a nightmare of epic proportions come alive. The manifesting characteristics of HIV/AIDS, as David Skal details in *V is for Vampire*, "weirdly echoed the classic motifs of vampire legends. A blood-borne wasting malady appears, each victim capable of creating others through vein-puncturing or unconventional forms of sex. Science is baffled. Self-appointed moral guardians come forth, waving religious talismans, insisting that the affliction is the work of the devil."[9] Also remarking on how wasting illnesses have been historically affixed to the occult, Susan Sontag writes that viral diseases on par with HIV/AIDS are often experienced as forms of demonic possession: "Tumors are 'malignant' or 'benign,' like forces—and many terrified cancer patients are disposed to seek out faith healers, to be exorcised."[10]

Between 1980 and 1989, over 150 vampire-related horror films were released both theatrically and direct to home video in the United States. Considering this sizable statistic, this chapter investigates how HIV/AIDS and its attendant specters of queer sexuality became one of the most prominent cultural connotations that informed the resurgence of the viral vampire film during the 1980s. While general correlations between HIV and screen horror have been pointed out by many scholars, my own inquiry seeks to explore a specific set of new issues.[11]

First, if blood is one of the prominent prerequisites that denotes the existence and reality of vampires, then a curious paradox appears across many 1980s horror films. Not only do vampires physically bite their victims less frequently, but a newly ambivalent rhetoric also emerges that questions the source, quality, and potential hazards of ingesting blood and other bodily fluids. If the cultural rhetoric of AIDS during the 1980s relied heavily on popular iconography from the horror film, imagining, as Jeffrey Bennett puts it, the "polluted stranger who wanders dangerously within the polity," then some vampire films shifted this fear in a new direction: Anybody's blood, vampire or otherwise, was suspect, a potentially dangerous source of contagion.[12] Whether vampire or human, straight or queer, male or female, everyone was now vulnerable to the deadly risks of infection.

Second, in light of the fact that most major reports on the initial viral demographics of HIV/AIDS were generated in major metropolitan centers like New York, San Francisco, and Los Angeles, much of the critical literature on the epidemic and its representations across American screen media have demonstrated similarly skewed emphases on the supposedly intrinsic urbanity of the disease. Like the meanderings of Michel de Certeau's phantasmatic *flâneur* or the clandestine crimes of Jack the Ripper, navigating the anonymous interstices of urban life was doubtlessly central to the transmission of HIV and the lives/deaths of its carriers, facilitated by easy access to sex in spaces like tearooms, bathhouses, and back rooms of gay bars. Yet the motifs of viral infection and contagious disease often present themselves in 1980s vampire films not only as theorizations of queer sexuality but also as projections of a mobile queer sexuality, broadening the scope of the transmissible threat beyond city limits. Indeed, at a time when both AIDS and queer sexuality were disavowed by many in the American heartland as exclusively urban phenomena, the rearticulation of all blood as potentially contagious made anyone, regardless of geographic locale, gender, or sexual orientation, subject to the changes it might cause. As such, viral vampirism in the 1980s horror film articulates queerness not just through same-sex relations but also by dramatizing the fact that "all heterosexual relations are also homosexual ones, once removed," highlighting the rhetorical turn of HIV/AIDS's sexual risk within the supposedly indomitable boundaries of heterosexual orientation at a time when this virus/syndrome was still imagined almost exclusively as an urban gay cancer.[13]

Finally, as the "Age(s)" in this chapter's title suggests, the horrific associations between HIV/AIDS and the paradoxically pathological and pleasurable valences of viral contagion have persisted well beyond the 1980s. Specifically, the chapter concludes with an exploration of the ways in which recent turns away from "safe sex" in some queer subcultures toward "barebacking," the practice of unprotected anal intercourse between men, imagines an occult form of sexual risk that embraces practices of promiscuity, sexual freedom, and eroticized ethics closely akin to that of vampirism. As Jean Rollin might put it, the "blessed malediction" of vampirism has been reimagined in the new millennium through the queer subcultural practice of "gifting" HIV toward creating new mechanisms of alliance: "a way of forming consanguinity with strangers or friends."[14]

Serpent of Old: Precedents of Queer Contagion in the Vampire Film

While the emergence of HIV/AIDS in the 1980s gave new viral, pathological, and epidemiological resonance to modern retellings of the vampire myth, the virus and its attendant immunosuppression was hardly the first epidemic to echo across vampire literature, drama, and/or film. The blight of incurable syphilis that cut a wide swath through London in the 1890s, for instance, "left its shadow on the literary conventions of Victorian vampirism: the obsession with blood contamination, the search for telltale lesions, the faith in antiscientific (read: quack) cures, and the demonization of prostitutes."[15] Indeed, some of the earliest superstitions related to the subjects of vampirism, witchcraft, and other occultly marvelous occurrences were doubtlessly fueled by "frightened responses to poorly understood medical phenomena. Plagues, wasting diseases, and invisible contagions were often attributed to the wrath of the recently dead, giving rise to an increasingly embellished mythology of fear and its attendant rituals of scapegoating and purification."[16] It is little coincidence that the source text for the overwhelming majority of vampire films, Bram Stoker's *Dracula*, was published in 1897, at a time when syphilis, tuberculosis, and other venereal diseases were making their own infectious impact on public discussions of sex and death in fin-de-siècle Europe.[17]

Throughout the early history of the cinema, occult iconography became a favored staple almost immediately, from Georges Méliès's *The Haunted Castle* (1896) and Robert Vignola's *The Vampire* (1913) to Carl Boese and Paul Wegener's *The Golem* (1920) and Robert Wiene's *The Cabinet of Dr. Caligari* (1920). But it wasn't until 1922 that the figure of the vampire would be decisively entrenched into film history with Prana-Film's release of F. W. Murnau's *Nosferatu: Eine Symphonie des Grauens* (*Nosferatu: A Symphony of Horror*), an unauthorized adaptation of Stoker's novel over which the author's estate, helmed by widow Florence Stoker, consequently sued and won an injunction that all prints of the film should be destroyed. Popular mythology has it that only one copy of Murnau's film survived destruction. One of the most expressionistic *Dracula* adaptations to date, *Nosferatu* partially unfolds as a retrospective, epistolary piecemeal chronicling the "Great Death" that afflicted the fictional town of Wisborg, Germany, during the 1830s. Yet in spite of its fictional mode, Murnau's film significantly had both historical and contemporary viral referents to draw on: the European outbreak of Asiatic cholera during the 1830s and the influenza pandemic that killed millions worldwide in the space of just one year between 1918 and 1919. As one introductory title card makes hauntingly clear, blood is the undeniable force that gives *Nosferatu*'s vampiric plague its viral sustenance and contagious vivacity: "Nosferatu—Does this word not sound like the deathbird calling your name at midnight? Beware you never say it—for then the pictures of life will fade to shadows, haunting dreams will climb forth from your heart and feed on your blood."

During his journey to the Transylvanian "land of phantoms" for the completion of a real estate transaction, young solicitor Hutter (Gustav von Wangenheim) finds a fortuitous book stowed in the night table of a room he has rented for the evening. "From the seed of Belial sprang the vampyre Nosferatu," the text forewarns, "who liveth and feedeth on human bloode. This unholy creature liveth in sinister caves, tombes, and coffins, which are filled with cursed dirt from the fields of the Black Death." Such an explicit association between an ancient occult force, the malicious malady that ravaged Europe between 1346 and 1353, and its perpetuation into the present becomes the foundation on which Hutter's nascent fears of the film's supernatural shadows are built. And indeed, given the vampiric subject in question, these fears are quite well founded.

Unlike Christopher Lee, Louis Jordan, Frank Langella, or more recent turns by Gerard Butler, Jonathan Rhys Meyers, and Claes Bang, Max Schreck's Count Orlok is a far cry from the urbane dandy or suave sophisticate vampire who charms his way into the ranks of high society with the aim of infecting it from the inside out. Instead, Schreck's heavy makeup, dreary accouterments, and bodily prostheses give him the appearance of an overgrown rat or bat (creatures often popularly associated with contagious disease) whose eyes, teeth, and claws have all been developed with the express purpose of feeding.[18] What's more, even the nomination of a masculine pronoun to describe Count Orlok betrays the fact that a knee-length tailcoat resembling a tight-fitting dress, elongated fingernails, and decorative fedora create a slippage not just between human and animal but also in the legibility of the count's gender. To this point, *Nosferatu* is remarkable not only for how explicitly its titular vampire and the rats that surround him are associated with contagion, infection, and viral pestilence but also for how little misdirection surrounding the queer valences of the occult Murnau attempts to create.[19]

From the time Hutter arrives at Castle Orlok, there's little doubt that its owner is a not-of-this-earth creature who consciously intends to seduce, stalk, and kill his guest. "Can we not stay together a little while longer, my lovely man?" the count implores Hutter tenderly after the solicitor has accidentally drawn blood from his finger. "It's still quite a long time until sunrise and I sleep by day, dear fellow . . . completely dead to the world." Later, when Orlok's transparent game of cat and mouse reaches its climax, the scene is constructed as a deadly, drawn-out tapestry of queer seduction vis-à-vis the Gothic art direction of Albin Grau, the German painter, architect, and avowed occultist who served as the film's producer.[20] Lurking through a mise-en-scène of shadows, skulls, and frightened facial close-ups, the shot-reverse shot pattern inches a menacing, open-mouthed Orlok ever closer to Hutter's bedchamber. Lending queer resonance to a scene of both seduction and suckling, Richard Dyer notes that it is "not just what the vampire does that makes it so readable in sexual terms, but the social space that it occupies. The act of vampirism takes place in private, at night, most archetypally in a bedroom—the same space which our society accords to the sex act."[21]

Count Orlok's subsequent descent from Transylvania into the town of Wisborg is framed as the invasion of a queer virus of which little is known to either scientists or laymen. As a local newspaper ominously reports, "A plague epidemic has broken out in Transylvania and in the Black Sea ports of Varna and Galaz. Masses of young people are dying. All victims appear to have the same strange wounds on their necks, the origin of which is still a mystery to doctors. The Dardanelles have been closed to all ships suspected of carrying the plague." Otherwise healthy young people are mysteriously dead. All victims share the same manifesting symptoms. No cause is readily apparent. Murnau's *Nosferatu* offers up one of the earliest sanguine supernatural nightmares that vampire myths still to be filmed would continue to reimagine.

Indeed, one of the most inadvertently prophetic of these reimaginings eerily anticipates the queer discursive turn that consistently conscribed early AIDS cases during the 1980s. "You can't trust your mother, your best friend, your next door neighbor . . . one minute they're perfectly normal THE NEXT . . . Pray it doesn't happen to YOU!" appears in bold font across the poster for David Cronenberg's *Rabid* (1977), the story of a woman who unintentionally becomes the harbinger of a nationwide epidemic. Starring porno chic starlet Marilyn Chambers in her first non-adult-film role, *Rabid* tells the tale of Rose (Chambers), a young woman who, after suffering a horrific motorcycle accident, is brought to the plastic surgery clinic of Dr. Dan Keloid (Howard Ryshpan). In an attempt to save Rose's life and test some of his own experimental procedures at the same time, Keloid genetically alters skin grafts taken from Rose's body and reinserts them, hoping to grow new native tissue.

However, in an epidemiologically queer twist on the archetypal mad scientist plot, Rose grows a pulsating orifice/vagina underneath her arm that also produces a penetrating organ/penis, transforming her into a deadly trans* predator who can only be nourished by human blood.[22] After each feeding attack, Rose's victims similarly turn into harbingers of this mysterious blood-borne illness, spreading the disease exponentially until it threatens to infect the entire population of Canada.

Like Count Orlok before her, Rose becomes a gender-bending, sexually subversive seducer who kisses and kills nearly everyone she comes into contact with. After escaping from Dr. Keloid's clinic and contaminating swaths of the Canadian countryside, Rose makes her way to Montréal and the apartment of her best friend, Mindy (Susan Roman). On the night of Rose's arrival, Mindy anxiously watches a television news report detailing the outbreak of this deadly epidemic. No cause has yet been determined, the interviewed doctor confesses, but what is clear is that the virus is spread through saliva, blood, and other bodily fluids, causing its victims to develop an insatiable desire to bite and infect others. The irony, of course, is that Mindy is drawn away from the broadcast at the precise moment that Rose knocks at her door.

Struggling for the remainder of the film to keep what's left of her human moral compass intact, Rose reluctantly capitulates to her hunger and attacks Mindy, only to be interrupted by Hart (Frank Moore), Rose's boyfriend, who has been frantically searching for her ever since she went missing from the Keloid clinic. Appalled not only that she would physically attack another woman but also her best friend, Hart and Rose struggle until she pushes him down a flight of stairs and knocks him unconscious. Regaining consciousness at the sound of a ringing phone, Hart hears the whimpers of a frightened Rose, who has locked herself in a room with her newest victim to see if she really is the monster Hart believes her to be. As the infected man wakes up, Hart listens in horror as Rose is attacked by one of her own kind. The film's contagious cautionary tale concludes the next morning as Rose's body is found by sanitation workers on top of a garbage heap and is thrown into the back of a truck.

Just four years after the release of *Rabid*, the queer specter of HIV/AIDS began to loom over the wreckage of the sexual revolution like the "pestilential image of Nosferatu had once presided over a decimated Germany."[23] This pathological association between aberrant sexuality and contagious disease was quickly paralleled on the plane of popular culture as images of gay people began to blur with images of vampires: "Homophobes had long held that gay people were evil predators with the Draculean power to corrupt and transform the sexually straight and virtuous."[24] Indeed, assessing the struggle between the cultural analysis of HIV/AIDS and its contemporary geopolitical activism, Douglas Crimp provides an important aide-mémoire: "AIDS does not exist apart from the practices that conceptualize it, represent it, and respond to it . . . this assertion does not contest the existence of viruses, antibodies, infections, or transmission routes . . . what it does contest is the notion that there is an underlying reality of AIDS, on which are constructed the representations, or the culture, or the politics of AIDS."[25]

What we would do well to recognize instead, according to Simon Watney, is that constellations of infectious clinical terminology indicate a "collapsing together of ideological concerns, which transform AIDS into a *malade imaginaire*—the viral personification of unorthodox deregulative desire, dressed up in the ghoulish likeness of degeneracy."[26] If Ellis Hanson's assertion is correct, that queer critics moralize movies to death by championing social realism over the polymorphous pleasures of sexual fantasy, then representations of HIV/AIDS do seem especially primed to incur reactionary assessments. Yet coming to terms with some of the darker and more abject representational meanings of HIV/AIDS is precisely what follows in the remainder of this chapter, not only to better understand how popular imaginations of viral contagion fueled the cultural resurgence of the vampire film during the 1980s, but also to recognize how these films' construction of their own "subversive otherness, [their] adventurous demand for sexual pleasure, [their] promiscuity, [their] funky sense of style, [and their] disregard for neoconservative 'family values'" present vital challenges to LGBTQ+ media studies' own "'positive images' campaign."[27] Death, disease, and occultly queer desires, in short, become tropes for what a perverse media culture can comprehend but neither heteronormative nor homonormative culture can.[28]

Sex and Seroconversion in the City

"One can analyze the microbe-like, singular and plural practices which an urbanistic system was supposed to administer or suppress, but which have outlived its decay; one can follow the swarming activity of these procedures that . . . have reinforced themselves into a proliferating illegitimacy."[29] Originally published the year before the first cases of HIV/AIDS were reported in the United States, Michel de Certeau's influential musings on the geographic and cultural practices of urban living have taken on haunting retrospective resonance in light of that epidemic: the modern city as a living organism constituted on a microbe-like organization that outlives its original, panoptic intentions and multiplies into swarms that thrive on the illicit actions of its citizens.[30] As Priscilla Wald makes clear in *Contagious: Cultures, Carriers, and the Outbreak Narrative*, concerns over the infectious nature of urban living have been part of both biological and sociological discourses since at least the turn of the 1900s. Indeed, the adoption of the term "social contagion" into popular parlance during the late nineteenth and early twentieth centuries—a term originally used to describe the hazards of tenement living and dramatized in the horrific stories of penny dreadfuls—"registered the inflection of bacteriology in the changing understanding of social interactions and community formation . . . and it marked an emerging conception of community formation that would be at once shaped and haunted by the multiple meanings of contagion."[31] In light of these concerns, it is little wonder that the "identification of a virus [has often] generated a viral narrative," and that the communicable, life-sapping qualities of vampirism have been taken up as particularly apt cultural metaphors in times of epidemic, and especially sexual, panic.[32] After all, vampires, like microbes, are not only capable of representing social and sexual bonds; they also create and enforce them.[33]

But how does the potentially contagious nature of city living relate to being queer, beyond the fact that homosexuality itself was once considered by some as a communicable disease? As George Chauncey maintains, processes of late nineteenth- and early twentieth-century urbanization resulted in the "breakdown of family and other social ties that kept an individual's behavior under control in smaller, more tightly organized and regulated towns . . . the emergence of an extensive and multifaceted gay . . . world was made possible in part by the development of distinctive forms of urban culture."[34] Like the vampire, whose fangs often hide behind the façade of a perfidious smile, city living allowed the urban queer to navigate the complex interstices of multiple social worlds and to lead a "double life: by day to hold a respectable job that any queer would have been denied, and by night to lead the life of a fairy on the Bowery."[35] This same duplicitous dynamic is also frequently foregrounded in the life of the queer vampire, whose artifices of normative gender and sexuality allow her/him to "pass" as not visibly identifiable as either queer or vampire.[36]

The rise of the modern contagious city staged a paradoxical drama between two distinct forms of individualism: "Its stimulation and anonymity at once liberated individuals from prior social conventions and inaugurated a free fall, forcing them to seek new means of distinction and self-definition."[37] It is precisely this dilemma, between the feted anonymity of urban spaces and compulsions toward community building as an instrument of survival, that has made queer sex in the city so historically significant. As Samuel Delaney considers in *Times Square Red, Times Square Blue*, "The general sexual activity in a city becomes anxiety-filled, class-bound, and choosy. This is precisely why public rest rooms, peep shows, sex movies, bars with grope rooms, and parks with enough greenery are necessary for a relaxed and friendly sexual atmosphere in a democratic metropolis."[38] What early sociologists and urban reformers called the social disorganization of the city, exemplified in anonymous encounters between strangers, can be queerly reconceptualized as one method of social reorganization vis-à-vis the construction of "an organized, multilayered, and self-conscious gay subculture, with its own meeting places, language, folklore, and moral codes."[39] Perhaps the most distinctive of these queer folkloric customs, sexual voracity, promiscuity, and the institutions of urban life that contributed to their acceleration, constructed a "sexual delivery system of unprecedented speed, efficiency, and volume."[40] Establishments like gay bathhouses, tearooms, and bars intended for cruising became epicenters for exacerbating the "mythical link between gay sex and death" almost immediately after HIV/AIDS entered the American public consciousness.[41] In a 1983 article from the *Los Angeles Times*, Alan Citron notes that "business at bathhouses, a hub for casual gay sex, is reportedly off by more than 50%. Leaders in the homosexual community say AIDS is the major topic of conversation among homosexual men, especially those who once engaged liberally in sex," now fearing that viral harbingers were "prowling the gay bars and bathhouses like vampires, infecting hundreds of unsuspecting sex partners with the deadly disease."[42]

Published in 1981, Whitley Strieber's *The Hunger* eerily anticipates the ways in which vampirism would become a touchstone for the pathological links between queer sex, urban living, and contagious disease as soon as HIV/AIDS began to haunt the American cultural imaginary later that year. The novel's protagonist, Miriam Blaylock, is an immortal vampire born before the time of Christ who lives, fucks, and feeds with her current partner, John. Descended from Lamia, the mythological bloodsucking queen of Libya, Miriam has remained ageless for millennia while ensnaring lovers with the promise of everlasting life. Searching for steady supplies of blood, the anonymity of urban spaces in which occasional disappearances are not uncommon, and the ability to generate a small community of their own kind that could pass undetected among the masses, Miriam and John settle in New York during the early part of the twentieth century.

Yet Miriam and John also have one rather large, eternal problem. Miriam's assurance of life everlasting is only partially accurate, and her "blessed malediction," to borrow from Jean Rollin, is not fully transferable within the limits of the penetrative blood exchange through which it is passed. Throughout the centuries, Miriam has been in the queer habit of "alternating men and women. Their sex was a matter of indifference to her," but the result has always been the same.[43] Miriam's lovers inevitably wither, weaken, and grow fragile, crumbling to little more than a pile of bone that is unable to wholly perish as their own contaminated blood turns against them. As such, one of the novel's central dramas charts John's race against time before he joins his predecessors, a community of corpses bound by their shared sanguine condition, in the coffins of Miriam's attic: "John could feel her [Miriam] in him. Her past seemed to whisper in his veins, her voice to jabber in his ears. In a sense, she haunted him; they all did. Was the hunger satisfied by their being or just their blood? John had often wondered if they knew, if they felt themselves in him. From the way he could hear them in his mind, he suspected that they did."[44]

In a 1985 *Time* exposé titled "AIDS: A Growing Threat," Claudia Wallis notes that it was the "virtual certainty of death from AIDS, once the syndrome has fully developed," that made the disease so frightening during the early years of its discovery, "along with the uncertainty of nearly everything else about it."[45] This assurance of impending demise is hauntingly foreshadowed throughout Strieber's novel as John begins to frantically acknowledge his own vampirism as an internal force that suddenly turns against him, like the immune systems of later HIV/AIDS patients: "This was the hardest part. How do you face it, the fact that the seed of death, hidden deep in the body, has started to grow?"[46] Desperately hoping to find a solution, John enlists the aid of Dr. Sarah Roberts, a young gerontologist whose high-profile epidemiological experiments with rhesus monkeys at one of New York's most prominent medical research facilities are intended to reveal, and ultimately to control, the very mechanisms of biological aging itself. Yet unlike some of her clinical predecessors in the horror genre, Sarah's reluctance to prove that the superstitions of yesterday can become the scientific realities of today ultimately dooms John. Indeed, the "failure of the cure, of finding relief from the torture of isolation," marks a much longer trajectory in popular culture's refiguring of the viral vampire that culminated during the early years of the AIDS crisis.[47]

John's star might be falling at this juncture, but Sarah's is just beginning to rise through the influence of Miriam, who intends to groom her to take John's place as her next lover. Comparable to the mechanisms of bat echolocation, or the eighteenth-century thought-transference experiments derived from the work of German doctor Franz Mesmer, the proximity afforded by New York's urban space, with only a few city blocks between Sarah's apartment and Miriam's palatial brownstone, allows the vampire to begin her stealthy seduction: "The next step in the infiltration of Sarah's life was to touch her. The human sense of touch had atrophied. They called it extrasensory perception, wrongly assuming it to be a means of reading thoughts. It was rather a means of sharing emotions."[48] Indeed, touch in *The Hunger* becomes precisely the sort of socially contagious metaphor for urbanity that, as Wald notes, expresses contact "as though it is physical—acting, that is, on the body without actual contact."[49]

Once Miriam finally manages to touch Sarah, the doctor's icy façade and pretense of a satisfying heterosexual relationship with coworker Dr. Tom Haver starts to disintegrate, as latent queer impulses emerge in their stead: "So that was what lay beneath the brilliance and the independence. Hunger, raw and unfulfilled, for a truly passionate lover. . . . Now that her inner self had been aroused, Sarah's hunger would grow and expand . . . as relentless as a cancer, until her present life would seem like a desert."[50] Hunger in the context of 1980s vampirism represents the negotiation of a dichotomy not unlike that of the urban queer's double life: a virus engendering a vacillation between sexual pleasure and pathology leading to the revelation of a true self. Like HIV/AIDS's later articulation by the religious right as an evidential smoking gun for homosexuality, this viral strain of vampirism "flushes out an identity that might have remained hidden from neighbors, jobmates, family, friends. It also confirms an identity."[51]

While touch is Miriam's introductory method of influencing new lovers, Sarah's queer identity is ultimately confirmed in the physical context of blood exchange. Surrendering herself to the clinical gaze of gerontolic experimentation, the sexual and sanguine intimacy that Miriam hopes to provoke reaches new heights inside Sarah's phlebotomy lab: "She inserted the needle. Miriam made another noise, one that was familiar to Sarah. It was her own little chortle, the one she always made when she was penetrated. To hear it under these circumstances, in the throat of another woman, was faintly revolting. . . . It was undeniably pleasurable and the very delight of it was what was so awful."[52] Stroking. Insertion. Penetration. Pleasure. If ever the letting of blood between two women took on resonances of queer sex, this exchange between Miriam and Sarah serves as a prime example.

During a blood transfusion later enacted in reverse in Miriam's bedroom, Sarah is formally initiated into her new viral vampiric life: "It was as if somebody else was living in her body, some wild being, driven by needs of which she herself was ignorant."[53] Miriam's blood attacking Sarah's healthy cells once again anticipates later articulations of how the HIV virus manifested: "So 'a host of opportunistic diseases, normally warded off by a healthy immune system, attacks the body,' whose integrity and vigor have been sapped by the sheer replication of 'alien product' that follows the collapse of its immunological defenses."[54] Fleeing in horror from Miriam's embrace, Sarah embarks on a frantic excursion through the New York cityscape in which her own newly heightened sense of touch overwhelms her with hundreds of voices that emanate from block to block. Unable to fully acquiesce to her new appetites for blood and queer sex, Sarah commits "suicide" at the novel's conclusion, joining John and the rest of the consanguineous community in the attic as Miriam lives on in search of her next victim.

While Strieber's novel explicitly engages the paradoxical pleasures of viral vampirism and its queer sexual expressions, Sarah's "death" at its denouement ultimately underscores the fact that some antinormative occult narratives, presenting the possibilities of fulfilling queer desires, may still enact their demonization and punishment.[55] Indeed, during the early 1980s, these overlapping concerns with pleasure and pathology, sexuality and sanguine ingestion, and death in its many guises were transformed across urban queer subcultures in the United States and UK as a fascination with the darkly perverse and sexualized appeals of the Gothic, particularly the rising tide of goth subculture that emerged in the "socioeconomic decline and Thatcherite politics of late 1970s Britain, on the heels of punk's infamous rebellion."[56] As Lauren Goodlad and Michael Bibby point out, goth subculture was a "discordant bricolage of hyperromantic elements" that "culled freely from Gothic literary-historical traditions; from vampire cults, horror flicks, and B-movie camp; from Celtic, Pagan, Egyptian, and Christian mythology... from oppositional sexual practices including queer, drag, porn, fetish, and B-D/S-M; from subterranean drug cultures; and from a historical canon of the gothic avant-garde."[57]

Among the hustle and bustle of urban cityscapes, goth subculture's flourishing in shadowy nightclubs and dimly lit bars cultivated a horrific materialization of the queer double life to which Chauncey refers: spaces in which thriving antiheteronormative sexualities and unconventional gender identities made it possible for queer men, women, and transpeople to come out and explore their interests and desires.[58] As former club kid Trevor M. Holmes observes, goth could be considered as "rather than a static noun, an activity, an active becoming-other of straight, singular gender norms. Think of *goth* as a verb, as in *to goth*. Rather like *to queer*."[59] Wed to an occult fascination with blood's powers over life and death, it is this polymorphously perverse ability of urban goth subcultures to queer that reverberates throughout some of the most virally resonant media culture in the early period of the AIDS crisis.

Released by MGM in 1983 and shown out of competition that year at the Cannes Film Festival, the screen adaptation of Strieber's novel was the first feature helmed by British director Tony Scott, who had previously made a successful career producing television commercials in the UK. The exceedingly stylized opening of *The Hunger*, a now-iconographic staple in queer goth subcultures, blends music video aesthetics with high-fashion photography, following Miriam (Catherine Deneuve) and John (David Bowie) through the bustling crowd of an urban goth nightclub where swirling smoke and strobe lights illuminate a live performance of postpunk band Bauhaus's "Bela Lugosi's Dead."[60] As Miriam and John survey the gyrating crowd from atop a flight of iron stairs, both of their gazes lock on a couple dancing suggestively below. The gaze of the vampire foregrounded in *The Hunger* is one of an intensified queer desire, scanning for sanguine sustenance and sexual fulfillment through the practice that Chauncey, Delaney, and so many others have pronounced as central to urban queer sex practices: cruising.[61]

The foursome's exit from the club, intercut with a tracking shot of a black limousine speeding toward Miriam and John's palatial lair, makes a point of highlighting the New York cityscape across the background of the coming dawn. The dangers of proximity within urban spaces, a palpable theme in Strieber's novel, are visibly rendered in Scott's film via Miriam and John's easy access to both sexual and sanguine fulfillment. As their seduction of the swinging couple begins, shots of two frantic rhesus monkeys jumping from wall to wall in a cage (we later learn that these are Sarah's gerontolic test subjects) are intercut with Miriam giving her male partner a lap dance while John is in the kitchen slowly caressing his female partner's bared breasts. As a techno musical crescendo reaches its climax, one of the rhesus monkeys violently attacks the other and bites its throat. At the same time, both Miriam and John unsheathe blades from ankh necklaces around their necks, slash the throats of their victims, and begin to eagerly imbibe.

The ankh, an iconic Egyptian hieroglyph symbolizing life, rapidly becomes laden with both the life-giving and life-taking properties of blood. Promiscuously queer cruising is no doubt the seduction strategy par excellence in *The Hunger*, yet the violent thrust with which the necklaces are thrown into a sink and the immediacy with which the blood begins to wash away creates a paradoxical imperative to cleanse these weapons of the very fluid they are designed to extract. What's more, the two mingling ankhs, representing an intertwined doubling of the traditional Western symbol for the female sex, not only recalls David Bowie's famously androgynous persona in both goth subculture's glam antecedent and his performance as John Blaylock but also foreshadows Miriam's seduction of Sarah, who is introduced as a lab-coat-wearing, short-hair-sporting dykish doctor in the following scene.

The female vampire who caresses and kills other women is, according to Barbara Creed, the most dynamic threat to the institution of heterosexuality represented across screen horror.[62] Similar to her male counterparts, yet doubly abject given her penetration of boundaries between women in order to allow blood/menstrual fluid to flow, the female-feeding woman vampire is always already queer because she "disrupts identity and order; driven by her lust for blood, she does not respect the dictates of the law which set down the rules of proper sexual conduct."[63] With the addition of the contagious viral metaphor, *The Hunger* presents a vision of queer female vampirism unlike any of its predecessors.

After John's rapid aging brings Dr. Roberts's experiments to both his and Miriam's attention, the transfusion of Miriam's contagious blood into Sarah's veins is staged as one of the most infamously queer seduction scenes in all of 1980s cinema. Like Schreck's Count Orlok and Chambers's Rose, Miriam is hardly a stranger to baiting her waiting prey, seducing Sarah with the "Flower Duet" from Delibes's *Lakmé* on piano:

SARAH: Is it a love song?
MIRIAM: I told you, it was sung by two women.
SARAH: Sounds like a love song.
MIRIAM: Then I suppose that's what it is.
SARAH: Are you making a pass at me, Mrs. Blaylock?
MIRIAM: Not that I'm aware of, Sarah.

But of course, a sexual advance is precisely what Miriam is making. Taken aback by her realization of what is potentially about to happen, Sarah spills a glass of sherry on her blouse, the perfect excuse for her to disrobe and accept Miriam's invitation to crawl into bed.

Amid shots of windblown muslin curtains and naked, intertwined bodies, Miriam performs cunnilingus, kisses and teases Sarah's nipples, and opens a vein in each of their arms in order to transfuse their blood. In an essay relating AIDS to spectacular images of queer abjection in 1980s media culture, Ellis Hanson explains, "When I speak of the vampire as the embodiment of evil sexuality, I speak of gay men and people with AIDS in the same breath. . . . I am talking about essentialist representations of men as vampiric: as sexually exotic, alien, unnatural, oral, anal, compulsive, violent, protean, polymorphic, polyvocal, polysemous, invisible, soulless, transient, superhumanly mobile, infectious, murderous, suicidal, and a threat to wife, children, home, and phallus."[64] Not only was HIV/AIDS routinely articulated as an urban pathology during the 1980s but, as Hanson's reflections reveal, it was also framed almost exclusively as a male issue. The HIV virus, as Simon Watney maintains, manifested itself in the popular imagination as affecting three particular constituencies that were "already feared and marginalized in the West—blacks, intravenous drug-users, and gay men."[65]

The Hunger's infamous coital scene between Deneuve and Sarandon has received much critical attention simply by virtue of representing same-sex desire on screen. However, within a more specific trajectory of queer occult horror, this scene is especially worthy of attention both because queer sexuality is explicitly linked to vampirism as a blood-borne pathogen that contaminates the cells of its victims and because the diffusion of that viral malady occurs within the milieu of a pleasurable sexual transaction between two women. To be sure, those few male characters in *The Hunger* are all impotent, "dull and ineffectual, and Sarah's lack of sexual interest in Tom becomes a running joke."[66] One of occult cinema's most explicit representations of seroconversion, a term popularized later in the 1980s to refer to the time frame when the body begins producing antibodies that reflect the presence of the HIV virus in the bloodstream, may thus belong not to a queer man but rather to a queer woman.

Relatedly, perhaps *The Hunger*'s most obvious derivation from Strieber's novel is the triumph engendered by the queer female vampire's viral abjection. As Sarah's hunger for blood becomes increasingly insatiable, she takes to the streets of New York on a similar hallucinatory journey as in the novel, where every city block brings her back to Miriam's spectral visage. Facing no choice but to return to the embrace of her queer creator, remaining both repulsed and fascinated by who and what she's quickly becoming, Sarah tears away Miriam's ankh and plunges it deep into her own throat in a desperate attempt at suicide. As Creed maintains, the bloody nature of queer female abjection that binds Sarah to Miriam is what gives this scene its particular significance: "Because the two women are kissing at the time, Sarah's blood spurts up and out from her mouth into Miriam's open mouth. . . . The two women, both vampires, appear to be drinking each other's blood. It is impossible to tell if the blood signals life or death. The film deliberately plays on this ambiguity, reinforcing the notion that lesbian desire is deadly."[67] But for whom is this ambiguous amalgamation of contaminated blood and queer sexual desire ultimately fatal?

Pining for the loss of yet another lover while carrying Sarah's still-bleeding body upstairs, Miriam is interrupted as an attic door suddenly swings open and the reinvigorated corpses of her previous partners descend for revenge. Forsaking Sarah to protect herself, Miriam is overcome and falls over a balcony to her "death." Yet the hunger, as both Strieber's novel and Scott's film make plain, is eternal. In the film's closing sequence, an establishing shot through another set of windswept curtains shows that it is Sarah, not Miriam, who has survived the deadly barrage. Embraced by a new female partner on the balcony of a high-rise apartment building that overlooks the skyline of another urban center, London, Sarah stares contemplatively out into the twilight as the camera pulls back and Miriam's cries for Sarah echo off-screen.

According to Andrea Weiss, the queer vampire film's fluctuating degrees of narrative closure profoundly affect the multiplicity of meanings such texts can generate and the extent to which queer viewers can find "alternative or oppositional meanings.... Hollywood films do not usually allow their lesbian characters to act on sexual desire. The horror film, in contrast, has an added punishment to mete out: the lesbian vampire is killed because of her active sexuality as well as her lesbianism."[68] Yet *The Hunger*'s conclusion provides a notable exception to this rule. Not only does Sarah survive, but it is her life, her agency, and her gaze that proves triumphant. Even more than the Karnstein trilogy's flirtation with the reversal of gendered power dynamics, *The Hunger* emphatically proves Hanson's earlier point: that the gaze is "forever in danger of appropriation and reconfiguration by the very lesbian vampire it seems to have dreamed into existence."

In *Variety*'s original appraisal of *The Hunger*, an unnamed staff writer pronounced that Tony Scott's background in television commercial production contributed to his first feature outing as "all visual and aural flash, although this modern vampire story looks so great, as do its three principal performers, and is so bizarre that it possesses a certain perverse appeal."[69] *The Hunger* does indeed play out as a paradoxical symphony of surfaces, with shadowy corners, smoky hallways, windswept curtains, and antique mirrors reflecting at every turn a tale of ageless beauty and blood-borne pathology in the 1980s urban metropolis. "It is against this surface impression of smooth, coherent perfection," Creed summarizes, that the film explores the "forces of abjection associated with blood, wounds and the decaying crumbling body."[70] Vampiric abjection in *The Hunger* is presented as a duplicitous masquerade, "a glamorous appeal to the senses, that renders the monstrous, the outcast, and the lesbian as a highly self-conscious mode" of pleasurable urban exoticism.[71] The abrupt degeneration of David Bowie's John Blaylock into a viral-ridden elderly invalid, for example, is particularly striking in light of the fact that the remainder of the film relies so heavily on a mise-en-scène of exquisite beauty.

The HIV/AIDS crisis of the 1980s was perhaps most significant, according to Priscilla Wald, for the ways in which it too became a pathological play of surfaces that made so-called deviant sex visible, entailing the vampiric-like penetration of the "familiarly wily, crafty, sinister invader, but this one, with particular cruelty, disabled the very defense mechanisms needed for the fight, leaving the body completely susceptible to all of the other marauders responsible for the physical devastation that constituted the syndrome."[72] *The Hunger* not only thematizes vampirism as a communicable, sexually transmitted virus but simultaneously contributes to demythologizing one of the well-worn myths surrounding queer urban life in the later context of the AIDS crisis: that the proximity engendered by city living presents an irresistible mecca of "virtual convenience stores for quick cavorting" situated in a consequence-free environment of limitless partners.[73] In place of this evanescent lore of urban hedonism, *The Hunger* not only sells chic clothing, chic furniture, and chic urban living, but perhaps most definitively, chic viral perversity.

Rural Retroviruses and Queer Anti-Urbanism

As recent queer theoretical scholarship has demonstrated, the overwhelming emphasis on urbanity as the supposed nexus of queer subject formation, sexual activity, and both physical and psychological death in the wake of HIV/AIDS has had a distinct impact on the ways in which contemporary debates about nonnormative sexualities, sexual politics, sexual practices, and sexual health have been and continue to be articulated. In his 2010 book *Another Country: Queer Anti-Urbanism*, Scott Herring begins with the following provocation: "I hate New York . . . It's not simply the city's awesome capacity to imagine itself as the be-all and end-all of modern queer life . . . What I really hate is the casualness with which this move is dispatched. . . . One horizon of possibility among the many . . . magnifies into the horizon of fantastic possibility for all."[74] Indeed, this horizon of ostensible opportunity has not only translated into the "make it someday" ethos with which so many queer pilgrims continue to emblazon their knapsacks en route to New York, San Francisco, Los Angeles, and so forth, but has also materialized as a formidable specter that haunts queer theoretical scholarship: "Much of queer studies wants desperately to be urban planning, even as so much of its theoretical architecture is already urban planned."[75] But what about those whose horizons of queer possibility point in different directions, toward a cornfield, a mountain, an abandoned resort, or a dusty roadside motel?

In contrast to cultures of metronormativity, some recent strains of queer theory have productively thought through the rural and the nonurban as "dynamic space[s] of inquiry and sexual vitality. Complicating geophobic claims that ruralized spaces are always and only hotbeds of hostility, cultural and socioeconomic poverty, religious fundamentalism, homophobia, racism, urbanoia, and social conservatism," queer anti-urbanism instead questions "knee-jerk assumptions that the 'rural' is a hate-filled space for queers as [it archives] the complex desires that contribute to any non-metropolitan identification."[76] At the height of AIDS's contagious paranoia in the mid- to late 1980s, the American vampire film similarly began meditating on an embryonic iteration of this queer anti-urban aesthetic, broadening its epidemiological horizons to demonstrate that the bloody abjection of viral vampirism could threaten and infect but also create polymorphously perverse pleasures in locations far removed from high-rises, blaring taxi horns, and the shimmer of city lights.

Released by Warner Bros. on July 31, 1987, *The Lost Boys* has become something of a cult classic among queer horror fans over the past thirty years. Leaving an unidentified city in a fully packed U-Haul after the settlement of a messy divorce, Lucy Emerson (Diane Wiest) and her sons, Michael (Jason Patric) and Sam (Corey Haim), travel to the sparsely populated seaside town of Santa Carla, California, to move in with Lucy's father. The tracking shots that accompany the film's credit sequence, following the Emerson's journey along a coastal highway, display little in the way of occupied civilization, making a special point of stopping behind a billboard with the spray-painted moniker "Murder Capitol of the World." This opening montage is edited to the sounds of "People Are Strange," the 1967 hit single by the Doors performed on the film's soundtrack by British postpunk band Echo & the Bunnymen.

And indeed, people are very strange in Santa Carla. On the way to Lucy's father's home, set far above the tiny town on an otherwise deserted hill, Michael, Sam, and their mother pass a smattering of residents ranging from leather-clad punks and strung-out junkies to dumpster-diving teenagers. Even Lucy's father has a rather eccentric and macabre sense of humor, pretending to lie dead of a heart attack on his front porch as his family arrives. Questioning their grandfather as to whether or not Santa Carla truly holds the distinction of being the "Murder Capitol of the World," the old man frankly responds, "If all the corpses buried around here were to stand up at once, we'd have one hell of a population problem."

Seeking any sort of adventure in what they believe to be the middle of absolutely nowhere, Michael and Sam are thrilled to discover that Santa Carla has a beach-adjacent boardwalk that becomes an active nocturnal scene of live music, mischief, and mayhem. During that night's entertainment, set to the performance of an all-male rock band whose lead singer sports a bare, oiled chest and leather pants tight enough to rival those of Olivia Newton John in *Grease*, Michael catches the eye of a beautiful young woman across the crowd. This exchange of glances appears to show that Michael is interested in Star (Jami Gertz) because he's sexually attracted to her, yet a closer look at its meeting "reveals something very queer indeed. Michael and Star's first looks at one another, which signal their sexual desire, take place at a beach-front concert and are repeatedly punctuated with shots of a sweaty, bare-chested, pumped-up male singer. These shots suggest that the female Star is being used to buffer or triangulate male homoerotic desires."[77] Furthermore, this triangulation expands into a queer quadrilateral when, unable to hold his brother's attention, Sam dejectedly declares: "I'm at the mercy of your sex glands, bud."

The exchanged glances between Michael and Star are ultimately what brings the Santa Carla stranger into the orbit of the titular lost boys, specifically that of their leader, David (Kiefer Sutherland). As Harry Benshoff notes, chief among the queer signifiers pressed into service by the mise-en-scène of *The Lost Boys* is the goth glam "'look' of the vampires themselves, a visual style lifted from punk and urban gay subcultures. Black leather, earrings for boys and other piercings, tattoos, facial stubble and/or goatee beards, and copious amounts of hair-bleach make this particular bunch of vampires look like gay male pin-ups."[78] Sweeping Star away on the back of his motorcycle, David dares Michael to follow the lost boys out into the night. Michael accepts the challenge and catches up to the group on his own bike, and the tracking shot that follows Michael and David's game of chicken across an abandoned rural landscape becomes a back-and-forth play of eye-focused queer intensity. "What could it mean for a man to engage the gaze of another man?" Hanson inquires. "In psychoanalytic terms, such a gaze would be a form of madness, an embrace of narcissism and death. The gay male gaze is the gaze of the male vampire: he with whom one is forbidden to identify."[79] Such engagement of illicit identification is taken to its suggestively queer peak when, after stopping short of plummeting over a jagged cliff, David seductively asks his prey, "How far are you willing to go, Michael?"

Unlike Sarah Roberts's vampiric transformation in *The Hunger*, Michael's viral metamorphosis in *The Lost Boys* doesn't take place among the chic urbanity of a thriving metropolis but rather amid its ruins. Leading Michael down into the bowels of a hollowed-out mountain, David declares that the lair of the lost boys used to be the most popular resort hotel in

Santa Carla when it was a humming tourist destination before being devastated by an earthquake that left the town practically abandoned. Among these ruins, David presents Michael with a jeweled bottle and invitation: "Drink some of this, Michael. Be one of us."

This mise-en-scène of death and desertion draws noticeable attention to what becomes Michael's subterranean moment of seroconversion. Looking around at Star, David, and the rest of the boys, Michael develops a sneaking suspicion, even before he drinks, that the bottle he's been handed is filled with blood. And it is this hunch that gives rise to a striking combination of aesthetic and narrative anxieties blurred into swirling images that begin to pass in slow motion. Whose blood is this? How did David procure it? What are the risks involved in its ingestion? Eventually bowing to the pressures that have him cornered, Michael drinks from the bottle and embarks on a hallucinatory voyage of swirling mists and intertwined male bodies, intimating queer sex and fluid exchange between Michael and David as the head vampire's smirking face is superimposed over the entire scene. Michael's seroconversion concludes with the lost boys and their new member hanging, like bats, beneath a railway bridge before floating down into an interminable miasma of fog.

In the context of the 1980s HIV/AIDS crisis, vampire mythology was frequently reworked across popular culture to offer a strategy for processing what David Skal calls the "widespread, inescapable reality of death at an early age . . . just as the younger generation of gay activists reclaimed the epithet 'queer' as a badge of honor . . . so was the negative vampire identification similarly embraced, rehabilitated, and defanged."[80] This dialectic between celebration and insecurity surrounding the perils and pleasures of youth, disease, and death became crystalized in *The Lost Boys*' tagline: "Sleep all day. Party all night. Never grow old. Never die. It's fun to be a vampire."

As Michael's viral symptoms begin to vampirically manifest as aversion to sunlight and hunger for blood, Sam quickly realizes that his brother is transforming into the same kind of invader anthropomorphized across 1980s media culture in reference to the HIV retrovirus: a contagious assailant that attacks from within. "You're a creature of the night, Michael," Sam exclaims, "just like out of a comic book! You're a vampire, Michael! My own brother, a goddamn, shit-sucking vampire!" Rehearsing a common homophobic slur through which the queer activity of analingus or "rimming" is assumed to inevitably produce sexually transmitted infections, Michael's bond with his normative family is threatened by his newly acquired psychological and physiological attachment to a queer family of lost boys. "With the exchange of 'normal,' human blood for the 'contaminated,' vampire blood," Katia Yurguis argues, the victim "stops being human, one of 'us,' and either by [her/his] own decision or by social rejection, undergoes a symbolic death. Similarly, when a person is tested for HIV antibodies and is diagnosed positive, [his/her] 'normal,' 'healthy' blood has mutated into 'contaminated,' 'sick' blood, like that of a vampire."[81]

Yet all is not lost for the Emerson family. Expanding *The Lost Boys'* queer trajectory through a viral reimagining of the conventional coming-out scene, Michael confesses to Sam that the malady that has begun to plague his body and change his appetites is unknown to him, but he promises that he will not act on these new desires and will do his best to expunge the virus as soon as possible. According to Stacey Abbott, vampirism in the context of HIV/AIDS and other viral maladies can be equated with "the body out of control; the act of becoming a vampire is increasingly portrayed as physical change to the body as opposed to resurrection from the dead," and *The Lost Boys* does indeed follow Michael's struggle "against his own transformation into a vampire as his body begins to rebel ... begins to act of its own accord."[82] What's more, there are strong suggestions that this scene of Michael's viral declaration and disavowal actually represents a double coming-out, juxtaposed alongside Sam's own significations of queer masculinity by sporting a "Born to Shop" T-shirt against a background pinup poster of a shirtless Rob Lowe in his bedroom. In this and other scenes throughout the film, *The Lost Boys* turns interwoven virally queer undertones into overtones, "taking the latent, the implied and the mysterious, and turning them into the loud and the obvious," as Dave Kehr of the *Chicago Tribune* said in his review.[83]

If Michael/David and Michael/Sam represent two of *The Lost Boys'* queer dyads, the solution to the film's viral dilemma is found in a third: the Frog Brothers. Edgar and Allen Frog, portrayed by Corey Feldman and Jamison Newlander, respectively, share a passion for all things occult, finishing each other's sentences, and manning their parents' comic book store on the Santa Carla boardwalk while moonlighting as local vampire hunters. Enlisted by Sam to rid the Emerson family of the lost boys' influence, Edgar, Allen, Sam, and the increasingly infectious Michael venture down into the abandoned resort in search of David and his minions. If the mise-en-scène of Michael's subterranean seroconversion represents an internalization of the vampire's queer malady, Edgar's staking of one of the lost boys represents the inverse, covering the young slayers in a torrent of contaminated blood as the vampire's body explodes in a horrific reversal of the film's ambivalence toward fluid exchange. In an even more grotesque sequence later that evening inside the Emerson home, Edgar and Allen hold each other tightly as one of the vampires is thrust into a bathtub filled with holy water and garlic, triggering a spectacular reaction between "his flesh and the holy water [that] causes the water to bubble and his flesh and blood [to infect] the house's entire plumbing system, as every sink, pipe and toilet explodes in a purple shower of blood, flesh, and other bodily liquids."[84] If the staking scene toward the conclusion of *The Hunger* solidifies the queer viral bond between Sarah and Miriam through the back-and-forth exchange of blood/menstrual fluid, a similar dynamic is at work in *The Lost Boys*, as the eruption of these male vampires' life-force becomes an abject substitute for the "little death/*la petit mort*" orgasmic release of semen covering other men.[85]

From his first queer encounter with David and the lost boys, Michael's viral seroconversion is dramatized as a battle between his human moral compass and the new, bloody desires of his body.[86] Paradoxically, however, it is only by fully embracing his vampirism that Michael is able to overcome David's strength, impale him on a set of deer antlers, and return to his human form. In contradistinction to the chic urban landscapes of *The Hunger*, *The Lost Boys* muses on the pleasurable and pathological possibilities of creating a nonurban queer viral vampire community shared among men. In fact, during a climactic moment of confession in which Lucy's love interest Max (Ed Herrmann) admits that all he's wanted was to turn the Emersons in order to create "one big happy family . . . your boys and my boys," it is revealed that Max, not David, is the leader of the lost boys. "Great," Edgar quips snidely, "the blood-sucking Brady Bunch!" But before Max's queer dream can be consummated, Lucy's father storms through the front façade of the house in his Jeep, launching an elongated stake through the air and into Max's chest.

While *The Lost Boys* does attempt to maintain a thin veil of two ostensibly heterosexual subplots, one between Lucy and Max and the other between Michael and Star, the film's focus remains squarely on the interactions and queer desires of the boys themselves.[87] Lamenting what this unique strain of queer contagion has done to his solitary seaside serenity, Lucy's father calmly grabs a Coke from the refrigerator and declares in a concluding line, "One thing about living in Santa Carla I never could stomach . . . all the damn vampires."

Released just two months after *The Lost Boys*, F/M Entertainment's *Near Dark* was the second feature directed by Kathryn Bigelow, who, along with Eric Red, coauthored its screenplay. Like much of the clamor that surrounded Bigelow's historic Oscar win for directing the Iraq-war-focused *The Hurt Locker* (2008), *Near Dark*'s significance as an independent occult success has been bolstered by the supposedly remarkable ability of a female director to fashion a film that, as Nina Auerbach puts it, is filled with "gratuitous macho slaughter Bigelow's camera relishes as much as her vampires do."[88] Underneath its surface machismo and insistent heteronormativity however, attempting "so strenuously to submerge its vampires in paternalistic morality that it makes us cry out for something new," *Near Dark* presents a panorama of virally queer vampirism and bloody ambivalence in ways that envision the phantasmatic consequences of rural contagion even more emphatically than *The Lost Boys*.[89]

As both popular press reviews and academic critics have noted, *Near Dark* is at least a tripartite generic hybrid: a Western and road film as much as a vampire movie. Through the centrality of contaminated blood's paradoxically infectious and life-giving properties during the course of the film, "the vampires' nocturnal existence, along with the recurring themes of immortality and inhuman predation, situate the narrative in the horror genre, while visuals of the rural heartland, from dusty vistas and farmland to roadhouses and pickup trucks, position the characters firmly in the Western tradition."[90] Indeed, Caleb Colton (Adrian Pasdar) is introduced in *Near Dark*'s opening sequence as a quintessential country boy, complete with cowboy hat, checkered shirt, and battered red pickup truck. Caleb's truck serves as a mobile signifier not only of his rugged life on an Oklahoma family farm but also as something of a poet's corner of sensitive introspection, as an establishing medium shot focuses on Caleb as a silhouetted, solitary figure staring contemplatively out into the twilight from the truck's bed. The subsequent long-distance tracking shot follows the truck traveling as a diminutive specter against a vast nightfall landscape of farms, hills, telephone wires, and country dirt roads.

Replicating a predominantly Western mise-en-scène, *Near Dark* places much of its visual attention on the rural horizon, as Caleb's truck is framed in long shot, "dwarfed by the expanse of the surrounding landscape . . . this emphasis on the horizon serves to draw attention to both the landscape and the significance of the sun as it rises and sets."[91] The visual and narrative motifs of the occult horror film are not absent across this rustic background but rather are rearticulated, within the contours of its many shadows, by Bigelow's camera.[92] Addressing a similar attitude toward nonurban horizons of perverse possibility, Herring argues that the rural, "at once a geographic entity and a performative space that has often been shunned, mocked, and discarded by the metropolitan-minded—can be a supreme site of queer critique given that stereotypical images of the region or the rural can be used for unexpected ends."[93] Placing *Near Dark* squarely in the middle of the American heartland shatters the normative expectation that viewers will not encounter familiarly horrific images from elsewhere, as Bigelow herself commented early in 1988.[94]

As evening falls and Caleb arrives in what can only be described as the late-1980s equivalent of a one-horse town, his attention is immediately drawn to a young woman eating an ice cream cone under the shadows of a nearby lamppost. Introducing himself with all the "howdy ma'am" charm that only years of country cliché could muster, Caleb's initial encounter with Mae (Jenny Wright) is filled with both sexual and vampiric double entendre:

CALEB: "Can I have a bite?"
MAE: "Bite?"
CALEB: "I'm just dyin' for a cone."
MAE: "Dyin'?"

Ironically, Caleb's imperious heterosexual advances are directed toward a woman whose pixie haircut, cutoff shirt, denim jacket, and refusal to acquiesce to male solicitations sets up a desiring tableau of crossed wires and queer misdirection: androgyny with a rustic tint. Mae even nominates herself as a not-of-this-world creature whose queerness sets her apart from all others: "You wanna know why you've never met a girl like me? Because I'll still be here when the light from that star gets down here to Earth . . . in a billion years." Indeed, Caleb may attempt to engage Mae's attentions not necessarily because he is sexually attracted to her but rather in light of his exasperation with the normative tedium of country living, exemplified by his earlier reflection, "I wish I may, I wish I might. Wish I was a thousand miles from here tonight." Perplexed yet enchanted by the obscurity of Mae's musings, Caleb finally does receive the kiss he pressingly requests, but its consequences are not at all what he bargained for.

Stumbling home across sunburned fields after Mae has drawn blood from his neck, Caleb begins to physically crumble with the rising sun, emitting pillars of smoke and exhibiting gruesome signs of a rapidly burning face, as, from afar, his young sister Sarah (Marcie Leeds) implores their father (Tim Thomerson) to help with his obvious illness. But just before Caleb reaches home, a dilapidated Winnebago filled with Mae and her traveling companions storms across the field, picks up Caleb, and races off. After introducing them as a nomadic clan who live and feed exclusively on the "open road or on the outskirts of cities, near railroad tracks, bus stations, and truck stops," reminiscent of the perverse rural families in *The Texas Chainsaw Massacre* (1974) and *The Hills Have Eyes* (1977), the remainder of *Near Dark* follows Mae, Jesse Hooker (Lance Henriksen), Severen (Bill Paxton), Diamondback (Jenette Goldstein), and the adolescent Homer (Joshua Miller) as they attempt to complete Caleb's seroconversion by persuading him to accept his new vampiric lifestyle.[95]

Although premised on a model of heteronormative desire, Caleb and Mae's performance of sexuality is both stunted and "careful—subtle and limited—and [their] sexual status indeterminate (viewers never see [them] have sex, so it is unclear if she and Caleb attain that level of intimacy while they are both vampires)."[96] Dramatizing seroconversion as even more visceral and "uncomfortably debilitating" than the process endured by Michael in *The Lost Boys*, *Near Dark* becomes feverishly obsessed with the viral malady that fights to overwhelm Caleb's appetites, sexual and otherwise.[97] Indeed, Mae's dogged insistence that Caleb has no other choice but to surrender to the viral blood now coursing through his veins relies on the distinctly queer pleasures of passive male submission frequently evoked in vampire fiction.[98] Refusing to ingest blood of his own accord, Caleb is forced to survive by employing Mae as an intermediary, accessing the blood of her victims by biting Mae's arm once her own feeding is complete. Within this queer dyad, then, Caleb becomes an indeterminate combination of both partner and pet.[99] As Bigelow's film makes plain, the play of "gender role, sexual position, active/passive is part of the structure of vampirism and lesbian/gay sexuality alike—unlike heterosexuality (at least at the level of representation) such play is the rule, not the exception."[100]

Yet *Near Dark*'s penultimate act seems to abandon, at least ostensibly, its flirtation with nonnormative sexual and gender transgressions by transforming Caleb into the consummate conquering hero who swoops in to rescue the damsel in distress. As Caleb's father liberates his son from the vampires during their respite at a deserted motel, both agree that this queer virus is something their Oklahoma heartland has never witnessed before:

> LOY: Caleb, those people back there, they wasn't normal. Normal folks, they don't spit out bullets when you shoot 'em, no sir.
>
> CALEB: I ain't a person anymore. I don't know what I am. I'm sick! . . . Daddy, you ever transfuse a person before?

Caleb is fortunate that his father, channeling the spirits of so many Van Helsings before him, possesses significant medical expertise as their town's veterinarian. And in a feat rarely if ever accomplished by characters in vampire cinema despite innumerable attempts, Dr. Colton's transfusion of Caleb, set among cattle and hay bales in the middle of their family barn, does prove successful and returns Caleb to his fully human state by expunging the queerly contaminated blood.

Following Caleb's rescue of his sister after the vampires have kidnapped her, Homer, Jesse, and Severen meet their respective ends in *Near Dark*'s final act through a spectacularized succession of gruesome deaths that viscerally invoke the somatic trauma of their viral condition set against the pastoral landscape of middle America. Once rid of his antagonists, Caleb rushes to Mae's aid before she also succumbs to the rays of the rising sun. After he implores his father to work another miracle, Mae too is successfully transfused as Caleb embraces her in a final freeze frame that fades to black.

Many commenters have read *Near Dark*'s ending as heteronormativity once again reigning supreme in the horror film, as monsters are vanquished and two persons heretofore gone astray have returned to their rightful roles in heterosexual coupling. However, the conclusion of the film actually presents something quite different. Rather than rejoicing in the fact that her hand is not being seared by the rays of the morning sun, Mae's contemplative marveling evokes instead a palpable register of remorse, reservation, and even regret. Caleb looks with a proud smile on his rescued partner, who is disoriented "as memories and long-conditioned responses to the danger of the sun collide with her new reality."[101] Yet as Cynthia Miller reminds us, Mae is completely unaware that her blood has been transfused, "that her dreams of immortality have been taken, without her consent. . . . With the life-giving transfusion of his blood, [Caleb] denies her the opportunity" to choose her own destiny.[102] The ambivalence surrounding the transactional exchange of blood in *Near Dark* is consequently a two-way street, as the expunging of contaminated blood may be as debilitating to some as its ingestion is to others. Indeed, if the link between vampirism and the HIV/AIDS crisis is simply that of a wasting malady, then the vampire's cure is "a blessing, but if it [also] contains immortality, secret strength, and forbidden identities, its domestication is a death more painful" than that of any human viral victim.[103] In this final image, then, Mae mourns for the marvelously queer world she's been forced to leave behind, wherein she and her perverse family reveled in nights "so bright, it'll blind you" and vast rural horizons so loud "it's deafening."

How to Have Consanguineous Community in an Epidemic

In April 1987, the *Chicago Tribune* article "Vampires Halted by AIDS Scare" reported the findings of one Dr. Josef Sperl, a "Vienna-based virologist," who argued that vampires were facing the "most serious threat to survival in the history of their breed."[104] The *Tribune*'s Clarence Petersen called the piece—originally published in the *Weekly World News*, an iteration of the *National Enquirer* then at its peak of tabloid sensationalism—a "step into an alien world" where there was "every indication that several of them [vampires] have already been infected with the AIDS virus and the rest of them are terrified they'll be next."[105] What's more, in a "frightening footnote," Sperl suggested that most vampires were at "especially high risk" of contracting HIV/AIDS due to the fact that most were "flaming homosexuals."[106] Regardless of whether Dr. Sperl and his discoveries were based on fact or fiction, Petersen's article and others like it demonstrate that the supposedly ill-fated identities of both the sexually active queer and the vampire were condensed into one of the most easily digestible media metaphors for HIV/AIDS in the epidemiological imagination of the 1980s, with both groups taking on the viral rhetoric of clearly defined "risk groups."

Across the 1980s vampire film, figures like Sarah Roberts, Michael Emerson, and Caleb Colton share many similar experiences during their immersion into an emergent rhetoric of bloody ambivalence, becoming involved with vampires who queer both their social and sexual lives, dramatize their seroconversions, and inspire habitual "What's happening to me?" breakdowns wherein the vampiric virus finally begins to manifest in unavoidable ways. Significantly, these seroconversions are explicitly framed as family affairs, initiations into viral communities through which members are both physically and psychologically bound. Yet no matter how powerfully these moments are framed by dialogue, music, and mise-en-scène as dark, deviant, and deadly, they nevertheless engender perversely queer pleasures that continue to thrill some nonnormative sexual subcultures: "That, on the basis of viral transmission, they can form relations and networks understood in terms of kinship—networks that represent an alternative to, even as they often resemble, normative heterosexual kinship."[107]

In October 2003, a panel discussion at the New York City Lesbian, Gay, Bisexual and Transgender Community Center focused on a topic that seemed wildly inimical to both the clinical and cultural strides made in the fight against HIV/AIDS over the previous twenty-two years: barebacking, the practice of unprotected anal intercourse between men, sometimes with the purposeful intent of facilitating HIV transmission.[108] As a demographic study discussed at the panel and reported in the *Advocate* revealed,

> [Of the] 518 gay and bisexual men surveyed, 204 reported having bareback sex in the previous three months. One quarter of those men engaging in anal sex without condoms were aware that they were HIV-positive at the time they had unsafe sex. The survey also showed that 47.9% of the men who had bareback sex said they did so because of the effectiveness of new anti-HIV medications, while 45.6% blamed AIDS fatigue and 48.9% said boring safer sex campaigns led to their behavior. About 40% of the men surveyed said bareback sex was a new "sexual and cultural" phenomenon in gay communities.[109]

Far from being apathetic to the presence of HIV, then, many gay men were beginning to make the virus "central to their erotic lives. They [were] having sex not only with other men but also with a virus . . . deliberately [incorporating] an invisible microbe into their sexual practices and relationships."[110] According to Tim Dean, the rise of barebacking as an identarian viral community "organized around the abandonment of condoms . . . organized around the giving and receiving of semen—is something new. The subculture of what is colloquially known as 'cum swapping' needs to be distinguished from gay sex practices that, before AIDS, never gave rise to subcultural communities."[111] What had gone wrong, the panel participants wondered? Had Randy Shilts's dark prophecy from *And the Band Played On*, that the "complete focus on the physical aspect of sex [meant] constantly devising new, more extreme sexual acts because the experience relied on heightened sensory rather than emotional stimulation," finally returned to haunt queers of the new millennium?[112] Would the gradual abandonment of condoms and the growth of barebacking communities engender a reappearance of the bloodsucking, body-fluid-exchanging pathological discourse that so heavily marked HIV/AIDS as vampirically queer during the 1980s?

As Dean writes in *Unlimited Intimacy: Reflections on the Subculture of Barebacking*, the emergence of subcultural community formation around unprotected anal intercourse between gay men has typically been viewed as a case of "pathological self-destructiveness or, at best, gross irresponsibility on the part of those who should know better."[113] This kind of sexual moralizing has, according to Michael Warner, become a lingua franca of contemporary queer sexual discourses: "Sooner or later, happily or unhappily, almost everyone fails to control his or her sex life. Perhaps as compensation, almost everyone sooner or later also succumbs to the temptation to control someone else's sex life. Most people cannot quite rid themselves of the sense that controlling the sex of others, far from being unethical, is where morality begins."[114] "You just met her and she gives you a present," Tom Haver polices Sarah Roberts snidely over dinner in *The Hunger* when sensing her queer infidelity. "Did you have something you wanted to tell me?"

As Warner, Douglas Crimp, Simon Watney, and others maintain, the overwhelming discursive labor centered on the viral contagion of HIV/AIDS has turned and continues to turn on the projected phantasm of "'promiscuity,' as if all non-gays were either monogamous or celibate and, more culpably still, as if AIDS were related to sex in a quantitative rather than qualitative way."[115] To be sure, HIV/AIDS often constructs a cultural screen of causality through which all forms of sexual practice aside from long-term monogamy are seen as promiscuous, therefore dangerous, and therefore deviant.[116] If much of the horror inspired by queer sex, especially the recent explosion of subcultural barebacking practices, revolves around the "too much, too often" characterization of insatiable sexual appetites and precarious mixtures of semen, blood, and other bodily fluids, so too does such indiscriminate conduct crystalize in the occultly queer sexualities of the vampire. For not only do both vampires and barebackers signify abjection by their refusal to respect "boundaries that separate persons, classes, races, and generations from each other," but they correspondingly create polymorphous forms of "socially unsanctioned sex or promiscuous mixing . . . because [they] muddle identification, contaminating one thing with another."[117] To recall Richard Dyer's interpretation, one doesn't have to read the boundary-breaking vampiric bond as sexual, "but an awful lot suggests that you should. . . . Biting itself is after all part of the repertoire of sexual acts; call it a kiss, and, when it is as deep a kiss as this, it is a sexual act; it is then by extension obviously analogous to other forms of oral sex acts, all of which . . . importantly involve contact not only with orifices but with body fluids as well."[118]

Akin to acts of unprotected anal intercourse and "cum swapping" between gay men, the vampire can forcefully propel her/himself and her/his partner toward the very limits of queer sexual desire. Even before Leo Bersani famously asked if the rectum was a grave in 1987, the mythology of the vampire expressed itself in anal-erotic terms, recognizing the "abjected space that gay men are obliged to inhabit; that space unspeakable or unnamable, itself defined as orifice, as a 'dark continent' . . . that gap bridge over or sutured together, where men cease to play dead and yet cease to accept the normative sexual role."[119] Bareback sex has thus become a sexually Gothicized activity par excellence, opening horizons beyond normative social patterns and rational decisions while acknowledging the irrational as a great liberator of feeling.[120] Indeed, barebacking has been taken up not just in dimly lit queer bathhouses, bars, and other outlets of both private and public sex but also by the gay pornography industry in such best-selling titles as *The Lust Boys* (Sierra Pacific, 1999), *Twink Blood* (BoyCrush, 2009), *Twinklight* (Gaylife Network, 2010), *Thirst* (MEN.com, 2016), and *Barebackula* (Lucas Entertainment, 2016).

To those for whom the Gothicized activity of barebacking represents a form of resistance to the "'logic of defilement'" that has historically marked both the sexually active queer and the vampire, unsheathed fucking and figurative or literal bloodsucking challenges "stereotypical narratives about homosexuality as a doomed identity," revealing in their stead newly emergent forms of sexual freedom.[121] Rather than wallowing in self-abasement, both the viral barebacker and the viral vampire endorse subcultural practices that continue to project a "familiar gay voice—it is the voice of that part of the gay liberation movement which set itself against respectability and fitting in, against monogamy and passing for straight . . . where depravity and degradation are validated; it is the voice that prizes gayness as outlawry and living on the edge."[122] This abject promiscuity credited to both the barebacker and the vampire presents an opportunity to refashion the ethics around which community formation can materialize—perverse permutations of sociability that hold queer cultures together.[123] Indeed, promiscuity has taught queer people many things, not only about the "pleasures of sex, but about the great multiplicity of those pleasures. It is that psychic preparation, that experimentation, that conscious work on our own sexualities that has allowed many of us to change our sexual behaviors."[124] These queer multiplicities are situated at the very heart of modern-day vampiric practice, wherein the vampire often solicits a cadre of willing blood donors of both sexes and, above all, develops relationships with them founded on respect, mutual self-care, the giving and receiving of blood, and the reciprocity of erotic gratification.[125] From Jean Rollin to Tony Scott and beyond, the "blessed malediction" of vampirism has been consistently coded as a "'dark gift' of blood, [playing] on the contradictory feelings of attraction and repulsion."[126] So too, among barebacking subcultures, has the intentional transmission of the HIV virus been refashioned as a gift, a "putative object of exchange," or a shared substance, permitting such bonds to be conceived in terms of kinship.[127]

Rather than being inscribed as pathological, self-destructive behaviors, promiscuous barebacking and promiscuous vampirism have been rearticulated as "promoting reciprocal care and self-protection . . . promiscuity, in other words, concerns more than new sex partners: it also concerns new ideas and new ways of doing things . . . unaccountable though it seems at first blush, [promiscuity] actually signals profound changes in the social organization of kinship and relationality."[128] Embracing the risks associated with unsheathed fucking and viral transmission, both barebacking and vampirism represent potential means to counteract health as an instrument of Foucauldian biopower: "If the desire to be healthy stems from the desire to be normal, then those who appreciate 'the trouble with normal' experience less pressure to conform to health mandates."[129] To borrow from Dean, the fantasies that animate both barebacking and vampiric subcultures, those limit-pushing, boundary-breaking sexual acts that can endure either literally or figuratively for life everlasting through the "gifting" of a virus, present some of the most morally challenging yet ethically innovative forms of unlimited queer intimacy.

Notes

1. Arlene Russo, *Vampire Nation* (Woodbury: Llewellyn, 2008), 73.
2. Cited in James Kinsella, *Covering the Plague: AIDS and the American Media* (New Brunswick: Rutgers University Press, 1989), 48.
3. Lawrence K. Altman, "Rare Cancer Seen In 41 Homosexuals," *New York Times*, July 3, 1981.
4. Ibid.
5. Ibid.

6. Deborah Lupton, *Moral Threats and Dangerous Desires: AIDS in the News Media* (London: Taylor & Francis, 1994), 121.
7. Lawrence K. Altman, "Clue Found on Homosexuals' Precancer Syndrome," *New York Times*, June 18, 1982.
8. Kinsella, 54.
9. David J. Skal, *V Is for Vampire: The A to Z Guide to Everything Undead* (New York: Plume, 1995), 5.
10. Susan Sontag, "Illness as Metaphor," in *Illness as Metaphor and AIDS and Its Metaphors* (New York: Anchor, 1989), 69.
11. See, for example, Nina Auerbach, *Our Vampires, Ourselves* (Chicago: University of Chicago Press, 1995); Harry M. Benshoff, *Monsters in the Closet: Homosexuality and the Horror Film* (Manchester: Manchester University Press, 1997); Richard Dyer, "Children of the Night: Vampirism as Homosexuality, Homosexuality as Vampirism," in *Sweet Dreams: Sexuality, Gender, and Popular Fiction*, ed. Susannah Radstone (London: Lawrence & Wishart, 1988): 47–72; Ellis Hanson, "Undead" in *Inside/Out: Lesbian Theories, Gay Theories*, ed. Diana Fuss (New York: Routledge, 1991): 324–40; Arlene Russo, *Vampire Nation* (Woodbury: Llewellyn, 2008); and David J. Skal, *The Monster Show: A Cultural History of Horror* (New York: Penguin, 1994).
12. Jeffrey A. Bennett, *Banning Queer Blood: Rhetorics of Citizenship, Contagion, and Resistance* (Tuscaloosa: University of Alabama Press, 2009), 3.
13. Susan Sontag, "AIDS and Its Metaphors," in *Illness as Metaphor and AIDS and Its Metaphors* (New York: Anchor, 1989), 161.
14. Tim Dean, *Unlimited Intimacy: Reflections on the Subculture of Barebacking* (Chicago: University of Chicago Press, 2009), 6.
15. Skal, 6.
16. Ibid., 5.
17. For an influential discussion of sex and death in fin-de-siècle Europe, see Judith Walkowitz, *City of Dreadful Delight: Narratives of Sexual Danger in Late-Victorian London* (Chicago: University of Chicago Press, 1992).
18. Skal, 48.
19. Although I don't wish to invoke the specter of the intentional fallacy, Murnau's own well-known queer sexuality is worthy of at least passing mention here.
20. Skal, 48.
21. Dyer, 55.
22. My use of trans* is borrowed from recent writings on the subject by Jack Halberstam, who argues that omitting suffixes like "-gender" or "-sexual" from "trans" and replacing it with an asterisk "modifies the meaning of transitivity by refusing to situate transition in relation to a destination, a final form, a specific shape, or an established configuration of desire and identity." See Halberstam, *Trans*: A Quick and Quirky Account of Gender Variability* (Berkeley: University of California Press, 2018).
23. Skal, 345.
24. Ibid., 346.
25. Douglas Crimp, "AIDS: Cultural Analysis/Cultural Activism," in *Melancholia and Moralism: Essays on AIDS and Queer Politics* (Cambridge, MA: MIT Press, 2002), 28.
26. Simon Watney, *Practices of Freedom: Selected Writings on HIV/AIDS* (Durham: Duke University Press, 1994), 11.

27. Ellis Hanson, "Lesbians Who Bite," in *Out Takes: Essays on Queer Theory and Film* (Durham: Duke University Press, 1999), 212.

28. Ibid., 199.

29. Michel de Certeau, *The Practice of Everyday Life*, trans. Steven Rendall (Berkeley: University of California Press, 1984), 96.

30. See also Michel Foucault's discussion of the "plague city" in *Discipline and Punish: The Birth of the Prison* (New York: Pantheon, 1977).

31. Priscilla Wald, *Contagious: Cultures, Carriers, and the Outbreak Narrative* (Durham: Duke University Press, 2008), 116–30.

32. Ibid., 216.

33. Ibid., 120.

34. Chauncey, *Gay New York: Gender, Urban Culture, and the Makings of the Gay Male World, 1890–1940* (New York: Basic, 1994), 132.

35. Ibid., 131.

36. Andrea Weiss, *Vampires & Violets: Lesbians in Film* (New York: Penguin, 1993), 91.

37. Wald, 130.

38. Samuel R. Delany, *Times Square Red, Times Square Blue* (New York: New York University Press, 1999), 127.

39. Ibid.

40. Sontag, 164.

41. Hanson, "Undead," 324.

42. Alan Citron, "Gays' Sex Life Haunted by AIDS Specter," *Los Angeles Times*, July 17, 1983.

43. Whitley Strieber, *The Hunger* (New York: William Morrow, 1981), 49.

44. Ibid., 58–59.

45. Claudia Wallis, "AIDS: A Growing Threat," *Time*, August 12, 1985.

46. Strieber, 55.

47. Nancy Gagnier, "The Authentic Dracula: Bram Stoker's Hold on Vampiric Genres," in *Goth: Undead Subculture*, ed. Lauren M. E. Goodlad and Michael Bibby (Durham: Duke University Press, 2007), 302.

48. Strieber, 81.

49. Wald, 133.

50. Strieber, 86.

51. Sontag, "AIDS and Its Metaphors," 113.

52. Strieber, 107–8.

53. Ibid., 170.

54. Sontag, "AIDS and Its Metaphors," 107.

55. Weiss, 103.

56. Lauren M. E. Goodlad and Michael Bibby, "Introduction," in *Goth: Undead Subculture*, ed. Lauren M. E. Goodlad and Michael Bibby (Durham: Duke University Press, 2007), 1.

57. Ibid., 2.

58. Trevor M. Holmes, "Peri Gothous: On the Art of Gothicizing Gender," in *Goth: Undead Subculture*, ed. Lauren M. E. Goodlad and Michael Bibby (Durham: Duke University Press, 2007), 79.

59. Ibid., 80.

60. Barbara Creed, *The Monstrous-Feminine: Film, Feminism, Psychoanalysis* (London: Routledge, 1993), 68.

61. Hanson, "Lesbians Who Bite," 214.
62. Creed, 61.
63. Ibid.
64. Hanson, "Undead," 325.
65. Simon Watney, *Policing Desire: Pornography, AIDS, and the Media* (Minneapolis: University of Minnesota Press, 1987), 8.
66. Hanson, "Lesbians Who Bite," 212.
67. Creed, 69.
68. Weiss, 103.
69. "The Hunger," *Variety*, April 27, 1983.
70. Creed, 68.
71. Hanson, "Lesbians Who Bite," 195.
72. Wald, 225.
73. Randy Shilts, *And the Band Played On: Politics, People, and the AIDS Epidemic* (New York: St. Martin's, 1987), 89.
74. Scott Herring, *Another Country: Queer Anti-Urbanism* (New York: New York University Press, 2010), 1.
75. Ibid., 5.
76. Ibid., 9.
77. Benshoff, 253.
78. Ibid.
79. Hanson, "Undead," 328.
80. Skal, 347–48.
81. Katia Yurguis, "The Dark Gift: Vampires in the AIDS Era," *Discoveries* 4 (Fall 2002): 5–6.
82. Stacey Abbott, *Celluloid Vampires: Life after Death in the Modern World* (Austin: University of Texas Press, 2007), 133.
83. Dave Kehr, "'The Lost Boys' a Vampire Film Thirsting for a Good Story," *Chicago Tribune*, July 31, 1987.
84. Abbott, 137.
85. Both Roland Barthes and Georges Bataille have used the "little death"/*la petit mort* metaphor in reference to the near-ecstatic feeling of subliminal unconsciousness following orgasm.
86. Abbott, 133.
87. Benshoff, 252.
88. Auerbach, 187.
89. Ibid.
90. Cynthia J. Miller, "Liberating the Vampire, but Not the Woman: Kathryn Bigelow's *Near Dark* (1987)," in *Dracula's Daughters: The Female Vampire on Film*, ed. Douglas Brode and Leah Deyneka (New York: Scarecrow, 2014), 273.
91. Abbott, 165.
92. Ibid.
93. Herring, 12–13.
94. Cited in Louise Gray, "Film: The Lady and the Vamps," *New Musical Express*, January 9, 1988.
95. Abbott, 168–69.
96. Miller, 272.

97. Auerbach, 189.
98. Dyer, 63.
99. Miller, 269.
100. Dyer, 64.
101. Miller, 280.
102. Ibid.
103. Auerbach, 192.
104. Clarence Petersen, "Vampires Halted by AIDS Scare," *Chicago Tribune*, April 30, 1987.
105. Ibid.
106. Ibid.
107. Dean, x.
108. Technically, barebacking can refer to any type of unprotected sexual intercourse, regardless of orientation. However, the term has been used almost exclusively in queer contexts.
109. "New York Panel Examines Rise in Barebacking," Advocate.com, October 28, 2003, http://www.advocate.com/health/health-news/2003/10/28/new-york-panel-examines-rise-barebacking-10298.
110. Dean, 17.
111. Ibid., 10.
112. Shilts, 24.
113. Dean, 2.
114. Michael Warner, *The Trouble with Normal: Sex, Politics, and the Ethics of Queer Life* (Cambridge: Harvard University Press, 2000), 1.
115. Watney, *Policing Desire: Pornography, AIDS, and the Media*, 12.
116. Sontag, "AIDS and Its Metaphors," 161.
117. Dean, 20.
118. Dyer, 54–55.
119. Hanson, "Undead," 325.
120. Robert B. Heilman, "Charlotte Brontë's 'New' Gothic," in *From Jane Austen to Joseph Conrad: Essays Collected in Memory of James T. Hillhouse*, ed. Robert C. Rathburn and Martin Steinmann Jr. (Minneapolis: University of Minnesota Press, 1958), 131.
121. Dean, 68.
122. Dyer, 69.
123. Warner, 35.
124. Douglas Crimp, "How to Have Promiscuity in an Epidemic," in *Melancholia and Moralism: Essays on AIDS and Queer Politics* (Cambridge: MIT Press, 2002), 64.
125. Russo, 74.
126. Yurguis, 1.
127. Dean, 78.
128. Ibid., 5–6.
129. Ibid., 66..

4

"NOW IS THE TIME, NOW IS THE HOUR, OURS IS THE MAGICK, OURS IS THE POWER"

Casting as Coming Out in Millennial Media

On June 30, 2016, millennial-targeted media site Mic.com ran a brief exposé entitled "The Secret Lives of Teen Witches on Tumblr." Found within the site's Connections, a division dedicated to discussing "our common problems and [answering] the less-obvious questions that people don't feel okay discussing with their friends, like sex, money, religion, family, aging, mental health, and more," Leigh Cuen's editorial details how young occult practitioners have increasingly harnessed the community-focused characteristics of social media, particularly platforms like Tumblr, to foster the formation of new magickal identities.[1] Founded in 2007 by tech entrepreneur David Karp, Tumblr advertises itself as a collection of hundreds of millions of different blogs, "filled with literally whatever," that are accessed by over half a billion visitors worldwide each month.[2] Although an initial encounter with Tumblr's rhizomatic organization can be difficult, diffuse, and disorienting, even the most cursory search of this microblogging museum reveals thousands of users whose on-site activity is dedicated solely to the practice of magick. In the space of just six months between January and June 2016, one Tumblr spokesperson reported the following numbers of original posts hashtagged (#) with occult vocabulary: #witchcraft (225,472), #witch (106,125), #wicca (87,937), #spells (50,293), #wiccan (28,563), #divination (26,494), and #coven (6,265).[3]

To say that social media outlets like Facebook, Twitter, Instagram, Snapchat, and Tumblr have changed the ways young people around the world foster their senses of self and relationships with others now seems, at least to many, simple common sense. Yet whereas platforms such as Facebook and Instagram have become steadily embroiled in debates over content moderation and subject matter censorship, Tumblr has continued the fight to remain a decidedly NSFW (not-safe-for-work) space should users choose to use the site for such purposes. Indeed, the platform's "literally whatever"/anything goes ethos is manifest most obviously in the circulation of both still and moving-image pornography, but also less conspicuously in the dissemination and cultivation of hobbies, habits, and lifestyles that many users may be reticent to reveal outside the boundaries of their online lives. For instance, as Cuen notes, new forms of magickal spellcasting have emerged on Tumblr that are specific to "digital teenage witchery, such as 'emojicraft,' or the practice of using emojis to cast spells and reblogs to charge it with the power of cooperation from hundreds of fellow online witches."[4] As such, the comparative anonymity of a life on Tumblr has allowed the site to become a paradigmatic platform for both curious and already-competent millennials to practice magick.

As demonstrated throughout previous chapters, the concurrent mediation of queerness and the occult has proved far more than a series of serendipitous coincidences over the past sixty years. And indeed, Tumblr is no exception to this trend. As scholars like Adrienne Shaw, Elisabeth Friedman, Alexander Cho, and others have noted, the internet's ability to connect people across divergent borders of geography, culture, and language has allowed minoritarian communities the ability to articulate senses of both community and self that might otherwise prove difficult, distressing, and even dangerous within normal daily interactions. For their part, queer Tumblr users "circulate porn, flirt, provide support to deal with homophobia as well as advice on coming out, disseminate news pertinent to LGBT communities, organize real-life meet-ups, post pictures of themselves, 'reblog' pictures of others, 'like' pictures of sexy men and women"[5] and, as blogs owned by users such as "magick-queer-bro," "agender-witch," "queer-magick," "craftingmagick," and "queerwitchcraft" reveal, curate magickal online spaces for "pagans, queers, heathens, fags, heretics, trans folx, faeries, dykes, genderfuckers, witches and you."[6] This final "you" acts as both statement and invitation, welcoming those with curiosity about the Craft to continue scrolling through.

As Alexander Cho argues, Tumblr's nonlinear, disjointed, and transient organization has engendered a uniquely queer relationship to temporality and affect.⁷ This incoherence has lent itself almost seamlessly to the simultaneous articulation of both queerness and the occult, even down to the diction of scholarly digital discourse that remains haunted by the language of the supernatural. For instance, navigating through Tumblr stimulates feelings of "*eerie dislocation*, it is *elusive*, a *shock* of dumbness, the sense that you may not be able to understand the (primarily visual) vocabulary being used around you, an *alien* architecture of affinity and attunement that at first glance *evades literal understanding* [emphases mine]."⁸ If both queerness and occultism have been united by a historical doubling down of secrecy, ephemerality, and the evasion of official archival records, then Tumblr may represent one of the newest media platforms through which queer magickal practitioners are able to turn "underground economies of expression and relation that traffic in code, affinity, and intuition" into a cyberpublic space decipherable and legible to those who, in typically queer fashion, are attuned to reading between the lines and cracking the code.⁹ As the *Sunday Times*' Victoria McKee simply puts it, "The computer has replaced the cauldron."¹⁰

Tumblr is only one recent instantiation within a much longer history of teenagers and adolescents latching on to alternative spiritualties and occult media culture in the spirit of rebellion. As Lynn Schofield Clark observes, experimentation with the occult, "from visits to cemeteries to sleepover séances . . . challenge authority. Teens know that adults consider such actions to be deviant and even dangerous; that is part of their appeal. Like séances and other supernatural activities, horror films and television programs give young viewers a chance to vicariously participate in rebellion."¹¹ One of the most significant of these rebellious activities, embedded within teen films of the 1990s and carried through to the current Tumblr blogs of "magick-queer-bro," "agender-witch," "queer-magick," "craftingmagick," "queerwitchcraft," and others, is the process of coming out, both as queer and as a witch.

If visual media offers pleasure and satisfaction to its viewers, it does so in part through its ability to symbolically work through and resolve communal conflicts that are often deeply troubling to our collective cultural psyche.¹² As such, this chapter contextualizes the sexual and spiritual comings out of young people in the new millennium as part of a longer history of teen-focused films that use the occult, specifically witchcraft, for the same purpose. To begin, I look to popular press discourse of the 1990s to reveal a renewed interest in occultism and New Age spiritualities, particularly the religious practices of Wicca, and the suggestive consistency with which commentators articulated this movement as a "coming out of the broom closet." From this revived metaphysical milieu, I investigate the ways in which this supernatural resurgence facilitated a reinvigorated industrial interest in producing both mainstream and independent occult cinema specifically marketed toward younger audiences, one of the most conspicuous ways that American media culture guided teen viewers toward finding their sexual and spiritual selves at the turn of the last century.

Coming Out of the Broom Closet

In a 2010 poll conducted by the UK LGBTQ+ rights organization Stonewall, fifteen hundred "already out" respondents were asked at approximately what age they first revealed their sexuality to others. The outcomes were reported as follows: those over age sixty (coming out ≈ age thirty-seven), those in their thirties (coming out ≈ age twenty-one), and those aged eighteen to twenty-four (coming out ≈ age seventeen).[13] The results, Stonewall deputy director of public affairs Ruth Hunt said, were clear: people have been coming out at younger and younger ages.[14] This trend is thrown into even sharper relief by the research findings of Ritch C. Savin-Williams and Lisa M. Diamond in a 2000 study published in *Archives of Sexual Behavior*: Sexual identity milestones (including first instances of same-sex attraction) are likely to occur for both sexes between ages eight and nine, while first disclosure typically averages around age eighteen.[15] Without drawing any definitive causal relationships from this data, it does seem, as Hunt observes, that the global circulation of media culture does have at least some correlation with this trend, as "young people today are given a lot more information about sexuality, and are more likely to see gay people in the public eye . . . with whom they could identify feelings they might be having."[16] With near-startling consistency, popular press discourse of the 1990s used this younger coming-out trend as a metaphor for a new generation of occult practitioners.

By September 1990, the *Los Angeles Times* estimated that the number of practicing goddess worshippers, the then-most popular form of witchcraft in the United States, numbered approximately one hundred thousand from coast to coast.[17] Considered a spiritual offshoot of feminism, women's rights, and contemporary LGBTQ+ activism, goddess worship offered "purpose behind the purpose of witchcraft, or Wicca (Old English for *witch*), a form of nature worship that has long been popular in alternative circles."[18] Like the occult heyday reported by the *Los Angeles Times*' Paul Steiger in 1969, magick was back in vogue at the end of the twentieth century and beginning of the new millennium. "It's hard to know the exact numbers," Melissa Block of NPR's *All Things Considered* reported in May 2004, "but Wicca is believed to be one of the fastest-growing religions among high school and college students."[19] Yet like those drawn to earlier Aquarian alternatives of the 1960s and 1970s, this generation of New Age witches was charged with sorting fact from popular fiction.

Although some forms of Euro-American witchcraft have taken the shape of black magick and devil worship over time, witches of the late twentieth century were adamant that their spiritual activities shared no relation to such "dark arts." Many practitioners were acutely concerned, as Rebecca Reisner of the *New York Times* reported, about the general public's "misconceptions about the faith. Wiccans place an emphasis on seasonal celebrations and stress the importance of the relationship between nature and human beings. But because it is part of the occult, some people have confused Wicca with Satanism, wrongly accusing Wiccans of espousing evil and performing sadistic rituals."[20] On the contrary, in 1974, the Council of American Witches adopted a document known as the Principles of Wiccan Beliefs, containing thirteen core values, ones worth citing in full to clarify exactly how modern witches continue to practice what they preach:

   I. We practice rites to attune ourselves with the natural rhythm of life forces marked by the phases of the Moon and the seasonal Quarters and Cross Quarter.
  II. We recognize that our intelligence gives us a unique responsibility toward our environment. We seek to live in harmony with Nature, in ecological balance offering fulfillment to life and consciousness within an evolutionary concept.
 III. We acknowledge a depth of power far greater than that apparent to the average person. Because it is far greater than ordinary, it is sometimes called supernatural, but we see it as lying within that which is naturally potential to all.
  IV. We conceive of the Creative Power in the universe as manifesting through polarity—as masculine and feminine—and that this same Creative Power lies in all people, and functions through the interaction of the masculine and feminine. We value neither above the other, knowing each to be supportive to the other. We value sex as pleasure, as the symbol and embodiment of life, and as one of the sources of energies used in magickal practice and religious worship.

V. We recognize both outer worlds and inner, or psychological, worlds sometimes known as the Spiritual World, the Collective Unconscious, Inner Planes, etc.—and we see in the interaction of these two dimensions the basis for paranormal phenomena and magickal exercises. We neglect neither dimension for the other, seeing both as necessary for our fulfillment.
VI. We do not recognize any authoritarian hierarchy, but do honor those who teach, respect those who share their greater knowledge and wisdom, and acknowledge those who have courageously given of themselves in leadership.
VII. We see religion, magick, and wisdom in living as being united in the way one views the world and lives within it—a world view and philosophy of life which we identify as Witchcraft—the Wiccan Way.
VIII. Calling oneself "Witch" does not make a Witch—but neither does heredity itself, nor the collecting of titles, degrees, and initiations. A Witch seeks to control the forces within her/himself that make life possible in order to live wisely and well without harm to others and in harmony with Nature.
IX. We believe in the affirmation and fulfillment of life in a continuation of evolution and development of consciousness giving meaning to the Universe we know and our personal role within it.
X. Our only animosity towards Christianity, or towards any other religion or philosophy of life, is to the extent that its institutions have claimed to be "the only way" and have sought to deny freedom to others and to suppress other ways of religious practice and belief.
XI. As American Witches, we are not threatened by debates on the history of the Craft, the origins of various terms, the legitimacy of various aspects of different traditions. We are concerned with our present and our future.
XII. We do not accept the concept of absolute evil, nor do we worship any entity known as "Satan" or "the Devil," as defined by the Christian traditions. We do not seek power through the suffering of others, nor accept that personal benefit can be derived only by denial to another.
XIII. We believe that we should seek within Nature that which is contributory to our health and wellbeing.[21]

Given these professed creeds, the espousal across popular press of the 1990s and early 2000s that witchcraft and Satanism were not reducible to each other is understandable. "We're a religion that's a legally recognized religion," Ravenswood Grove Coven high priestess Bonnie Nadeau told Susan Pearsall of the *New York Times* in October 1994, "but because of 800 years of propaganda, lies and persecution, many witches will never allow you to know who or what they are."[22]

Witchcraft has undeniably suffered, according to the *Age*'s Andrew Masterson, "predictably bad press since 1484, when Pope Innocent VIII issued a Papal Bull declaring the belief heretical. Since then, practitioners of the Craft, as it is known, have regularly (and sometimes fatally) been accused of almost every piece of hideous conduct imaginable."[23] This negative public image has, paradoxically, been exacerbated from both without and within. Practices like human sacrifice and devil-worshipping orgies may never be on most magickal dockets, as any true Wiccan will attest, yet much of the misunderstanding surrounding contemporary witchcraft's magickal rites can be attributed to the father of modern Wicca, English civil servant Gerald Gardner. In 1951, when the British Witchcraft Act of 1736 was finally repealed, Gardner broke away from organizations like the Hermetic Order of the Golden Dawn and formed his own coven that made nudism and sexual exhibitionism central tenets of magickal conduct, even going so far as to introduce the practice of scourging, "or flogging . . . as a method of symbolic purification."[24] As Masterson notes, Gardner's style of witchcraft enjoyed remarkable popularity in Great Britain and the United States during the 1960s and 1970s among young people, "but for most adherents the attraction lay in its salaciousness rather than its beliefs. Its influence quickly waned. The interest in Wicca has now taken on a more serious, genuine aspect and has continued to grow."[25]

To be sure, part of this growth, as articulated across the pages of the *New York Times*, the *Sunday Times*, the *Age*, and on the airwaves of NPR, has been and continues to be the often-challenging process of coming out of the broom closet. "The witches coming out of the closet for Halloween this month look more like Hollywood sex symbols than horrid old hags," Victoria McKee of the *Sunday Times* reported in 1998.[26] "Interest in Wicca and all the Neo-Pagan religions is at an all-time high," practitioner Layla Morgan Wilde wrote in a *New York Times* letter to the editor in 2002. "The only way we can dispel the myths and stereotypes surrounding witches is to come out of the 'broom closet.'"[27] For those in Australia who sought the company of other magickal practitioners to work toward social justice for witches, the *Age* reported in March 2004, "Pagan Awareness Network and the Pagan Alliance are just a few Melbourne organizations for those who want to come out of the 'broom closet.'"[28]

The consistency of such "coming out of the broom closet" rhetoric was equally matched by a knowingness, sometimes covert and sometimes more obvious, of how revived interest in the occult dovetailed with the increasing public visibility of young LGBTQ+ peoples and queer culture writ large. The very power of the word "witch," Margot Adler writes in her bestselling *Drawing Down the Moon: Witches, Druids, Goddess-Worshippers and Other Pagans in America*, "lies in its imprecision. It is not merely a word, but an archetype, a cluster of powerful images. It resonates in the mind and . . . takes us down to deep places . . . the witch is the changer of definitions and relationships."[29] Consider how Annamarie Jagose demarcates the term "queer" as "very much a category in the process of formation. It is not simply that queer has yet to solidify and take on a more consistent profile but rather that its definitional indeterminacy, its elasticity, is one of its constituent characteristics," and it is easy to see how queerness; youth, vis-à-vis processes of formation, development, and becoming; and occult figures like the witch have made and continue to make opportune bedfellows.[30]

During the 1990s and into the new millennium, most young witches turned to the Craft when traditional Judeo-Christian religions didn't satisfy their needs. As Clark observes, "Rather than asking about religion's decline among young people . . . more and more people are interested in how religion and spirituality are continuing in an increasingly religiously plural world, and how they are changing in relation to the highly mediated cultural and historical context in which they are found."[31] As Jessica, a young Wiccan interviewed by Melissa Block on NPR's *All Things Considered*, puts it, "It's hard because [with] Christianity, [if] you feel lost, you go to church. And there's set paths. Like, you have the Bible. You have church. They tell you what to do. They tell you how you should live your life. And this is so open, and it just seems like it would be so much easier just to be something orthodox."[32] Yet the deceptively seductive ease of traditional orthodoxy is belied, Jessica confesses, by the fact that witchcraft "really gives you some power. I mean, you make stuff happen for your life, and you're not waiting around for your parents or your teachers or anything else to make stuff happen for you. You're doing it."[33] Indeed, much of the appeal of modern occultism can be explained in direct relation to the desire of young people to explore aspects of their lives in ways apart from those sanctioned by both adults and orthodox religions.[34] As many first-person accounts corroborate, practicing nonnormatively sanctioned spiritualities goes hand in hand with the simultaneous disclosure of queer sexualities.

When Jody, a shamanic witch, first came out of the sexual closet, his spiritual beliefs directly inflected his search for a new identity:

When I first "came out," I experienced this rush—"I can finally love, I can finally have sex, I can finally express myself." But in many ways the gay culture did not serve my needs. I felt that, in many ways, it was an oppressive parody of straight culture. It takes place primarily in bars, where music is loud and people are not encouraged to talk, or form bonds or care for each other. It imitates the worst of heterosexual culture. I found I had to become a different person to get laid, and I didn't like that at all. I became ashamed and I wondered, "Is this the best we have to offer?"[35]

Indeed, one of the original principles behind the most high-profile magickal group of gay men, known as the Radical Faeries and of which Arthur Evans was a founding member, was that there had to be something beyond assimilation to living queerly, "a totally different view of the world, with different goals and different spiritual values than the 'straight' world."[36] As a gay male, young witch Brian told Helen Berger and Douglas Ezzy in their 2007 book *Teenage Witches: Magical Youth and the Search for the Self*, "I have always had a—if you will—kinship with feminism and its teachings because I didn't identify with a normal male image. So in that respect I always identified with females and I had always seen the inequalities between males and females in our society. Wicca has opened me up to understanding the female side of divinity better."[37] "Shake it up and shake it out," Wiccan practitioner Michael G. Lloyd advises young witches and queers. "Be hermetic, be mercurial, react, reject, rebel, look outside the bone box, look up the Goddess' skirt, be more than they'll let you be, breathe the free air, fight the good fight, seize the day, brave the elements, bust a nut, and live! All magick is an act of rebellion against the status quo."[38]

Such rebelliously queer witches make up one of the most dynamic demographics of what Jason Louv calls the millennial phenomenon of Generation Hex: a new crop of young people who are not only delving into witchcraft and occultism in numbers previously unmatched but who are "coming to magical consciousness at a time when it has never been easier to find and link up with people of like minds and experience."[39] Witches are strange characters, Louv confesses: "You'd have to be a little odd to try to become something that's not supposed to be real."[40] Substitute "queer" for both "strange" and "odd" and the meaning remains the same or, perhaps, becomes even more precise. Like so much about what it means to come out in queer culture, witchcraft and magick have been filtered through various visual media to present young people with alternative ways of knowing, ways of doing, and ways of being.

"Now Is the Time, Now Is the Hour, Ours Is the Magick, Ours Is the Power": Pop-influenced Paganism in 1990s Teen Cinema

Although spells, rituals, and other magickal practices became increasingly commodified, packaged, and marketed to multiple youth audiences after their importation into North America during the height of midcentury countercultural fervor, this practice had earlier precedents. As Kevin Heffernan notes, the beginning of the 1950s witnessed the first time in US history that teenagers possessed enough discretionary income to become a targeted demographic for the entertainment industry.[41] Sales of products like comic books and rock and roll records, as well as attendance at movie theaters (especially for horror films), were all bolstered by the rising youth market, echoing what has always proved true of the confluence between popular culture and the occult: each was met with backlash from parents, educators, clergy members, and civic authorities due to their promises of diversion, dissension, rebellion, and revolt.[42] Combined with increased social paranoia about the rise of the "juvenile delinquent," specters of the monstrous, supernatural adolescent and the demonic child became staples of the American horror film.[43]

Yet both genres and markets are cyclical, and interest in youth-targeted occult entertainment steadily waned throughout the late 1970s and into the 1980s. This drought changed dramatically, however, during the 1990s, when the post-Reagan economic boom once again gave teenagers an unprecedented amount of spending power that attracted the attention of the culture industries in general and fueled the resurgence of magick in popular media in particular. In 1998, for instance, a *New York Times*/CBS News poll of American teens found that 49 percent of respondents claimed to have a part-time job, "reinforcing the general perception that teenagers possessed the financial means to become good consumers."[44] Consequently, as Valerie Wee observes, film studios began to produce an increasing number of "'teenpics'—films directly and specifically aimed at the teen movie-going audience. At the same time, the newly launched WB broadcast television network began targeting the narrow teen/youth demographic. . . . Teenagers were back on Hollywood's radar. A new millennial teen cycle had arrived."[45] By 1998, what had been a $10 billion teen market in 1959 had morphed into a $122 billion market forty years later.[46]

In 1996, eager to capitalize on the growing industrial interest in both occultism and youth markets, Columbia Pictures released a sleeper-hit film that would provide a blueprint for nearly all teen occult media that came after: *The Craft*. As the film opens, three young women, later identified as Nancy Downs (Fairuza Balk), Bonnie (Neve Campbell), and Rochelle (Rachel True), are seated in an outdoor gazebo, holding hands and chanting while surrounded by various magickal paraphernalia: candles, spices, pentagrams, oils, and so forth. Prior to the development of Wicca as a legitimized religion in North America, Tanice Foltz observes, witches were generally portrayed in one of two stereotypical ways in mainstream media: "Either they were ugly, old hags who used their powers for evil, or those portrayed as beautiful covertly used their magical powers to 'catch' or keep a man or to maintain peace (as well as traditional gender roles) within their homes."[47] With the Wicca craze of the 1990s coming into full bloom, however, representations of young female witches like those in *The Craft* began to change and were often characterized by "attractive, youthful, strong, and independent females who openly use their magical powers to fight against evil for the greater good."[48] Indeed, how Nancy, Bonnie, and Rochelle look is just as significant as the words invoked in their repeated mantra: "Now is the time, now is the hour, ours is the magick, ours is the power."

To own agency and control over one's power, identity, and inner strength, as these three young women seek to do, has always been part of Wicca as a religious practice and is central to millennial media's occult coming-out narratives. As Berger and Ezzy observe, Wiccan practitioners believe that their religion provides them with many benefits, specifically "self-empowerment, a sense of connection with nature, and answers to existential questions."[49] On the whole, teens want more control in their lives, and they feel that Wicca can give it to them.[50] Indeed, "self-transformation through magical and ritual practices has always been one element in Witchcraft: Witches identify areas of their personalities or lives that require change, and focus on changing those things both magically and in the mundane world."[51] This focus, characteristic of witchcraft, is immediately invoked in *The Craft* and leads to a politics of self-transformation that challenges the hegemonic power of contemporary gender and sexual norms for young people.[52]

For as much as Nancy, Bonnie, and Rochelle attempt to magickally change the world around them, the full potential of their powers remains stunted without a fourth member to "call the corners" of nature's compass: North, South, East, and West. Enter Sarah Bailey (Robin Tunney), a young woman with her own magickal past who arrives in California and happens

Fig. 4.1. Promotional cast photo for *The Craft* (1996)

to enroll at the same private Catholic high school as Nancy, Bonnie, and Rochelle. As Sarah is introduced to the cultural hierarchies of St. Benedict's Academy, one of the first things she learns from football star Chris Hooker (Skeet Ulrich) is about the so-called Bitches of Eastwick, referencing the rumors that the three women in question are witches with possible lesbian tendencies.

Although Sarah is initially distrustful of forming close friendships in her new environment, she's eventually seduced by the homosocial sisterhood that Nancy, Bonnie, and Rochelle offer. Specifically, this friendship is one that emphatically sets itself apart from the toxic, normative gender roles and heterosexual imperatives that run throughout St. Benedict's. The girls are all outsiders, Roger Ebert writes in his original review, and "their classmates don't like them, which seems strange, since they have messy hair, slather on black lipstick, wear leather dog collars, smoke a lot, have rings piercing many of the penetrable parts of their bodies, [and] sneer constantly."[53] As director Andrew Fleming recalls, this image (fig. 4.1) was precisely the film's inspiration: "The point was to embrace the other . . . to the people who were on the margins . . . to make it about them."[54] Indeed, these young women take their nonnormative outsider status, specifically when it comes to relationships, quite seriously. Nancy, for example, constantly confesses her fervent distaste for men, largely as a byproduct of an abusive stepfather and a previously disastrous liaison with Chris: "He spreads disease. I speak from personal experience."

It is immediately after this confession that Sarah decides to accompany the three girls to the local occult gift shop, where Nancy, Bonnie, and Rochelle often congregate to gather, and more specifically steal, magickal supplies. It is also here that Sarah meets Lirio (Assumpta Serna), the shop's proprietor, who immediately senses Sarah's magickal abilities. On their way home, the four girls are attacked by a homeless man who wanders out into the middle of a crowded boulevard to chase after them. The shot-reverse shots that follow imply a sense of frenetic and collective telekinetic power that eventually causes a car to run the man over. Quickly fleeing the scene, the girls are equal parts frightened and ecstatic about what they've just witnessed, as Bonnie exclaims, "This is it, guys. North, South, East, and West. We can make things happen."

And make things happen they do. Looking to seal their union as a coven, the girls take a bus out of town to perform an initiation ritual in the countryside. As their driver politely reminds them to "watch out for those weirdoes," Nancy cheekily responds, "We are the weirdoes, mister." For as much as they may be ostracized misfits and social outcasts, these girls find unmatched solace in their homosocial bonds, kissing each other gently to cement their sisterhood while sharing a chalice of wine laced with a drop of each of their blood. This magickal invocation ultimately sends a flurry of butterflies down from the sky to surround them, presumably a sign that the nature deity they worship (Manon) has heard their call.

As Annette Hill details in *Paranormal Media: Audiences, Spirits, and Magic in Popular Culture*, paranormal beliefs such as "divinatory arts, psi processes, esoteric systems of magic, new age therapies, Eastern mystico-religious beliefs and Judeo-Christian religious beliefs are represented . . . as personal empowerment."[55] Indeed, the ability to come out and find one's true self through magick is perhaps the most obvious trope of witchcraft that *The Craft* invokes. As Rob Latham elegantly puts it, shimmers of the supernatural across popular youth media culture often function as "redemptive deliverance from an otherwise brutally impoverished experience, thus remarking the stubborn persistence of a utopian impulse even in this bleakest of contexts."[56] Contemporary magick is, in and of itself, its own coming-out process, demonstrating that "what is visible is the manifestation of the invisible; it is the use of one's understanding of the invisible to affect change in the visible. How to negotiate unmanifest realms, while keeping oneself grounded in the manifest, is the Work (and Play) of a lifetime."[57]

It is here, however, that *The Craft* begins to diverge from verifiable Wiccan teachings and venture squarely into the realm of Hollywood horror.

Although Ebert registers his confusion as to why these four girls, "who could outgross David Copperfield in Vegas . . . limit their amazing powers to getting even," their queerly outcast status is precisely what the film seeks to critique through magick.[58] As Clark observes, an important appeal of "confronting the stories of the supernatural in teen culture . . . may have references to a need to feel competent and powerful in the face of powers beyond one's control."[59] In every scene that has something to do with witchcraft, director Fleming recalls, "the whole idea is that underneath it is the possibility that there's a universality to it . . . that it mirrored experimentation with drugs or sex . . . the scenes should be universally about being a teenager and finding out the limits of your powers."[60] Halfway into what starts out as a celebration of "adolescent nonconformity and female independence," Stephen Holden of the New York Times remarks, The Craft "reverses its attitude and makes the spells cast by its four teen-age witches come back to haunt them."[61]

Perhaps the most obvious and indeed queer of these magickal repercussions dooms Sarah's relationship with Chris. After a first date where, in stereotypical teen boy fashion, Chris attempts yet ultimately fails to "get laid," Sarah's name becomes persona non grata around the halls of St. Benedict's. In her own attempt to get even, Sarah casts a spell on Chris to make him fall madly in love with her, not actually intending the relationship to go anywhere and having her own fun by rebuffing Chris's advances at every turn. But Chris's intense infatuation turns dark one evening as he aggressively attempts to rape Sarah in his car. When Sarah escapes his grasp and runs to her three coven mates for help, Nancy decides that Chris must pay for his trespasses. Finding him at a nearby party, Nancy transforms herself into Sarah's likeness and leads Chris into an upstairs bedroom in order to seduce him. But before things progress too far, the real Sarah arrives and forces Nancy to reveal herself. It is at this point that Nancy's queer fury is finally unleashed on Chris: "The only way you know how to treat women is by treating them like whores when you're the whore! And that's gonna stop! Do you understand? Do you understand what I'm saying?" With a sudden gust of wind, the french doors of the bedroom are blown open and Chris is propelled over the balcony to his death.

While characters in millennial occult media may shift from good to evil as the result of magickal experiences over time or spells cast with immediate effects, a "strong contrast between good and evil behavior pervades their story lines, with social responsibility a taken-for-granted value that drives the characters to embrace danger out of concern for the welfare of others."⁶² Indeed, while Nancy may "save" her magickal sister with the best of intentions, her drunk with power behavior eventually begins to taint Bonnie and Rochelle as well, causing Sarah to sense an impending swell of danger and question her loyalty to the coven. This decision does not, of course, sit well with the other girls, who begin to frantically invade Sarah's dreams and torture her through them.

This magickal cat and mouse game eventually culminates in the film's finale, during which Nancy and Sarah square off against each other, with Sarah ultimately proving triumphant and Nancy being sent to the psychiatric ward of a hospital for clinical observation. While none of these young women would be best classified as children, the simultaneous combination of desire and dread that they engender is well informed by Andrew Scahill's work on the figure of the "revolting child" in horror cinema. Teen occult films like *The Craft* present a phantasmatic space to "circumnavigate emotive experiences of queerness: secrecy, rejection, rage, alienation, revolt, and community."⁶³ More specifically, Scahill finds a dual-edged salience within this type of queerness: "These are figures that are 'revolting,' which is to say, repellant. They are bodies that violate natural laws and order. . . . But these figures are also bodies in revolt: they traffic in the rhetoric and representational force of the youth movement and the nature of the 'rebel,' a figure at once prized as distinctly American and yet vilified as disruptive and antithetic to the harmonious community."⁶⁴ In the film's penultimate scene, as Bonnie and Rochelle come to apologize to Sarah for their previous behavior, the latter makes a tree limb fall inches from the other two, a reminder, over the crescendoing rock soundtrack, that the power Sarah has found within herself is not to be trifled with. *The Craft* thus helped to usher in a queer era of what Michael Lloyd calls "pop-influenced Paganism: a time characterized by fluid and rapid growth and a multiplicity and diversity of ideas. There are arguably more solitary practitioners than members of formal groups at this point in time. No one holds the keys to the kingdom; or, rather, everyone does."⁶⁵

As Sarah Banet-Weiser argues in her 2007 study of teen markets and consumer citizenship, "The rise of the youth market and the increasing sophistication of market trends for youth audiences indicate that consumption habits have come to be one of the most profound elements in basic definitions of youth identity. It is through this interpretive community of consumers that the definition of a nation is sustained, with young people as the 'citizens' of the nation."⁶⁶ In this way, millennial occult films like *The Craft* and its ilk helped to sustain an interpretive media nation of queer coming-out witches that became an aggressively targeted demographic for both mainstream and independent entertainment outlets in the United States. As Banet-Weiser continues, "This move, from the world of politics to the world of media as constitutive sites for national and personal identity, is one that follows a more general consumerist trajectory in U.S. culture... quite simply, people who are underrepresented within political and cultural realms are often recognized as lucrative markets in consumer culture, where willingness to buy products is what really 'counts.'"⁶⁷ For as much as brand loyalty may function as a particular kind of citizenship practice, loyalty in terms of genre may be an even more powerful point of cathexis for certain marginalized groups. As Caralyn Bolte observes, such consistent views originating from the sociocultural margins "most incisively highlights the fissures in our cultural fabric and, in the process of constructing and presenting such vocal commentary, reevaluates the definition of desire."⁶⁸

Take, for example, the case of the independent *Little Witches*, a film co-produced by Le Monde Entertainment and Planet Productions and released just seven months after *The Craft*, in December 1996. As the film opens in an unnamed location in 1896, a magickal ritual is taking place in a dark underground dungeon. A swirling 360° pan reveals a coven of topless female witches chanting praises to a female deity, dancing, and caressing each other around what appears to be an ancient well that begins to emit smoke and colored vapors. Before the ritual is completed and the unknown force within the well is summoned forth, however, a group of women claiming to be the Guardians of the Lord suddenly arrives to halt the blasphemy, imprison the witches, and set fire to the temple. From this aborted ritual, the film quickly fast-forwards one hundred years to present-day California and the Catholic boarding school Santa Carlita Academy, where Faith (Mimi Rose), Jamie (Sheeri Rappaport), Kelsey (Clea DuVall), Nicole (Zoe Alexander), Gina (Lalaneya Hamilton), and Erica (Melissa Taub) are all attending their mandatory weekly confessions. Immediately singled out as the "bad girl" of the group, Jamie is given twenty minutes' penance for graphically confessing her masturbatory fantasies to the priest.

For as much as *Little Witches* may unfold as a cookie-cutter down-market impersonation of *The Craft*, it is little coincidence that both films take place in high schools, particularly Catholic institutions, where invocations of witchcraft, magick, and the occult are coded as especially transgressive and taboo. Indeed, as we've seen, if occultism has historically been tied to issues of sexual nonnormativity and erotic anxiety, placing films like *The Craft* and *Little Witches* in sexually riven environments like high schools only further exacerbates these themes. Schooling, as Christine Jarvis argues, "constructs much of young people's social and cultural environment and is intimately connected with many of their fears and anxieties. Schools set the criteria for success and failure. . . . Part of the horror in the horror genre is based on exaggerated versions of these fears."[69] Like the young women of *The Craft*, the primary fear circling around *Little Witches* is the adolescent fear of not fitting in, a theme that manifests as Faith, Jamie, Kelsey, Nicole, Gina, and Erica are the only girls who haven't traveled away from Santa Carlita on the school's spring break. Yet as the queer pleasures of witchcraft are gradually invoked, the imperative to fit in to Santa Carlita's social hierarchies seems much less alluring. The fact that each of these girls stands outside of but is not completely alien to the school's sociosexual structures "offers credibility to their critique that normally wouldn't exist. These former insiders can see, now that they are outside the world that they once occupied, what doesn't work; their unique perspective encourages their audiences, through the audience's association with these exiled protagonists, to similarly interrogate the worlds in which they live."[70]

To be sure, the girls' staycation ultimately proves far more interesting than a typical tropical holiday. As construction work on the school is being completed, the crew finds a mysterious underground crypt that appears to have been sealed off for decades, the same one used in the ritual that opened the film. Warned by their teacher Sister Sherilyn (Jennifer Rubin) that the crypt is dangerous and strictly off limits, the girls, of course, decide to rebuke authority and explore the subterranean space one evening. As Jarvis contends, the most meaningful actions of millennial occult films like *Little Witches* are often set in "marginal spaces—the corridors, locker rooms and basements between and beneath the orderly classroom. In these liminal spaces, repressed energies emerge in the shape of fantastical monsters or murderers. Forces of chaos break through the very fabric of the school building, demonstrating the ultimate inability of the adult world and its rules to protect young people."[71] While the girls don't run into any monsters or murderers in this particular crypt, they do happen on a tattered old book written in Latin that only Faith—singled out, as her name might suggest, as the film's smart, reluctant follower—can decode: "Whoever reads aloud from this poisonous book will be condemned as the Devil's mistress . . . it's a book of magic or something."

Predictably, the magick that has lain latent inside this book makes the queerness bubbling around the shadows of *Little Witches* quickly boil to the surface. One day, for example, Faith and Jamie, who are sharing a room over break, happen to notice a crew of shirtless male construction workers just outside their window. As if compelled by an otherworldly force, Jamie blasts the radio in the room, ostensibly to attract the attention of the men, and begins a slowly seductive striptease while Faith watches aghast. Even still, the slow-motion camerawork and eye-line matches between Faith and Jamie turning around to watch her queers what otherwise appears as a definitively heteronormative exercise. Is Jamie performing for the men or for Faith, whose face queerly mixes both aversion and arousal? This ambiguity is further reinforced by their conversation immediately after Jamie's performance. As Faith confesses that she's a virgin, Jamie hatches a plan to make her over. "Do you think I'm pretty?" Faith asks, to which Jamie winkingly responds, "Yeah I do. I think you got potential."

Whatever force possessed Faith during this exhibitionist performance only continues to ramp up the queer magick of *Little Witches*. Enticed by promises of power and eternal life that the book they found provides, the girls attempt to resurrect the witches who perished underneath the school one hundred years earlier. After a preliminary botched attempt, Jamie suggests that the girls all strip naked to rid themselves of anything modern. The girls' nakedness and homoerotic dancing does begin to summon powers that make thunder roll and lightning crash, but the ritual is quickly disrupted as one of the walls of the temple caves in.

As with *The Craft*, it is here that *Little Witches* takes a turn firmly into the realm of fantastical horror as it rushes toward its finale. As the witch chosen to lead the coven and resurrect the aforementioned ancient being, Jamie uses magick to summon all of the girls to the crypt except Faith, who, like Sarah in *The Craft*, has not been seduced by the encroaching evil and vows to stop the scheme. As the girls take another turn dancing naked around the crypt's well, smoke and colored vapors once again begin to materialize, along with a hideous demon. But before the demon can fully emerge, Faith arrives just in time to shove a consecrated host into each of the girls' mouths and push Jamie down the well and into the demon's open arms.

As the 1990s waned toward the dawn of a new millennium, the age at which young people around the world were coming out as queer, as witches, and as queer witches fell significantly, due in no small part to the ways in which film, television, books, magazines, and digital media spread information far and wide on a global scale. Especially in the case of millennial magickal practices, "the media play[ed] a more significant part in Witchcraft than in most other religions. . . . Movies and television shows have become increasingly important, particularly since the 1990s, in putting a benign public face on Witchcraft, even if they have trivialized the religion."[72] Yet herein lies a significant paradox. As Foltz puts it, while representations of witchcraft and magick in millennial media do occasionally forward negative stereotypes and perpetuate "unrealistic views, in other cases authentic information is relayed that might contribute to a better understanding of Witches. The dilemma is that commodification can result in a greater understanding of the religion as well as one that is distorted and inaccurate."[73] Regardless of whether any individual representation of witchcraft is high or low on the scale of verisimilitude, there's little question that the booming interest in occultism and New Age magick during the 1990s went hand in hand with the increased coming out of global queer youth, a time in one's life that, as Sharon Ross and Louisa Stein explain, may be inherently queer itself, a period during which bodies begin to exhibit "sexual development and adult characteristics and yet when one has little social power . . . an inherently contradictory, transgressive experience."[74]

Notes

1. Leigh Cuen, "The Secret Lives of Teen Witches on Tumblr," Mic.Com (blog), June 30, 2016, https://mic.com/articles/147283/the-secret-lives-of-teen-witches-on-tumblr#.W5nFO3Uw6.
2. https://www.tumblr.com/.
3. Cuen.
4. Ibid.
5. Alexander Cho, "Queer Reverb: Tumblr, Affect, Time," in *Networked Affect*, ed. Ken Hillis, Susanna Passonen, and Michael Petit (Cambridge: MIT Press, 2015), 43–57.
6. http://queerwitchcraft.tumblr.com/.
7. Cho, 47.
8. Ibid.
9. Ibid.
10. Victoria McKee, "Wicca's World," *Sunday Times*, October 4, 1998.

11. Lynn Schofield Clark, *From Angels to Aliens: Teenagers, the Media, and the Supernatural* (New York: Oxford University Press, 2003), 63.

12. Ibid.

13. Cited in Rachel Williams, "People Coming Out as Gay at Younger Age, Research Shows," Guardian (blog), November 15, 2010, https://www.theguardian.com/world/2010/nov/15/gay-people-coming-out-younger-age.

14. Ibid.

15. Ritch Savin-Williams and Lisa M. Diamond, "Sexual Identity Trajectories Among Sexual-Minority Youths: Gender Comparisons," *Archives of Sexual Behavior* 29, no. 6 (December 2000): 607.

16. Williams.

17. Irene Lacher, "She Worship: Return of the Great Goddess," *Los Angeles Times*, September 19, 1990.

18. Ibid.

19. Melissa Block, "Profile: Teen-Age Wiccans," *All Things Considered* (NPR, May 13, 2004).

20. Rebecca Reisner, "Witchcraft Held as Nothing to Fear," *New York Times*, November 25, 1990.

21. Council of American Witches, "Principles of Wiccan Beliefs," Sacred-Texts.Com (blog), 1974, http://sacred-texts.com/bos/bos056.htm.

22. Cited in Susan Pearsall, "Ancient Belief, Ancient Ritual," *New York Times*, October 30, 1994.

23. Andrew Masterson, "Witches Revive Pagan Blessing," *Age*, February 28, 1998.

24. Ibid.

25. Ibid.

26. McKee.

27. Layla Morgan Wilde, "Out of the Broom Closet, Even in the Suburbs," *New York Times*, November 3, 2002.

28. Claire Halliday, "Strange Brew," *Age*, March 23, 2004.

29. Margot Adler, *Drawing Down the Moon: Witches, Druids, Goddess-Worshippers and Other Pagans in America* (New York: Penguin, 2006), 40–42.

30. Annamarie Jagose, *Queer Theory: An Introduction* (New York: New York University Press, 1996), 1.

31. Clark, 5.

32. Cited in Block.

33. Ibid.

34. Clark, 7.

35. Cited in Adler, 357–58.

36. Ibid., 360.

37. Cited in Helen Berger and Douglas Ezzy, *Teenage Witches: Magical Youth and the Search for the Self* (New Brunswick: Rutgers University Press, 2007), 179.

38. Cited in Adler, 370.

39. Jason Louv, "Introduction: Towards an Ultraculture," in *Generation Hex*, ed. Jason Louv (New York: Disinformation Company, 2005), 9.

40. Ibid.

41. Kevin Heffernan, *Ghouls, Gimmicks, and Gold: Horror Films and the American Movie Business, 1953–1968* (Durham: Duke University Press, 2004), 57.

42. Ibid.
43. Ibid., 67.
44. Valerie Wee, *Teen Media: Hollywood and the Youth Market in the Digital Age* (Jefferson: McFarland, 2010), 30.
45. Ibid., 6.
46. Ibid., 27.
47. Tanice Foltz, "The Commodification of Witchcraft," in *Witchcraft and Magic: Contemporary North America*, ed. Helen Berger (Philadelphia: University of Pennsylvania Press, 2005), 137.
48. Ibid.
49. Berger and Ezzy, 23.
50. Foltz, 153.
51. Berger and Ezzy, 33.
52. Ibid., 172–73.
53. Roger Ebert, "The Craft," RogerEbert.Com (blog), May 3, 1996, http://www.rogerebert.com/reviews/the-craft-1996.
54. Andrew Fleming, *The Craft*, Blu-ray (Shout! Factory, 2019).
55. Annette Hill, *Paranormal Media: Audiences, Spirits and Magic in Popular Culture* (London: Routledge, 2011), 57.
56. Rob Latham, *Consuming Youth: Vampires, Cyborgs, and the Culture of Consumption* (Chicago: University of Chicago Press, 2002), 136.
57. Louv, 9.
58. Ebert.
59. Clark, 6.
60. Fleming.
61. Stephen Holden, "The Craft," New York Times (blog), May 3, 1996, http://www.nytimes.com/library/filmarchive/the_craft.html.
62. Clark, 57.
63. Andrew Scahill, *The Revolting Child in Horror Cinema: Youth Rebellion and Queer Spectatorship* (New York: Palgrave Macmillan, 2015), 3.
64. Ibid., 5.
65. Cited in Adler, 367.
66. Sarah Banet-Weiser, *Kids Rule!: Nickelodeon and Consumer Citizenship* (Durham: Duke University Press, 2007) 10.
67. Ibid., 12–26.
68. Caralyn Bolte, "'Normal Is the Watchword': Exiling Cultural Anxieties and Redefining Desire from the Margins," in *Teen Television: Essays on Programming and Fandom*, ed. Sharon Ross and Louisa Stein (Jefferson: McFarland, 2008), 94.
69. Christine Jarvis, "School Is Hell: Gendered Fears in Teenage Horror," *Educational Studies* 27, no. 3 (2001): 257.
70. Bolte, 99.
71. Jarvis, 258.
72. Berger and Ezzy, 38.
73. Foltz, 150.
74. Sharon Ross and Louisa Stein, "Introduction: Watching Teen TV," in *Teen Television: Essays on Programming and Fandom*, ed. Sharon Ross and Louisa Stein (Jefferson: McFarland, 2008), 7.

5

"HOLD ME, THRILL ME, KISS ME, KILL ME"

The Ambivalent Queer of Occult Cable TV

On March 10, 1997, I waited with bated breath in my family's living room for the premiere of the WB's newest midseason pickup. Adapted from a 1992 film of the same name, *Buffy the Vampire Slayer* (The WB, 1997–2001; UPN, 2001–3) follows the life of Buffy Summers (Sarah Michelle Gellar) through the supernatural trials and tribulations of living in the Hellmouth town of Sunnydale, California. Surrounded by what became known in both the series and popular press as a "Scooby gang" for the new millennium, including human and nonhuman characters such as Rupert Giles (Anthony Head), Xander Harris (Nicholas Brendon), Willow Rosenberg (Alyson Hannigan), Spike (James Marsters), and Angel (David Boreanaz), *Buffy the Vampire Slayer* now sits among some of the most iconic texts of cult television, often mentioned in the same breath as Mark Frost and David Lynch's *Twin Peaks* (ABC, 1990–91; Showtime, 2017) and Chris Carter's *The X-Files* (FOX, 1993–2018).

Even the then-eleven-year-old me knew something about *Buffy* was different. I was an occult aficionado already well versed in the canon of Universal monster movies and Hammer horror films, but the vampires, witches, werewolves, and other occultly marvelous creatures that populated Joss Whedon's supernatural story world were not what I was accustomed to. Here were depictions of strong women, not damsels in distress, who didn't crumble in the face of adversity, but rather flexed both their physical and mental muscles to vanquish their foes. Also here were dashingly attractive yet sensitive men who didn't rely solely on machismo to survive. But perhaps most importantly, *Buffy* introduced me to some of the first characters on television that I recognized as queer, individuals whose genders and sexualities became intimately entwined with their lot as occult outcasts.[1]

Since the turn of the 1990s, television has become perhaps the most conspicuous media marker of a new era of LGBTQ+ visibility: "While much has been made of the recent wave of gay-themed films, it is really the more prosaic medium of television that has beamed gay life (or a televisual version of it) into millions of homes across this country [the US] and abroad."[2] It may indeed be one thing to watch explicit representations of LGBTQ+ life projected within the walls of a local art house cinema, but it is quite another to have them "return to your living room week after week, insinuating themselves into the very fabric of the American home."[3] Yet despite this tempting triumphalist teleology, often celebrated in the annual "Where We Are on TV" report published by the Gay & Lesbian Alliance Against Defamation (GLAAD), the historical struggle for queer representation on television cannot and should not be reduced to a quantitative measure of "us" that has finally arrived on-screen. Instead, more critical space needs to be cleared in order to account for representational fits and starts, peaks and valleys, and complex questions of industrial, demographic, and generic specificity.

During the "Golden Age" of American network television, programmers at ABC, CBS, and NBC largely viewed their audiences as masses of family-oriented entities, consequently orchestrating a schedule likely to be palatable to the broadest range of viewers, a strategy that CBS vice president of programming Paul Klein once described as that of "least objectionable programming."[4] This was indeed broadcasting in its most literal sense, wherein networks selected programs that would reach a heterogeneous mass audience, but whose address was directed predominantly toward white, heterosexual, and middle-class viewers.[5] Within this mass cultural milieu, neither queer storylines nor occult narratives (one prominent exception to the latter being CBS's *The Twilight Zone*) were especially high on the list of network executives hoping to entice a maximum number of viewers with acceptable programming. To wit, as Lorna Jowett and Stacey Abbott explain, televisual horror has often been considered in "bad taste or to be excessively violent and this is one reason there has been little consideration of TV horror, since TV itself is assumed to be a mainstream medium that cannot sustain the graphic nature (visual or thematic) of horror's subject matter."[6] And for their part, when either openly or coded LGBTQ+ characters did appear on screen during the network era, queer men were most often trotted out in stereotypical fashion as the "swishy, effeminate queen/ hairdresser/interior decorator" of situation comedies, while queer women were largely relegated to the hackneyed roles of asexual schoolmarms or exaggeratedly butch caricatures played for laughs.[7]

Assessing the academic terrain of television studies in the early 2000s, John Caldwell provides the field with an important aide-mémoire: "Studying television's 'production of culture' is simply no longer entirely convincing if one does not also talk about television's 'culture of production.'"[8] Indeed, television's historical characterizations as a domestic (and increasingly nondomestic) technology, a set of industrial practices, and a sociocultural meaning-maker have and continue to exist in dialogic conversation. Simply put, what appears on television has everything to do with the ever-changing fluctuations of the industry that put it there and vice versa. And perhaps this reciprocal relationship has never been more clearly illuminated than over the past thirty-five years of the medium's history. As Caldwell summarizes, "The advent of new programming and delivery systems . . . broke [the network oligopoly] and opened American television screens to many more emerging companies. . . . This climate of increased diversification suggested to fiscal conservatives what had long been a mantra of the television industry and the NAB: a free market, not regulation, was the only way to ensure diversity of programming."[9] In their attempt to combat a downward spiral of diminishing viewership numbers, this era of fragmentation and rechanneling saw influential network series such as *Dallas* (CBS, 1978–91), *Hill Street Blues* (NBC, 1981–87), *Dynasty* (ABC, 1981–89), *St. Elsewhere* (NBC, 1982–88), and *thirtysomething* (ABC, 1987–91) inaugurate the circulation of a cultural and industrial buzzword that still retains so much cachet today: quality.[10]

In the context of the US television industry, described by Jane Feuer as a community of "profit-minded capitalists interested in 'delivering' audiences . . . the term quality describes the demographics of the audience. Delivering a quality audience means delivering whatever demographic advertisers seek, or in the case of premium cable, attracting an audience with enough disposable income to pay extra for TV."[11] Not surprisingly, discourses of televisual quality have taken on significant resonance in the arenas of race, ethnicity, class, and especially gender and sexuality. As Michael Newman and Elana Levine argue in *Legitimating Television: Media Convergence and Cultural Status*, the development of American TV's quality identity and cultural elevation has relied on rhetorical flourishes of uplift and change, embracing a narrative of progress that "naturalizes classed and gendered hierarchies with its assumption that moving forward means a shift away from the feminized past toward a more masculinized future."[12]

Even still, this masculinization and presumptive heteronormitivizing of quality television has also been built on a set of queer paradoxes. In the increasingly competitive era of 1990s niche market advertising and programming, network executives began to incorporate LGBTQ+ material into their prime time lineups in order to attract an audience of what Ron Becker labels "upscale, college-educated and socially liberal adults."[13] For as much as conversations about quality television had always been about targeting certain audience demographics, the term also became increasingly applicable to certain types of programming that were variously considered edgy, risqué, groundbreaking, sophisticated, original, taboo, and so forth. Including LGBTQ+ material in prime time programming was one maneuver intended to up the quality ante.

In this way, American network television has been historically defined more by the limits of what it cannot show than what it can. Beholden to the content restriction and censorship standards of the FCC, networked queerness in the 1990s and beyond continued to be filtered most often through a set of "safe" generic conventions, especially sustained reliance on situation comedies. As Anna McCarthy notes of Ellen DeGeneres's infamous coming-out in both her personal and ABC on-screen life during the spring of 1997, the comedienne's self-fashioning as a queer trailblazer upheld visions of what might be called the "liberal progressive narrative of TV history. A key element in popular and professional understandings of the history of the sitcom's 'evolution,' this is the idea of the genre as a mirror of broader currents of social change. This narrative often consists of whiggish tales in which the sitcom form became [ever] more socially responsible."[14] Resonances of Hanson's earlier-cited thoughts inspired by the lesbian vampire film reverberate throughout McCarthy's findings. We might say, then, that one of the difficulties for some viewers in digesting most mainstream LGBTQ+ material on network television has been its own "cold shower of political correctness—its preoccupation with a narrow politics of representation and its search for so-called positive or accurate images, which, when they finally do appear, are often dull anyway."[15] So where could viewers seeking depictions of a more complex queerness at the dawn of the new millennium turn?

In *Gothic: Transmutations of Horror in Late Twentieth Century Art*, Christoph Grunenberg argues that the years immediately preceding and following the turn of the new millennium witnessed a renewed fascination with the supernatural and the occult, from "'high' literature to 'schlock' science fiction, mystery and romance novels . . . and, most pronounced, making its daily appearance in film and television, where an obsession with sex . . . has developed into one of the most popular categories in [visual] entertainment."[16] As such, this chapter investigates these renewed enchantments with occult sexualities since the late 1990s, turning to the ways in which their mediation through cable television has extended more provocative and challenging considerations of queerness than those found on American networks. Specifically, I examine what I term the "ambivalent queer" of occult cable TV as presented on premium cable outlets such as Showtime and here!. Since viewers cannot simply stumble on these channels but must choose to subscribe through cable or streaming providers, they are not bound by the same FCC regulations that impact other channels and do not need "broad appeal but rather [target] niche audiences interested in 'quality television.' As a result [they are] able to offer writers and series creators a great deal of autonomy and creative control, leading to series . . . being praised as stylistically, generically and narratively provocative and transgressive, often breaking social, cultural and televisual taboos."[17]

Horror on contemporary television, as Jowett and Abbott maintain, must do more than be gory in order to be provocative.[18] While series like *The Hunger* (Showtime, 1997–2000) and *Dante's Cove* (here!, 2005–7) don't forsake shocks of blood and bodily violence, their more complex innovations within the millennial television marketplace can be found in (1) queering discursive formations of quality cable programming against those that posit the genre as overwhelmingly straight, masculinist exercises in social realism (e.g., *The Sopranos* [HBO, 1999–2007], *Breaking Bad* [AMC, 2008–13], *Mad Men* [AMC, 2007–15], etc.); (2) promoting increasingly intersecting themes, motifs, and narratives among horror and LGBTQ+ television; and (3) utilizing occultism to refract morally and ethically ambivalent characters and relationships that broaden the horizons of contemporary televised queerness beyond a narrow politics of positivist representation.

As Lynne Joyrich notes, American television's positioning within and between conflicting spaces of social and psychic life saturate its representations of sexuality with ambivalence, and this is "all the more noticeable in television's representations of gay and lesbian sexualities. It is no surprise then that the . . . tension between the fictional and the real . . . is particularly noteworthy in television's treatment of queer subjects."[19] What's more, this queer ambivalence has the potential to be especially exacerbated through occultism as, according to Helen Wheatley, there is no "*straight* connection between representation and reality when it comes to the construction and reception of television fiction and fantasy [emphasis mine]."[20] Ultimately, then, the ambivalent queer of occult cable TV complicates a set of assumptions that Amy Villarejo points to as stymieing LGBTQ+ representations and their criticism across popular visual culture, namely that television mimetically reflects its viewers; that it ought to do so; that it has an obligation toward positivist and diverse representations; or that such representations automatically lead to progressive political change.[21]

You Can't Do That on Television: The Evolution of US Cable

Director Tony Scott once said the following in an interview about his feature-film debut: "My daughter's been watching this thing called MTV. . . . I'm going to do an MTV [-style] movie . . . I stole from Helmut Newton's erotica. His pictures tell a story. They're always erotic and sexy and perverse and strange and fucked-up."[22] Indeed, as previously explored, one of the elements consistently emphasized in original reviews of *The Hunger* was its excessive visual style married to a queer viral perversity, all dressed up in the fragmentary garb of postmodern rock-video aesthetics. As Scott's reflections make plain, the film's deliberate flourishes of histrionic eroticism were no accident. A new influence called cable was beginning to circulate throughout 1980s American popular culture, inflecting the visual and thematic possibilities of myriad media forms.

Originally designed as an ancillary technology to boost the signal strength of broadcast networks and their affiliates in rural areas, cable television in the United States began to come into its own during the mid-1970s. According to Erik Barnouw, cable started courting its own share of the television market during this period by presenting supplemental offerings such as studio catalog feature films, live sporting events, and eventually original programming: "During the 1970s the number of local US cable systems grew to some four thousand, with more than fifteen million homes subscribing . . . [this growth] revolutionized the cable industry and suddenly changed the shape of American television."[23] In 1970, the American cable industry included 2,490 systems, 4.5 million subscribers, and was seen in 7.6 percent of US households.[24] By 1980, those statistics had climbed to 4,225, 15.2 million, and 19.9 percent respectively, and 9,575, 54.8 million, and 59 percent by 1990.[25]

From an industrial perspective, the phenomenal advancement of American cable systems and their new horizons of programming possibilities were abetted by similarly innovative technological developments, including the introduction of DBS (direct broadcast satellite), pay-per-view, the VCR, and a two-decade, push-and-pull struggle between networks, cable providers, and government regulators that attempted to make the US television landscape more competitive and diverse than it had previously been under the oligopolistic reign of the Big Three. In 1970, for example, the FCC famously issued the Financial Interest and Syndication Rules, better known as fin-syn, which prohibited ABC, CBS, and NBC from having any financial interest or ownership stake in their prime time programming. Fin-syn also strictly policed network participation in syndication, "considerably eroding the networks' control of their own industry and making them dependent on the Hollywood studios for product."[26] At the beginning of the 1971–72 season, the FCC also implemented the Prime Time Access Rule, better known as PTAR, which prohibited "network-affiliated television stations in the top fifty television markets from broadcasting more than three hours of network or 'off-network' (i.e., rerun) programmes during the four prime-time viewing hours."[27] As Amanda Lotz details in *The Television Will Be Revolutionized*, the rise of independent production under the auspices of both fin-syn and PTAR engendered a spirited environment of competition between networks and cable systems in which programming decisions were increasingly made based on content, since many financial considerations had been legislated away.[28]

Paradoxically, however, the range of programming options supposedly encouraged by the adoption of fin-syn and PTAR would eventually come to fruition most strikingly within the deregulatory climate of the 1980s and 1990s. In May 1981, President Ronald Reagan appointed Mark Fowler as chair of the FCC. Concurring with Reagan that the federal government should "get out of the way with respect to regulating the broadcasting industry, allowing for a marketplace approach instead," Fowler's laissez-faire FCC began a campaign of eradicating most existing regulatory prohibitions for television.[29] By the end of 1985, the FCC had reviewed, changed, and/or eliminated 89 percent of the agency's approximately nine hundred mass media rules.[30]

Beyond fin-syn and PTAR, which were repealed in 1993 and 1996, respectively, many of the broadcasting guidelines revisited by the FCC during this period centered on the ability of the federal government to regulate programming content, specifically regarding what was and was not permissible concerning on-air violence, profanity, and sexuality. While constitutional protection under the First Amendment has always guarded against "governmental interference with 'the press' and the FCC is specifically prohibited from preemptory censorship of broadcasts," First Amendment protections have never applied directly to radio or television, "owing to the government's role in licensing all broadcast stations."[31] Since broadcasters transmit signals via publicly owned over-the-air spectrums, networks and their affiliates have always been bound by FCC regulations, including content indecency standards, if they wish to be granted and retain broadcast licenses. These licenses are "issued for and held accountable to the public good or, more specifically, ill-defined community standards—a constantly changing and highly variable target."[32]

As previously discussed, community standards have served as tenuous yet enduring juridical scapegoats for policing charges of obscenity at least since the *Roth* decision in 1957. And indeed, five years earlier, the National Association of Broadcasters issued its own Television Code[33] that urged networks and their affiliates to air "sufficient amounts of educational and cultural programming," simultaneously creating an NAB review board designed to field viewer concerns and an official code seal doled out for respecting content restrictions, and prompting the establishment of Standards and Practices departments at all three major networks.[34] These censorial bodies, as confirmed through internal network documents such as Bernardine McKenna's earlier-cited ABC memo for *Dark Shadows*, were charged to be on the lookout for any manner of objectionable material involving profanity, violence, and/or sexual indecency (including references to homosexual behavior). Yet during the administrate reign of Fowler's FCC, mirroring the abandonment of the PCA seal and the years leading up to the adoption of the new MPAA rating system in 1968, the authority of the NAB Television Code had all but vanished. Networks and affiliates could certainly still risk alienating their ever-important revenue stream from advertisers by broadcasting risqué content, but control of objectionable material was largely left to program producers and network programmers.[35]

Within this flurry of industrial and legislative debate surrounding the permissible limits of network television content, cable was simultaneously separating itself from broadcast TV, primarily in the "private and selective nature of its transmission [cable operates through a subscription-based or pay-per-view model] . . . cable operators began to argue that they possessed different First Amendment rights than broadcasters."[36] Simply put, the legal logic of this double standard is that "over-the-air broadcasts are inescapable—if you have a television with a functioning antenna, you're bound to pick up NBC, CBS, and ABC. Cable service, on the other hand, requires a monthly fee. Paying your monthly cable bill is tantamount to acknowledging that you know what you're getting into"—bad words, gruesome deaths, steamy sex, and all.[37] What's more, because it was initially developed as a supplemental technology intended to improve network broadcasting and was not considered a "common carrier," the FCC saw no need to regulate cable in its nascent stages, since it was not conceived as a discrete content provider. Yet as more independent cable systems began to come online in the 1970s, discussions about whose interests new channels like HBO (launched in 1972), Showtime (launched in 1976), and the Movie Channel (launched in 1979) served and what they could and could not show became more vocal.

Histories of the American television industry agree almost universally that the remarkable rise of cable, in addition to the adoption of new technologies like the VCR (later DVR), remote control, and pay-per-view, irrevocably changed both the economic and sociocultural possibilities of the medium. "Television as we knew it," according to Lotz, "understood as a mass medium capable of reaching a broad, heterogeneous audience and speaking to the culture as a whole—is no longer the norm in the United States."[38] From the network era to the multichannel transition to the postnetwork era and beyond, an ever-increasing ubiquity of programming options has progressively transformed television from an electronic public sphere to an "electronic newsstand through which a diverse and segmented society pursues deliberately targeted interests. The US television audience now can rarely be categorized as a mass audience; instead, it is more accurately understood as a collection of niche audiences."[39] Indeed, both the industrial and scholarly attention paid to this "narrowcasting" phenomenon, within which discrete and isolated subsections of the television audience are sequestered as demographics that can be delivered more easily to certain advertisers and/or cable subscription systems, has significantly transformed television's industrial logics and has required a fundamental reassessment of how the medium operates as a cultural institution.[40]

The amplified partitioning of the American television audience among innumerable texts, channels, and distribution platforms may have lessened the ability of an individual network or program to reinforce a certain set of beliefs within a broad audience, but narrowcasting has hardly precluded television's function as what Horace Newcomb and Paul M. Hirsch famously termed a "cultural forum."[41] Regardless of era or technological manifestation, television has always been not just the "box in the corner" but also those behaviors, beliefs, and cultural practices associated with its use.[42] As such, the rise of cable, the consequent turn to niche marketing, and the expanding horizons of programming content intensified the critical discourse of television's possibilities among certain industrial actors, audiences, and demographics, creating a "subcultural forum when it reproduces a similar experience as the electronic public sphere, but among more narrow groups that share particular cultural affinities or tastes."[43]

By the early 1980s, niche marketing was indeed becoming the *technique à la mode* of the culture industries: "Audience segmentation was cutting-edge, and more and more advertising agencies tied their clients' campaigns to the targeting bandwagon. . . . Instead of trying to avoid or smooth over any differences that may have existed among people with different social experiences, target marketing exploited them in order to forge more intense connections between a product and its consumer."[44] And one of the most lucrative niches that both advertisers and television networks began to aggressively court was LGBTQ+ Americans. Reported (albeit reductively) to be more affluent, upwardly mobile, and well educated than their heterosexual counterparts, LGBTQ+ consumers were increasingly seen as an untapped source of revenue willing to swear both allegiance and spending power to networks and advertisers who served their interests. Analyzing its ubiquity across popular culture, Samuel Chambers argues that heteronormativity emphasizes the extent to which everyone, "straight or queer, will be judged, measured, probed, and evaluated from the perspective of the heterosexual norm . . . it goes almost without saying (but not quite) that the sort of identity reversal achieved by airing a show with primary gay characters has important effects."[45] Even still, the inauguration of what Becker terms "gay chic" did not take off in the 1980s and 1990s simply because the appeal of nonheterosexual representations across popular culture was limited to those who self-identified as such. Instead, LGBTQ+ programming material was advantageous for both television and advertising executives and for many viewers, regardless of sexual orientation, for whom "watching prime-time TV with a gay twist spoke to specific political values and offered some convenient ways to establish a 'hip' identity . . . homosexuality fit so comfortably with the socially liberal, fiscally conservative politics many 'sophisticated,' well educated and upscale Americans found resonant in [their] neoliberal political climate."[46]

Throughout this book, I've considered the consistent yet contingent ways that Euro-American film and television industries have historically articulated queerness not only as horrific, supernatural, monstrous, otherworldly, and deviant, but also as relatedly profane, obscene, indecent, and sexually explicit, regardless of whether anyone's clothing is coming off. Mirroring the earlier rise of porno chic, the domesticated turn toward both direct-to-video cinema and cable television during the 1980s and 1990s made "mature" and/or "adults only" content a primary tool of both marketing and cultural differentiation.[47] Indeed, central among emergent trends on cable TV was the use of "sex, nudity, violence, risqué language, and cutting-edge visual style to make a program 'edgy'—one of the buzzwords of the era."[48] In a 1989 survey of viewer preferences conducted by the Roper Center for Public Opinion, cable drastically outperformed network television in categories such as "educational, cultural, and entertainment programming. The survey's largest margins of difference, however, involved questions of mature content; respondents clearly believed that cable programming offered viewers more sex (71 percent to 6 percent), more violence (58 percent to 11 percent), and more profanity (69 percent to 7 percent)."[49]

In light of content restrictions placed on network programming, early original cable series like HBO's *Real Sex* (1990–2009) and Showtime's *Red Shoe Diaries* (1992–99) aggressively targeted sexually liberal audiences, both straight and queer, with an eye toward reimagining television not simply as a "forum for family programming or discussion of social issues related to sex but as a sexual technology that could be used as an adjunct to sexual practice, a kind of virtual sex toy."[50] This redefinition of cable as a sexual technology did not, however, go uncontested. In 1996, a new congressional Telecommunications Act was introduced that dictated provisions for governing the transmission of indecency on television and the exploding medium of the internet. Title V of the Telecommunications Act, better known as the Communications Decency Act (CDA), required any multichannel television provider to "scramble the audio and video signals of all sexually explicit, adult-oriented programming to prevent reception of the signals by nonsubscribers."[51] A separate clause of the CDA also mandated the establishment of a "voluntary age-based ratings system established for programming content that is broadcast ahead of the television program's signal," including a requirement that all television sets must contain a V-chip that would give parents the ability to prevent offensive programming from entering the home.[52] The V was originally short for "violence," but it also covered profanity and sex, and legislation of the V-chip was intended to maintain industrial self-regulation as the primary means of circumscribing media content, consequently minimizing direct state intervention.[53] As David Silverman asserts, with most networks already employing fewer and fewer censors, the ratings system established by the CDA actually allowed television producers to put "more and more objectionable material on television, arguing that the V-chip, not a Standards and Practices Department, is the new gatekeeper."[54]

While resisting the urge to indulge overly triumphalist teleology, it is difficult to dispute that sexuality on US television has become more explicit over the past thirty-five years. According to Brent Bozell, conservative pundit and founder of the Media Research Center and Conservative Communications Center, audiences are increasingly exposed to "more direct references to genitalia, prostitution, pornography, oral sex, kinky practices, masturbation, and depictions of nudity during primetime viewing hours."[55] Yet these representational changes are symptomatic not only of the shifting tastes and interests among certain demographics of the television audience but also have a clear industrial logic undergirding them. If, as Michel Foucault reminds us, the cultural repression of sexuality actually doubles back on itself as a paradoxical incitement to confessional discourse,[56] attempts to control broadcasting standards and patrol television for obscenity, indecency, and profanity have analogously incited proliferating discourses of the illicit.[57]

In fact, courting illicit, risqué, and controversial programming has become intentionally institutionalized by subscription cable channels like HBO, Showtime, and Cinemax, embedded in their original programming, and has become a distinctive feature of both their cultural cachets and quality brand labels: "Contentious subject matter and edgy scripts containing adult themes are predicated on risk-taking that strains broadcasting limits. . . . Pushing the limits of respectability, of daring to say/do what cannot be said/done elsewhere on the networks, is entwined with being esoteric, groundbreaking and risk-taking."[58] Even if the brief industrial history recounted here advances an understanding of how cable became a major player across the US television landscape and consciously packaged mature content in contradistinction to network fare, focused attention still needs to be paid to the particularities of this programming. It is not enough to simply say that certain segments of American television became more sexually explicit, more violent, or even more queer. Instead, a different kind of analysis is required to investigate in what kinds of programming these trends have been most substantial, what types of narratives audiences have become particularly invested in, and what genres serve as privileged sites for the risk-taking with which cable television has become so well known. As the following examinations of Showtime and here! demonstrate, LGBTQ+ sexualities and the occult have worked in tandem to create queer characters and story worlds that would be simply untenable within network venues. Indeed, these cable outlets often succeed precisely when they offer up programming that gratifies the interests of niche audiences whose interests and tastes go otherwise unserved.

Skeletons in (and out of) the Closet at Showtime

In an April 29, 1996, article for *Variety*, trade columnist Joe Flint reported that according to its parent conglomerate Viacom, revenues for cable juggernaut Showtime the previous year were "$622.1 million, compared with $589.2 million for 1994. Its cash flow margin went from 9% to 12% and its earnings went from $52.6 million to $75.8 million. The subscriber base for Showtime Networks Inc., which includes services Showtime, Flix and the Movie Channel, grew 11%, from 13.3 million subs in 1994 to 14.5 million last year."[59] Many of Showtime's economic and industrial successes on the eve of its twentieth anniversary were attributed to the channel's gradual halting of studio feature recycling and consequent turn toward revenue gambling on original programming that was considered edgy, risqué, taboo-pushing, and controversial. Between 1995 and 1999, Showtime's base of subscribers nearly doubled, to 22.3 million.[60]

Showtime's growth in the 1990s was due, at least in part, to a succession of softcore anthology series immersed in binary-dismantling worlds of sexual fantasy, where normative dichotomies of either/or were replaced by queer multiplicities of both/and.[61] Indeed, beginning with *Red Shoe Diaries* (1992–99), one of the trademarks of softcore cable anthologies became their critical meditations on sexual difference, with narratives that were "continually testing the limits of what is 'gender appropriate' ... [their] anxieties accompanying the representation of sex leave the construction of heterosexuality unstable," dissolving normative boundaries and laying bare the social construction of gender and sexuality.[62] Yet none of this is to say that *Red Shoe Diaries* and its progeny are de facto transgressive and/or sexually progressive. On the contrary, as Nina Martin, David Andrews, and others recount, early erotic anthologies' near-inevitable expression of erotic fulfillment through returns to compulsory heterosexuality often bracket their potentially liberating moments.[63] Even still, *Red Shoe Diaries* was instrumental in establishing what we might recognize as Showtime's signature queer vision, not only through later episodes in which female-on-female sex is imagined as a potentially viable, if somewhat ephemeral, alternative to heterosexual romance but also in its expression of queer critique as divorced from sexual object choice.

Premiering in June 1992, *Red Shoe Diaries* was only the third original series that Showtime ever produced. Written and often directed by Zalman King, who became a softcore pioneer in the 1980s with steamy theatrical successes such as *Two Moon Junction* (1988) and *Wild Orchid* (1989), *Red Shoe Diaries* stars David Duchovny as Jake Winters, a bereaved man whose adulterous fiancée recently committed suicide. Attempting to understand why she took her own life, Jake takes out a classified ad in a local newspaper, asking anonymous women to write to him in order to confess their deepest, darkest sexual fantasies. While Jake's backstory and voice-over serve as loosely contiguous narrative frames, each week's episode is dedicated to a different cast of characters in singular diegetic spaces. All of these stories are thematically bound, however, as sexual bildungsromans: journeys of edification and self-discovery through which central female protagonists work toward erotic fulfillment.

With recurring narratives of adultery, sexual betrayal, crime, and occasional murder, *Red Shoe Diaries* rarely engages with the occult, although many of its episodes feature stylistic flourishes of magickal realism through "ambiguous shadows that dance across the screen . . . created through soft-focus cinematography and chiaroscuro lighting" that were culled from the pages of Gothic novels.[64] Even still, the series's combination of sexual fantasies and suspense worked together to create a generically adjacent hybrid on which Showtime's later anthologies would build: the erotic thriller, a "contemporary form of soft-core pornography that, as opposed to hardcore, male-oriented porn, deals specifically with the sexual subjectivity of women and the social construction of gender."[65]

By the late 1990s, shored up by the success of King's anthology, Showtime was successfully billing itself as the industry trailblazer in sexual television. Not only were series like *Red Shoe Diaries*, *Beverly Hills Bordello* (1996–98), *Hot Springs Hotel* (1998–2000), *Love Street* (1994–96), and

Women: Stories of Passion (1996–99) featuring nudity and sexual dialogue that were unimaginable under the content restrictions of network programming, but, according to Jowett and Abbott, Showtime actually "out-HBO'd HBO," the longtime cable frontrunner, in what was permissible on subscription TV.[66] At the same time, Showtime was also beginning to enjoy solid returns on original programming that fused its established interest in sexuality with a budding curiosity about the occult, such as *Poltergeist: The Legacy* (1996–99), a reimagined version of *The Outer Limits* (1995–2000), and the anthology series *The Hunger* (1997–2000). The latter was billed in industry trades as a "weekly half-hour that intermingles 'the erotic and the bizarre.' Its storylines will be culled from horror pulp fiction of the past and center on characters who hit speed bumps on the road to carnal adventure,"[67] wherein "insatiable desires [turn] into nightmares."[68] If Tony Scott envisioned *The Hunger* as a film done in what was the then-edgy style of MTV circa 1983, this new collaboration with brother Ridley (both were executive producers on the series) finally saw that vision come full circle to cable.

Showtime's two-season run of *The Hunger* shares no narrative continuities with Scott's film, but rather reappropriates its stylized investigation of the erotic associations between the occult and dismantling normative genders and sexual practices, consequently creating ambivalent, multidimensional characters that broaden the horizons of televised queerness. This representational expansion is accomplished most obviously in the series through the Gothic trope of the doppelgänger. Consider, for instance, the July 20, 1997, episode "Ménage à Trois." Steph Reynolds (Lena Headey), a mild-mannered live-in nurse, is dispatched to the home of Miss Gati (Karen Black), a brash, eccentric, wheelchair-bound invalid with a penchant for duplicitous grins and chain-smoking. Scrutinizing Steph while assessing her eye-catching innocence, Miss Gati cryptically declares that Steph will suit her needs nicely. During this initial meeting, Miss Gati also introduces Steph to the other member of her household: live-in handyman Jerry (Daniel Craig). As days go by, Steph and Jerry gradually bond over the peculiar habits of their employer, especially a basement closet housing an extensive collection of fetish costumes, dildos, and other assorted sex paraphernalia, "remnants of a once promiscuous past."

Inside Miss Gati's home, time is marked not by clocks or watches but by thrice-daily injections of morphine administered to Miss Gati by Steph. These shots not only alleviate Miss Gati's discomfort but also visibly alter her typically confrontational demeanor. After every injection, the camera lingers in close-up on Miss Gati's face, as her flickering eyelids and gradual smile of gratification connote the initiation of a euphoric trance. One evening, however, this spell escapes Miss Gati's body in a process perhaps best termed "trance transference." After her employer asks her to sit awhile and hold her hand until the pain subsides, Steph's typically stoic expression suddenly turns to lustful inquisitiveness. Up until this juncture, Steph and Jerry have enjoyed mild flirtation, but the former's sense of professionalism has kept the latter at arm's length. Changing into a see-through negligee that allows full access to her nude body, Steph leaves Miss Gati and goes directly to a noticeably surprised Jerry's room, where she climbs on top of him, disrobes, and proceeds to have her aggressive way with him.

According to Eve Sedgwick, the doppelgänger of Gothic horror represents a "mirrored monstrosity" between two subjects typically unveiled through a process of "fleshly autograph[ing]" that is uniquely female.[69] Jeffrey Sconce similarly echoes this point by citing the belief, long held in the annals of Western thought, that women are somehow more sensitive to the vibrations and spiritual stirrings of the occult.[70] By way of Miss Gati's touch, something new has indeed been written on, in, and throughout Steph's body, a parasitic reciprocity between the two that only grows more obvious, more perverse, and more queer.

If television has historically reflected the sociocultural confinement of women, queers, and especially queer women back to themselves, as Amy Villarejo argues, then television "in itself and in what it means is gender identification, and by extension sexual being."[71] As such, TV is "one of the— if not *the* most—gendered and sexualized repetition apparatuses of modern technoscience," the quintessentially modern implantation of gendered and sexualized sociality.[72] While Villarejo is primarily concerned with the phenomenology of spectatorship and the potentially queer interactions between viewer and text, the pride of place given to television as a repetitive technology of sexual and gender mimesis is equally fitting in a narrative context, even more so considering the representational latitude afforded to cable. During another trance transference in "Ménage à Trois," for example, Steph wears nothing but a neck brace (mirroring the paralytic disability of her employer) while forcefully fucking Jerry in the basement closet of sexual curiosities. The haunting suspicion that Miss Gati is somehow influencing Steph's behavior is wholly confirmed as her subterranean tryst is intercut with close-ups of her employer upstairs in a transcendental state now visually highlighted by facial expressions that connote synchronized orgiastic ecstasy. As Lynne Joyrich maintains, television's positioning within and between conflicting spaces of social and psychic life often saturate its representations of sexuality, even presumptive heterosexuality, with ambivalence.[73] In "Ménage à Trois," these clashing social, psychic, and physical spaces are visually represented and queered via occult means. Indeed, through the juxtaposition of Steph and Jerry with Miss Gati, what superficially appears as a straight sexual encounter becomes something much more supernaturally complex.

In the episode's climax, Steph slowly saunters into Jerry's room, now fully possessed by her employer. Not only have her hairstyle and eye color completely changed, but her voice has also fully morphed into that of Miss Gati. Terrified at the culmination of the transformation he's witnessed, Jerry unsuccessfully attempts to escape before Steph throws him against a wall and kills him. The episode concludes with a prospective new handyman entering the house as Steph greets him from the top of the stairs wearing a tight red dress and high-heeled shoes, and smoking a cigarette.

Just as homosexuality requires heterosexuality as a contrasting definitional referent, epistemologies of sexuality, especially queer sexualities, often exist in dialectical relation, "specific knowledges that simultaneously both illuminate and obscure, produced by specific discourses and modes of signification . . . and rather than identities always already existing, even if in the shadows, waiting to be brought to view, subjectivities and sexualities are only formed (and deformed; formed as deformed) through those specific knowledges."[74] Indeed, in "Ménage à Trois," Miss Gati's occult understanding of trance transference both conceals queerness (her direct relationship with Steph is never a sexual one) and also serves to highlight it, as she phantasmatically possesses the body of another woman as a means to sexual pleasure while also using that body as a queer conduit to create the occult threesome referenced in the episode's title.

As series creator Jeff Fazio once noted, "Most people want the formula that they've seen before. And the reason Tony Scott came to [cable] is he said he didn't want to do what people expected. What had been seen."[75] Echoing these observations, Giovanni Ribisi, star of *The Hunger*'s second season premiere, said, "I think it's a lot more free . . . it doesn't really fit the criteria or the standard of what is required or what people think is required in television."[76] If occultism, queerness, and explicit sexuality have all usually existed outside the bounds of normative mass media fare, Joyrich is quite right in arguing that "bringing what typically exists outside TV's representational space into its very core creates an epistemological crisis that threatens . . . to blow this space up."[77] On cable series like *The Hunger*, however, this haunting threat is rearticulated as an ambivalent source of both narrative and visual pleasure. Miss Gati may well be a witch or psychic vampire who co-opts Steph's body as an instrument for her own erotic gratification, but her interwoven ways of both sexual and supernatural knowing are never rebuked. Indeed, as Robin Wood argues of contemporary horror, the queer monster is typically not destroyed by the film's (or in this case, television episode's) conclusion, and that is precisely part of the pleasure.

If the entwined epistemologies of sexuality and the occult that provide the driving force behind "Ménage à Trois" work to both conceal and express queerness through the figure of the doppelgänger, *The Hunger*'s February 20, 2000, episode, "Double," uses the same trope toward slightly different ends. As the episode opens, an unnamed woman happens on a portrait of herself in the window of an art gallery, recounting through interior monologue, "That's the woman who's going to kill me." That evening, the same woman hides in the shadows across from the gallery while observing her exact double, Lisette (Lori Petty), an up-and-coming artist, arriving at the opening of a new exhibition. For years, Lisette has been haunted by nightmares of herself walking down the ward of an old hospital. As these dreams grow more vivid, continuing to disturb not only her own sleep but also that of her partner Danielle (Daniela Akerblom), Lisette vows to work more intently with her psychiatrist, Dr. Fuller (Larry Day), to unearth answers.

Under hypnosis at Dr. Fuller's office, Lisette recounts her recurring nightmares in intense detail: she is a nurse on the smallpox ward of a hospital and is convinced that one of the dying patients is scheming to possess her body. Waking her from the trance, Dr. Fuller inquires whether Lisette ever studied medical history. There hasn't been a smallpox epidemic in the city since the 1890s, Dr. Fuller recounts, yet Lisette speaks of it in such detail that it is almost as if she was there. Curious to know more about the epidemic and her possibly metaphysical connections to it, Lisette sets out to do some research.

Asleep at her computer that evening, Lisette is visited by the doppelgänger, who has been steadily spying on her. These two bodies cannot continue to exist in the same place at the same time, the doppelgänger's voice-over relates, so Lisette must die. The attempted murder is thwarted, however, when a magickally glowing protective shield prevents the doppelgänger from getting close enough to strangle Lisette. Eager to hatch an alternative plan, the doppelgänger leaves a website up on Lisette's computer that discusses rebirth and reincarnation. Finally connecting the logical dots, Lisette tells a skeptical Dr. Fuller the next day that what she's been experiencing are actually memories of her own death.

Through a combination of shifting narrative perspectives (the plot unfolds from both Lisette and her doppelgänger's point of view) and Lisette's gradual recollection of her own death and eventual reincarnation, "Double" fuses what Sconce calls two of the "best-known, most-hackneyed, and thus most-parodied" televisual conventions: the amnesia plot and the evil-twin plot.[78] Yet unlike sitcoms or soap operas that typically employ these devices in the service of camped-up laughs, "Double" uses them as occult meditations on the ambiguous boundaries of the queer closet. Ghosts, according to Samuel Chambers, are floating signifiers of a closeted existence, "entities that can never fully regain a material existence, nor can they (at least not yet) enter a completely spiritual realm that leaves the material world behind."[79] To borrow from Sedgwick and Joyrich, the epistemology of the closet/console is structured by a spectral recognition of both concealment and clarification, employing both/and rather than either/or logics. In "Double," this point is made plain through flashbacks from the perspective of Lisette's doppelgänger, wherein the spirit possessing the body of the female hospital patient does indeed vacate that vessel and possess Lisette-as-nurse. A literal floating signifier, the malevolent spirit of "Double" both is and is not the person it possesses.

Suggestively, this both/and ambivalence extends to each of the episode's female-on-female sex scenes, particularly the climactic one in which Lisette's doppelgänger (disguised as Lisette) and Danielle make love. Later, in the episode's penultimate sequence, Lisette finally confronts the doppelgänger in her living room. Both scream for help, and each tries to convince Danielle that she is the real Lisette. Danielle rushes at them, pushes their bodies together, and causes both to disappear in a cloud of smoke. Yet out of this haze rises the malevolent spirit, still active, who enters Danielle's body. The episode concludes with the possessed Danielle smiling in a mirror as the spirit's ventriloquized voice-over muses over its new body and decides that it will stay until it gets bored or sees another figure more to its liking.

Considering why Ellen DeGeneres's ABC sitcom failed shortly after its infamous two-part coming-out episode, Anna McCarthy argues that fear of a "quotidian, ongoing lesbian life on TV suggests that although the network could support queer television as 'must see TV,' it could not sanction a lesbian invasion of serial television's more modest form of history-making, its ongoing, regularly scheduled place in televisual flow."[80] Echoing this analysis, Glyn Davis and Gary Needham maintain that as television regularly configures queerness as "excessive, as spectacle, as interruption, sexual alterity cannot be accommodated by the medium into its dominant and pervasive time structures—regulated chronotypes which are intricately interwoven with its representational protocols."[81] In the case of Showtime, the "one-off" episodic structure of the anthology drama may indeed have been the most conducive format to representing both queerness and the occult on a nonidentarian cable channel.

Even still, *The Hunger* provocatively imagines what Michele Aaron calls the "new queer" of the 1990s and new millennium, not merely "an umbrella term for all that is, positively, not straight, or narrow. It is [rather] an oppositional stance intimately bound to an anti-normative trajectory."[82] In the worlds of both "Ménage à Trois" and "Double," the occult works to refract queer identities as ambivalent, as both duplicitous and harshly honest, conniving yet resourceful, and decidedly antiassimilationist in relation to both heterosexual and even some mainstream LGBTQ+ norms. "Queer cannot throw off its nasty history nor should it," Aaron argues, "for it is its nasty history that keeps it on its toes, keeps it daring, dancing, and not only astute to the nastiness of the present, but capable of undermining it."[83]

During its original run between July 1997 and March 2000, *The Hunger* was the only original series on Showtime tempting any sort of explicit sexual representation that was not consequently lumped into the category of "Adult Drama" or "Adult Comedy" by the network. As detailed above, Showtime's engagement with the anthology drama format, allowing queer characters and storylines to ebb and flow without the requisite restraints of seriality, may have been a conscious industrial move toward dualcasting, defined by Katherine Sender simply as the simultaneous targeting of two specific audiences.[84] As such, Showtime was able to widen the swath of both its occult and sexual appeals by tailoring narratives to serve a variety of orientations and interests. And while the erotic anthology proved conducive to bringing the "new queer" to television, the potential allures of programming that was all queer, all the time were further exacerbated by occult cable series still to come.

Hedonistic Queer Horror on here!

Following its momentum in airing modestly queer programming throughout the 1990s and early 2000s, Showtime announced in January 2002 that it was planning to partner with fellow Viacom subsidiary MTV on a new project: a cable channel aimed exclusively at the interests of LGBTQ+ audiences. "This isn't a very big departure for Viacom," Robert Knight of the conservative Culture & Family Institute noted, "because they've been promoting the homosexual agenda on MTV and other outlets for a long time. What makes this new is that a whole network is devoted to it."[85] Developers of this new channel, the aptly named Outlet, hoped to capitalize on both the niche demographic expertise that MTV had established since the mid-1980s and the queer-friendly reputation cultivated by Showtime.[86] Like PrideVision, a similar LGBTQ+ channel launched in the top four Canadian cable markets in September 2001, revenue for Outlet was originally intended to come from both subscription fees and advertising. But by 2004, a struggling US economy and aggressive ad market had postponed Outlet's premiere.

In February of that same year, MTV announced that Showtime had dropped out as a partner on the project and that the vision for Outlet had transformed into "an entirely ad-supported channel as part of a package that includes MTV, MTV2, VH1, Nickelodeon, and other channels. Changing the launch plan for the planned gay channel from a partial pay-for-service to a fully ad-supported and bundled channel meant that the channel would be available to all subscribers at a particular tier, not just those who opt in."[87] Historically, this strategy has been characteristic of most major media conglomerates in addressing issues of representational diversity: "Rather than dispersing taste niches and community viewpoints across competing channels, the new conglomerates have mastered the ability to include this diverse pantheon of tastes and perspectives within components or 'tiers' of the very same conglomerate."[88] In the case of Outlet and other intraconglomerate LGBTQ+ channels, however, this strategy ultimately proved fatal, as MSOs (multiple-system operators) such as Cox, Comcast, and Time Warner were disinclined to take on programming bundles that included a queer network for fear of alienating subscribers who had no wish to view such content.[89] A different approach to programming specifically for LGBTQ+ audiences was in order.

In the summer of 2003, DirecTV became the first US distributor to ink a deal to carry here!, a new pay-per-view channel directed specifically at the interests of LGBTQ+ audiences. Founded by Paul Colichman and Stephen P. Jarchow, here! is a division of their Regent Entertainment Group, which had previously seen success among LGBTQ+ audiences as a producer of films such as the Academy Award-winning *Gods and Monsters* (1998). In a July 8, 2003, article for *Daily Variety*, John Dempsey reported that Colichman's goal for here! was ultimately to turn it into a "24-hour-a-day cable network targeted to gays and lesbians. He [Colichman] deliberately decided against beginning with a 24-hour channel because of the barriers that prevented two proposed 24-hour nets [Outlet and an American version of PrideVision] from being launched last year despite elaborate pitches by their owners to cable operators and satellite distributors."[90] Charging $3.99 apiece for a catalog of independently produced queer feature films that rotated each month, executives at here! hoped to capitalize on a lucrative segment of the LGBTQ+ marketplace, "an affluent, underserved niche group with lots of buying power, an estimated $450 billion to $600 billion in annual disposable income, who have been starving for TV programming relevant to their lives."[91]

This pay-per-view model finally did prove profitable enough that here! expanded from an exclusively video-on-demand satellite service offered by DirecTV and Dish Network into a twenty-four-hour premium cable network on October 1, 2004, initially carried by Cablevision and the now-defunct Adelphia Communications Corporation. According to Karen Flischel, executive vice president and general manager, here!'s combination of video on demand, subscription video on demand, and continuous programming attempted to make the network available in a variety of ways that would "accommodate a variety of cable operators . . . for some that meant a linear channel, for others that meant transactional [video on demand]."[92] In its linear iteration, as reported by *Multichannel News*'s Linda Moss, here! took up an industrial model popularized by the Playboy Channel: "Subscribers can buy a program block or upgrade to the 24-hour linear feed for a monthly subscription fee."[93]

here!'s resolution to include a twenty-four-hour linear feed as part of its service offerings signaled that the company's success could no longer rest solely in the hands of independently produced feature films. The channel simply needed more and different types of content. Mirroring the trajectories of other premium cable networks, Colichman noted that "what we are focusing on is original, exclusive, story-form programming... we view our world as the world of Showtime and HBO."[94] If much of the trade press coverage of here!'s launch as a fully fledged LGBTQ+ cable network banged the drum of belatedness, the question still remained as to what kinds of queer representation the network would program. According to Jeffrey Garber, president of the queer-friendly advertising agency OpusComm Group, "Every minority is happy at first just to see itself portrayed [on television] ... it's only after time that they get impatient with one-dimensional portrayals and start looking for more realistic depictions."[95] Echoing this sentiment, as reported by *Daily Variety*'s Stuart Levine, Colichman was adamant that the mission of here!'s original programming was to "ensure that the gay characters seen throughout the channel are realistic, not the glossed-over or patronized versions often depicted in broadcast television. 'Our battle every day is to make sure we are showing an authentic look at the lives of our viewers.... We are the gay HBO. We set our sights very high.'"[96]

here!'s rhetorical trade-press flourishes on the eve of its twenty-four-hour launch smacked repeatedly of realism, community relevance, and appeals to verisimilitude. "What does it mean to be queer in the twenty-first century?" was the predominant question the channel seemed to pose. Given these concerns, it is curious that here!'s first original scripted series was billed, in the words of cast member Zara Taylor, as a "sexy, horror, gay and lesbian soap opera."[97] Premiering October 7, 2005, *Dante's Cove* began as a two-part miniseries, a blend of "*Sex and the City* meets *Dark Shadows* meets *The O.C.* meets *Buffy the Vampire Slayer* with a little bit of *Melrose Place* thrown in there."[98] While anxiously awaiting her marriage to wealthy entrepreneur Ambrosius Vallin (William Gregory Lee) in the year 1840, Grace Neville (Tracy Scoggins) becomes restless and uncertain of her fiancé's fidelity. She is eager to surrender her virginity to the man she loves, but Ambrosius reminds Grace that they mustn't spoil their wedding night and assures her that he has "absolutely no interest in other women." The irony of this promise is addressed as, on Grace's exit, Ambrosius's valet Raymond (Dylan Jordan) enters the drawing room, disrobes, and begins to receive oral sex from his employer. Recalling that she left her gloves on top of a soon-to-be ironic set piece, Ambrosius's copy of *Dante's Inferno*, Grace reenters the room just in time to witness Raymond bending Ambrosius over an armchair while penetrating him from behind. Grace's anger directed toward this queer mise-en-scène is matched only by her indignation that her fiancé would engage in such perversely emasculating behavior.

As Ambrosius scrambles for a quick explanation, Grace's eyes unexpectedly turn bright red and the fully nude, semierect Raymond begins to convulse uncontrollably on the floor.

Unbeknownst to Ambrosius, Grace is one of a long line of local witches who practice an ancient magickal art known as Tresum. Chaining up her fiancé in the basement of her mother's estate, Grace gives Ambrosius a final ultimatum: renounce his queer ways and come back to her or forever be doomed to rot in his own personal circle of hell on earth. After he swears that he would rather suffer an eternity alone than live a lie with her, Grace places a curse on her beloved: only the kiss of a young man will set him free. As Tracy Scoggins notes of the series's inspiration, *Dante's Cove* "pays a certain homage to shows that have come before," its thematic material and soap opera conventions culled most obviously from the frames of both *Dark Shadows* and NBC's *Passions* (1999–2008).[99] Indeed, borrowing from the former, Grace and Ambrosius are clearly characterized as the Angelique Bouchard and Barnabas Collins for the twenty-first century. As Darren Elliot-Smith and others contend, spectators must often make the primary leap of reading the "symbolic homosexual" within the supernatural milieu of Gothic texts like *Dark Shadows*.[100] Yet while that series's own ellipses and aphoristic misdirections hardly negate its nonnormativity, *Dante's Cove* makes Ambrosius's and other characters' struggles with their own queer gender and sexual identities entirely explicit.

In *Cable Guys: Television and Masculinities in the Twenty-First Century*, Amanda Lotz argues that the transformation of television's norms regarding the representation of gay men "from absence to occasional pathologized or mocked characters to a context where gay identity is banal and being closeted is pathologized . . . marks a trajectory of amazing speed and indicates a clear contestation of heteronormativity unquestionably relevant to the analysis of televised masculinities."[101] Indeed, if queer occult soap operas such as *Dante's Cove* and its spin-off *The Lair* (2007–9) render obvious any attempt at subtextual queer reference, the question then becomes this: "When monstrousness as a metaphor for the threat that homosexuality poses to heteronormativity ceases to be coded and instead becomes open, what does it mean?"[102] One prominent meaning can be found in the ways these series refract nonnormative sexualities through conventions of the occult in order to illuminate ambivalent horizons of contemporary queer masculinities and relationships between men.

From Ambrosius's subterranean imprisonment, *Dante's Cove* advances over 150 years to present-day Venice Beach, California, where Toby Moraitis (Charlie David) and Kevin Archer (Gregory Michael) enjoy one final lovemaking session during a fading summer fling. Encouraging Kevin to run away from his mother and homophobic stepfather, Toby doesn't understand why his lover can't simply be honest with everyone about his sexuality. For Toby, the series's hardworking gentleman with a heart of gold, being a man means being open, authentic, and true to oneself without compromise, an ethos the younger Kevin simply isn't ready to fully embrace. However, after tempers flare later that evening at the Archer house and his appalled stepfather smacks him across the face and uses the slur "faggot," Kevin catches the next bus out of town to join Toby, who has left for his winter job on the island of Dante's Cove.

Kevin's arrival at the Hotel Dante, a queer male reframing of the Gothic ingénue's entrance into a mysterious new world, is presaged by supernatural visions of both a shirtless and shackled Ambrosius and a magickal tome known as the Book of Tresum. These dreams are provisionally overlooked, however, as Kevin is welcomed into the local fold by Toby's friends: Van (Nadine Nicole Heimann), a local lesbian artist with her own soon-to-be-discovered magickal abilities; Cory (Josh Berresford), the Hotel Dante's "resident slut"; and Adam (Stephen Amell), a would-be straight man whose own repressed love for his high school best friend, Toby, eventually bubbles to the surface. Considering the history of minority sexual representation on television, one of the most noteworthy elements of *Dante's Cove* and a network like here! is their queer ubiquity. "If gays on TV (and in mainstream film) have too often been relegated to the token roles of sidekick, accessory, neighbor, on view for heterosexuals within a largely heterosexual world," Suzanna Danuta Walters argues, "here gays are the only show in town."[103] In fact, the only straight character with a speaking part throughout the entire series run of *Dante's Cove* is Grace, and nightly parties at the Hotel Dante, featuring little else than same-sex couples involved in various levels of erotic behavior set against racing strobe lights and bass-pumping trance music from composer Eric Allaman, are only one instance of how this series emphatically reverses the typically desexed plight of the televised queer.

As Jowett and Abbott explain of horror on contemporary television, it is no mistake that such narrative spaces are often set in isolated communities, "divorced in many ways from the larger world," where common codes of realism, morality, and plausibility are replaced by logics (or perhaps illogics) of the occult.[104] Indeed, both *Dante's Cove* and *The Lair* make conscious efforts to construct clear dichotomies between the mainland and their insulated island settings. According to cast member Charlie David, the thematic outlook of *Dante's Cove* can be best described as a process of occult rationalization: "OK, this is where we live. We're in Dante's Cove. It's a little nuts around here. There's ghost children and warlocks and witches . . . and it's more coming to terms with what the reality of living here is like."[105] In the context of queer horror on here!, sexuality itself should also be added to the list of normative codes that are disrupted, as *Dante's Cove* never questions that nearly every resident of this island presents somewhere on the LGBTQ+ spectrum. As director Sam Irvin explains, the "overall theme of our series is that there's just a complete acceptance" of the reality of these alternative lifestyles, both sexual and supernatural.[106]

Since his arrival at the Hotel Dante, Kevin has been presented not only with a plethora of new queer friends but also with assorted legends and continuing dreams of the island's haunting by a horde of occult forces. One evening, following an ethereal voice down into the basement of the hotel, Kevin finds a usually padlocked cellar door inexplicably ajar. What he finds below is the aging body of Ambrosius Vallin, who is magickally brought back to youthful vitality after stealing a kiss from Kevin in what becomes a prescient milieu of queer Gothic bondage and S&M. Ambrosius's release from his subterranean prison is the catalyst that propels the remainder of *Dante's Cove*'s three-year, twelve-episode run, including subplots ranging from Toby and Kevin's struggle to keep their relationship alive in the face of Ambrosius's unrelenting advances toward the latter to Grace's own resurrection and schemes to enact continued revenge on Ambrosius to the arrival of a thought-to-be-vanquished dark magickal force that threatens to destroy every resident of the island.

By the time *Dante's Cove* premiered in October 2005, Regent Entertainment was no stranger to backing queer occult horror productions, as the company had previously produced the first installment, then distributed the second installment of the direct-to-video vampire/witchcraft franchise *The Brotherhood*, directed by Roger Corman protégé David DeCoteau. As such, when asked why here! decided to make its first original series a "sexy show with elements of magick,"[107] CEO Colichman provided a revealing response:

> The horror genre has always been an important part of the gay and lesbian community. The reason horror and gay people have always gone hand in hand is that the gay community felt like they were monsters among everyone

else. There was a sense of alienation. And really horror deals with alienation. ... So what we did was take a very traditional genre, the horror soap, and populated that world with out gay and lesbian characters so that we could combine a genre that was comfortable to people who had been feeling alienated with people who were not alienated from themselves, people who had a strong sense of who they were, and a community that was all about being gay and lesbian.[108]

Of the many queer endeavors that occult media since the 1960s have engaged in, one of the most significant is destabilizing the dichotomy between realism and fantasy. There is, as Helen Wheatley reminds us, no "straight connection between representation and reality when it comes to the construction and reception of television fiction and fantasy." As such, Colichman's reflections are a fitting illustration of the ways in which occult horror has historically intersected with nonnormative sexual politics in order to turn the alienation of the sexual Other into a potential rallying point for both queer media production and community formation. Yet trade press coverage of here!'s launch and the eventual success of *Dante's Cove* provides an instructive industrial and sociocultural paradox vis-à-vis what types of representation have carved out the viable contours of televising queerness on cable.

From coverage in *Daily Variety*, *Multichannel News*, and other industry trades, representatives from here! made one thing abundantly clear about the network's launch: sexually explicit media would be emphatically eschewed. "We want mainstream, middle-of-the-road programming for gays and lesbians from the age of 16 on up," Colichman said, "if people want porno, let them take it off the Internet."[109] As previously noted, here! built its video-on-demand, subscription video-on-demand, and twenty-four-hour linear feed services around the Playboy Channel model of allowing subscribers access to a variety of programming options, several of whose transactional natures made the on-demand connotation of sexual gratification almost too obvious. As such, attempting to curtail stereotypical imaginings of gay men in particular as sexually voracious, representatives from here! may simply have been protesting too much, especially given that full-frontal male nudity appears within the first five minutes of *Dante's Cove*'s premiere episode. "It's not adult content, it's not erotica," Colichman affirmed, "but it is designed for a mature audience that pays for it and wants it."[110]

But how then did here! intend to negotiate this balance, consciously avoiding the ominous specter of pornography while still assuring viewers that they would receive their mature money's worth? In a dismissive yet ultimately apropos question posed by Andrea Lafferty, the executive director of the Traditional Values Coalition, "What are they going to do, have homosexuals knitting?"¹¹¹ Sexually explicit visual culture has always had to serve, according to Thomas Waugh, not only as "stroke material" for queers but also as "our family snapshots and wedding albums, as our cultural history and political validation."¹¹² Such materials have a privileged relationship with queer cultures due to their unique combination of "indexical (motivated) and iconic qualities . . . [resembling] the living flesh of everyday sexual experience (iconic) but also [testifying] to the existence of that flesh (indexical)," thereby unleashing the psychological potential for polymorphously perverse identifications and fantasies.¹¹³ In turn, after the first-season success of *Dante's Cove*, Colichman and here! began to change their representational tune: "We had to uncensor ourselves, to some extent. To allow us to have the same level of sexuality that other premium cable channels like Showtime and HBO have. And we had to allow that same level for our own community."¹¹⁴ This struggle to uncensor here! and *Dante's Cove* was particularly compounded by three interrelated factors: (1) a long-standing double standard of representing nudity in popular culture (i.e., that female nudity is somehow less transgressive than male, easier to program, etc.); (2) that so much ambivalence directed toward queer cultures has been inspired precisely because sex and sexuality, let alone nonnormative sexual practices, are things supposedly best kept private; and (3) that representing queer sexualities as promiscuous, polyamorous, and even pleasurably dangerous could be construed as politically irresponsible, trafficking in stereotype, and culturally counterproductive.

Nevertheless, as McCabe and Akass maintain, discourses of the illicit, whether sexual or otherwise, have become integral to the contemporary quality television landscape as "compelling story-telling, key to creating complex and morally ambivalent protagonists, [and] vital to dramatic verisimilitude."¹¹⁵ My interrogation of the occult sexualities of *Dante's Cove* is neither intended to argue how illicit the series is nor to demonstrate how it represents a de facto progressive example of queer representation on television. Rather, the series's latitude in representing male nudity and sex between men works in tandem with both its magickal milieu and serial structure to provide a genderqueer counteraction within the occult horror genre, demonstrating that magick can be as masculine as it is feminine, and to demonstrate how this reconsideration paints a potentially pleasurable portrait of ambivalent queer relationships set against a plaguing imperative toward assimilationist, positivist, and even sexually sanitized representations that continue to contour network programming. As F. Hollis Griffin argues, "Cinema, television, and online media that are created for sexual minorities frequently give short shrift to desire's multiplicities by privileging an identity-based definition of sexuality over and above a more fluid one rooted in acts."[116]

In *Dante's Cove*'s second season, the series's occult mythology shores up a well-defined dichotomy between female magick's association with powers of the moon and water and masculine magick with powers of the sun. As Elliot-Smith notes, this gender war stages a "struggle between the power of feminine witchcraft and its masculine counterpart," queering the pugnacious metaphor as the stereotypically stronger power of the sun is overcome by the "traditionally weaker feminine moon."[117] Indeed, throughout their jockeying to sabotage each other's plans and enact petty revenge schemes, Ambrosius and Grace constantly spar about which gender is Tresum's rightful heir. For her part, Grace refuses to believe that a man, "and not even a real one," could possibly have mastered such powers and continually attempts to shame Ambrosius with emasculating accusations of impotency. Such multivalent slights (i.e., that magick is not fit for men and even less so for queer men) are ones that Ambrosius emphatically endeavors to turn on their heads.

Ambrosius's modus operandi thus becomes demonstrating how his masculinity and sex appeal toward other men can be enhanced by his command of Tresum's magickal forces. For instance, after one especially emasculating conversation with Grace, Ambrosius returns home, takes off his shirt, and stands in front of a full-length mirror while unbuttoning his pants, slowly reaching inside to pleasure himself. This magickal masturbatory act not only summons spectral visions of a fully nude Kevin but also physically beckons Cory, previously enslaved to do Ambrosius's bidding, who sinks to his knees and orally pleasures his master before Ambrosius penetrates him from behind. As director Sam Irvin notes, "Ambrosius in *Dante's Cove* is the Barnabas Collins or Dracula for the new millennium. He's got a very sort of darkly sexual romantic side to him," a side revealed to be increasingly enigmatic and ambivalent as Ambrosius becomes the series's quintessential antihero.[118]

Indeed, Ambrosius's station as the seductively enchanting villain of *Dante's Cove* is underscored most obviously through his relationship with Kevin. Since being released from his subterranean prison, Ambrosius believes that he and Kevin are destined to be together. While Kevin does show signs of flirtatious attraction toward Ambrosius despite his professed love for Toby, this seduction turns dark when Ambrosius threatens Toby's life unless Kevin agrees to become his requisite aspirant during a magickal solstice ceremony in the second-season finale. Diana, Grace's sister and Ambrosius's own Tresum mentor (Thea Gill), temporarily vanquishes him during this ritual, but Ambrosius quickly returns to whisk Kevin away, reminding his aspirant that his pledge binds him indefinitely.

Up until this juncture, *Dante's Cove*'s codes of gender and sexual ethics are presented as fairly straightforward: masculinity remains figured as stereotypically aggressive and assertive, and magick aids in amplifying manipulative, scheming, and devious qualities so that wicked figures like Ambrosius may obtain what they desire at any cost. Relatedly, the sociosexual binary between insertive/masculine/top and receptive/feminine/bottom roles is also almost exclusively upheld both outside and within the island's same-sex bedrooms. As Nguyen Tan Hoang contends of gender roles and queer sexual representation, "Assuming the bottom position . . . has acquired a host of negative associations, including being weak or humiliated. For a man to get anally penetrated by another man signals the ultimate act of emasculation. In a patriarchal society, to bottom is akin to being penetrated and dominated like a woman. It is to be lacking in power or to surrender one's power to the top."[119] Relatedly, in a well-known essay intimately invested in queer horrors, Leo Bersani argues that human bodies are constructed in ways such that "it is, or at least has been, almost impossible not to associate mastery and subordination with the experience of our most intense pleasures. This is first of all a question of positioning . . . being on top can never be just a question of a physical position—either for the person on top or for the one on the bottom."[120] As such, one's physical arrangement in sexual life is inextricably linked to significations of gendered power that map themselves onto our psychic lives: "It is perhaps primarily the degeneration of the sexual into a relationship that condemns sexuality to becoming a struggle for power. . . . It is the self that swells with excitement at the idea of being on top, the self that makes of the inevitable play of thrusts and relinquishments in sex an argument for the natural authority of one sex over the other."[121] Within contemporary queer cultures, the extrapolation of insertive/dominant/top/masculine and penetrative/submissive/bottom/feminine onto specifically gay and lesbian relationships has been defined by Lisa Duggan as one of the primary pillars of homonormative culture.[122]

Yet in *Dante's Cove*'s third season, magick increasingly begins to destabilize these homonormative positions. In the final season premiere, for instance, Kevin and Ambrosius have forceful sex standing up in an outdoor shower. Up until this moment, Ambrosius has only ever been the insertive sexual actor with his partners, a point consistent with figuring his masculinity in the normative manner previously described. However, Kevin's bondage to Ambrosius has paradoxically flipped their sexual roles, as Kevin forcefully penetrates Ambrosius from behind with encouraging groans, asking if he is "close" and ready to "cum." As Walters maintains, two of the chief complaints about LGBTQ+ representations on television—"that gays are token, isolated from other gay people, and that gays are desexualized, denied the pleasures of the flesh"—are contested in a series like *Dante's Cove* that proudly wears its sexual identities on its sleeve.[123] Indeed, these explicit flourishes of simulated sex and orgasmic release are a first for the series and continue throughout its final season.

Kevin's newfound contention to be the man on top in his relationship with Ambrosius is about more than sexual egalitarianism, however. *Dante's Cove*'s third season reveals that sex is actually a way for the powers of Tresum to transfer from person to person. And this revelation extends the series's queer ambivalences in suggestive ways. For example, the questionable morality and dubious ethics heretofore attributed to Ambrosius steadily begin to inflect the thought-to-be-incorruptible Kevin. After each of their lovemaking sessions, Kevin steals away while his partner is asleep to read the Book of Tresum and discover more of its magickal secrets. As a new practitioner drunk with power, Kevin intends to use Tresum against Ambrosius to escape from his bondage and return to Toby.

With seeds of deceitful desire planted since its first season, the erotic triangulation between Kevin, Toby, and Ambrosius raises a set of questions that propel *Dante's Cove* beyond a narrow, positivist politics of queer representation: Can someone be forced into love? Must both sexual and romantic relationships between men be built on equality and egalitarianism? What is the place of promiscuity in queer life? How does surrendering to another shift the power dynamics of a relationship? After Kevin finally conjures enough magickal strength to overcome Ambrosius, he returns to Toby expecting to be greeted with all the praises reserved for masculine heroism. Instead, what he finds is a distant former lover whose patience has run dry. Casting a spell to pull Toby away from Adam, who has finally come out about both his sexuality and years-long love for his best friend,

Kevin falters when Toby reminds him that true love has nothing to do with possession. "He [Adam] doesn't even know magick," Kevin indignantly declares. "I'm the one who can give you what you want!"

At the same time that Kevin attempts to salvage his relationship with Toby, Ambrosius endeavors to reclaim his own superiority in order to win Kevin back. This undertaking is supported with the aid of Griffen (Jensen Atwood), a bisexual consort of the Tresum Council sent to Dante's Cove with the mission of making sure that magick on the island doesn't run amuck. Gradually seducing Ambrosius, Griffen introduces him to the power that sex can have in siphoning magickal energy from others but reminds him, akin to Toby's warning to Kevin, that such transactions shouldn't be about possessive domination. However, when a local sex club known as the Lair presents Ambrosius with an endless supply of naked men whose vitalities are free for the taking, the temptations of power quickly become too great.

All this circular jockeying for power and supremacy eventually culminates in *Dante's Cove*'s series finale, when Ambrosius, Kevin, Toby, Grace, and Griffen prevent a malevolent magickal force known as the House of Shadows from taking over the island. During an elongated battle sequence, Toby suffers the same fate as Adam in the penultimate episode, being pulled into a mystical nether realm from which there is little hope of escape. It is also during this final mêlée that, on the brink of death, Kevin and Ambrosius rekindle their love. In the closing scene, Ambrosius and Kevin lie naked in bed discussing everything they've been through. Even though Ambrosius reminds him that he's free to leave at any time, Kevin assures him that there's nowhere else he'd rather be. As the couple kisses and begins to make love, the camera pans to a mirror that superimposes Kevin and Ambrosius with Toby and Adam trapped in their magickal prison.

In Elliott-Smith's analysis of *Dante's Cove*, the series presents a homonormative vision of queer life that foregrounds assimilation and conformity, with almost exclusively white, chiseled Adonises curbing any substantive leanings toward political provocation or sexual radicalism.[124] Yet while racial and bodily diversity may be far from *Dante's Cove*'s representational forte, the series does foreground a demonstrable ambivalence surrounding queer identities and sexualities. As Samuel Chambers writes, in distinction to "lesbian and gay studies' effort to affirm and sometimes reify what it often took as some sort of 'given'—namely gay identity or sexual orientation," queerness starts from an impulse to "question, problematise, or even disclaim the very idea of a fixed, abiding notion of identity."[125] Indeed, throughout their relationship on *Dante's Cove*, Ambrosius and Kevin are enigmatically drawn to each other precisely because their ambivalent natures resist any notions of finality and/or fixity. Both are concurrently kind and cruel, conniving and sincere, loving and selfish, top and bottom, masculine and feminine, as their relationship televises what Bersani argues are some of the inestimable values of queer sex—"at least in certain of its ineradicable aspects—[as] anticommunal, antiegalitarian, antinurturing, antiloving."[126] Rekindling the relationship between Kevin and Ambrosius as a deliberate juxtaposition over the more normatively nurturing Toby and Adam presents a version of queer masculinity that "advertises the risk of the sexual itself as the risk of self-dismissal, of losing sight of the self," and in so doing proposes and provocatively represents magickal *jouissance* as a burgeoning horizon of contemporary queerness.[127]

According to Michael Newman and Elana Levine, no form of televised storytelling has been more celebrated over the past thirty-five years than serialized drama: "Taking a broad narrative scope and parceling out storytelling in regular installments [has] function[ed] to elevate television above its historical status as intellectually worthless mass culture."[128] Yet despite both the industrial and cultural enthusiasm for serialization, such lionizing has rarely made flattering reference to the genre that pioneered serialized television narrative: the soap opera.[129] As previously noted, contemporary discourses of televisual quality have been increasingly beholden to gender and sexual specificities as markers of cultural distinction, as the presence of soapy elements such as "domestic settings, drawn-out family and relationship narratives, and heightened emotional sensibility helps determine a given program's place on a scale of distinction within the category of Quality TV."[130] In the context of LGBTQ+ cable on here!, however, such traditionally feminized soap content continues to be reworked through a more fluid lens in order to challenge both the gender and sexual norms of long-form television storytelling.

Soon after *Dante's Cove*'s third-season finale aired on December 21, 2007, here! announced that the series would be brought back for a fourth season, one that has yet to materialize. Ever since, the fates of Kevin, Ambrosius, Toby, and Adam have been left to speculation. According to Glyn Davis and Gary Needham, the cancelled TV series, hanging without resolution, "could be seen as one of the queerest aspects of television programming and experience. The sense of conclusion and satisfaction delivered by the closed text—which arguably serves to valourise conservative and patriarchal ideologies—is not provided, replaced instead by a formless open-ended yearning, a realm of possibilities without barricades."[131] In the case of *Dante's Cove*, this open-ended yearning is both left hanging and reworked in a spin-off series, *The Lair*, following the goings on inside the island's local sex club that has been taken over by a coven of gay male vampire witches. As such, both of these series not only employ conventions of the occult to paint increasingly ambivalent portraits of contemporary queer masculinities and relationships between men, but also serve to destabilize the very definition of seriality itself in the postnetwork era.

Notes

1. For a more in-depth queer analysis of *Buffy the Vampire Slayer*, see Allison McCracken, "At Stake: Angel's Body, Fantasy Masculinity, and Queer Desire in Teen Television," in *Undead TV: Essays on* Buffy the Vampire Slayer, ed. Elana Levine and Lisa Parks (Durham: Duke University Press, 2007): 116–44.

2. Suzanna Danuta Walters, *All the Rage: The Story of Gay Visibility in America* (Chicago: University of Chicago Press, 2001), 59.

3. Ibid.

4. Cited in Amanda D. Lotz, *The Television Will Be Revolutionized* (New York: New York University Press, 2007), 11.

5. Ibid.

6. Lorna Jowett and Stacey Abbott, *TV Horror: Investigating the Dark Side of the Small Screen* (London: I. B. Tauris, 2013), 2.

7. Walters, 61.

8. John Caldwell, "Convergence Television: Aggregating Form and Repurposing Content in the Culture of Conglomeration," in *Television After TV: Essays on a Medium in Transition*, ed. Lynn Spigel and Jan Olsson (Durham: Duke University Press, 2004), 45.

9. Ibid., 66.

10. According to Ron Becker, "After reaching all-time highs in the 1979–1980 season in which ABC, CBS, and NBC together captured a 56.5 rating and 90 percent of prime-time audiences, network ratings and market share steadily dropped year by year. Between 1980 and 1990, the networks' portion of the prime-time audience dropped 28 percent to a 39.7 rating and a 65 share. By the end of the 1990s, the Big 3's share of prime-time viewers was half of what it had been at the end of the 1970s (27.0/43)." See Becker, *Gay TV and Straight America* (New Brunswick, NJ: Rutgers University Press, 2006), 87.

11. Jane Feuer, "HBO and the Concept of Quality TV," in *Quality TV: Contemporary American Television and Beyond*, ed. Janet McCabe and Kim Akass (London: I. B. Tauris, 2007), 147.

12. Michael Z. Newman and Elana Levine, *Legitimating Television: Media Convergence and Cultural Status* (New York: Routledge, 2012), 10–11.

13. Becker, 81.

14. Anna McCarthy, "'Must See' Queer TV: History and Serial Form in *Ellen*," in *Quality Popular Television: Cult TV, The Industry and Fans*, ed. Mark Jancovich and James Lyons (London: British Film Institute, 2003), 90.

15. Ellis Hanson, "Lesbians Who Bite," in *Out Takes: Essays on Queer Theory and Film*, ed. Ellis Hanson (Durham: Duke University Press, 1999), 191.

16. Christoph Grunenberg, *Gothic: Transmutations of Horror in Late Twentieth Century Art* (Cambridge: MIT Press, 1997), 210.

17. Jowett and Abbott, 11.

18. Ibid., 135.

19. Lynne Joyrich, "Epistemology of the Console," in *Queer TV: Theories, Histories, Politics*, ed. Glyn Davis and Gary Needham (New York: Routledge, 2009), 24.

20. Helen Wheatley, *Gothic Television* (Manchester: Manchester University Press, 2006), 154.

21. Amy Villarejo, *Ethereal Queer: Television, Historicity, Desire* (Durham: Duke University Press, 2014), 3.

22. Adam Smith, "Tony Scott On Tony Scott," Empire Online, August 20, 2012, https://www.empireonline.com/movies/features/tony-scott-tony-scott/.

23. Erik Barnouw, *Tube of Plenty: The Evolution of American Television* (New York: Oxford University Press, 1990), 493–94.

24. Patrick Parsons, *Blue Skies: A History of Cable Television* (Philadelphia: Temple University Press, 2008), 702.

25. Ibid.

26. Jennifer Holt, "Vertical Vision: Deregulation, Industrial Economy and Prime-Time Design," in *Quality Popular Television: Cult TV, The Industry and Fans*, ed. Mark Jancovich and James Lyons (London: British Film Institute, 2003), 14.

27. Ibid.

28. Lotz, *The Television Will Be Revolutionized*, 86.

29. David S. Silverman, *You Can't Air That: Four Cases of Controversy and Censorship in American Television Programming* (Syracuse: Syracuse University Press, 2007), 21.

30. Holt, 12.

31. Silverman, 3.

32. Ibid.

33. For an in-depth discussion of the NAB's Television Code, see Deborah Jaramillo, *The Television Code: Regulating the Screen to Safeguard the Industry* (Austin: University of Texas Press, 2018).

34. Silverman, 7.

35. Ibid., 24.

36. Luke Stadel, "Cable, Pornography, and the Reinvention of Television, 1982–1989," *Cinema Journal* 53, no. 3 (Spring 2014): 53.

37. Brendan Koerner, "Can the FCC Regulate HBO?," *Slate*, February 12, 2004.

38. Lotz, *The Television Will Be Revolutionized*, 2.

39. Ibid., 5.

40. Ibid.

41. See Horace Newcomb and Paul M. Hirsch, "Television as a Cultural Forum," in *Television: The Critical View*, ed. Horace Newcomb, 6th ed. (New York: Oxford University Press, 2000), 561–73.

42. Lotz, *The Television Will Be Revolutionized*, 29.
43. Ibid., 43.
44. Becker, 83–84.
45. Samuel A. Chambers, *The Queer Politics of Television* (London: I. B. Tauris, 2009), 35–36.
46. Becker, 108.
47. For discussions of direct-to-video cinema and sexuality, see David Andrews, *Soft in the Middle: The Contemporary Softcore Feature in Its Contexts* (Columbus: Ohio State University Press, 2006); Nina K. Martin, *Sexy Thrills: Undressing the Erotic Thriller* (Urbana: University of Illinois Press, 2007); and Linda Ruth Williams, *The Erotic Thriller in Contemporary Cinema* (Bloomington: Indiana University Press, 2005).
48. Becker, 98.
49. Cited in Ibid., 96.
50. Stadel, 57.
51. Parsons, 634–35.
52. Silverman, 26.
53. Ibid.
54. Ibid., 27.
55. Cited in Janet McCabe and Kim Akass, "Sex, Swearing and Respectability: Courting Controversy, HBO's Original Programming and Producing Quality TV," in *Quality TV: Contemporary American Television and Beyond*, ed. Janet McCabe and Kim Akass (London: I. B. Tauris, 2007), 65.
56. See Foucault's discussion of "the repressive hypothesis" in *The History of Sexuality, Vol. 1: An Introduction*, trans. Robert Hurley (New York: Vintage, 1990).
57. McCabe and Akass, 64.
58. Ibid., 67.
59. Joe Flint, "Spotlight: Showtime Twenty Years—Cable's Heavyweight," *Variety*, April 29, 1996.
60. Andrews, 168.
61. The television anthology format can be defined as a "freestanding, original teleplay [broadcast] each week." See Newman and Levine, 21.
62. Andrews, 14.
63. Martin, 47.
64. Ibid., 28.
65. Ibid., 2.
66. Jowett and Abbott, 11.
67. Ray Richmond, "22 Episodes Sate Showtime's 'Hunger,'" *Variety*, May 13, 1996.
68. Colin Brown, "Scott Brothers Create Hunger," *Screen International*, November 22, 1996.
69. Eve Sedgwick, *The Coherence of Gothic Conventions* (New York: Methuen, 1980), viii.
70. Jeffrey Sconce, *Haunted Media: Electronic Presence from Telegraphy to Television* (Durham: Duke University Press, 2000), 46.
71. Villarejo, 46–47.
72. Ibid., 7.
73. Joyrich, 24.
74. Ibid.

75. Jeff Fazio, *The Hunger*: Season 1, DVD, n.d.
76. Giovanni Ribisi, *The Hunger*: Season 2, DVD, n.d.
77. Joyrich, 20.
78. Jeffrey Sconce, "What If?: Charting Television's New Textual Boundaries," in *Television After TV: Essays on a Medium in Transition*, ed. Lynn Spigel and Jan Olsson (Durham: Duke University Press, 2004), 101.
79. Chambers, 41.
80. McCarthy, 91.
81. Glyn Davis and Gary Needham, "Introduction: The Pleasures of the Tube," in *Queer TV: Theories, Histories, Politics*, ed. Glyn Davis and Gary Needham (New York: Routledge, 2009), 7.
82. Michele Aaron, "Towards Queer Television Theory: Bigger Pictures sans the Sweet Queer-After," in *Queer TV: Theories, Histories, Politics*, ed. Glyn Davis and Gary Needham (New York: Routledge, 2009), 64.
83. Ibid.
84. Katherine Sender, "Dualcasting: Bravo's Gay Programming and the Quest for Women Audiences," in *Cable Visions: Television Beyond Broadcasting*, ed. Sarah Banet-Weiser, Cynthia Chris, and Anthony Freitas (New York: New York University Press, 2007), 314.
85. Cited in Linda Moss, "Pushing the Boundaries: Fledgling Nets Will Supply a Groundswell of Gay Fare," *Multichannel News*, October 18, 2004.
86. Anthony Freitas, "Gay Programming, Gay Publics: Public and Private Tensions in Lesbian and Gay Cable Channels," in *Cable Visions: Television Beyond Broadcasting*, ed. Sarah Banet-Weiser, Cynthia Chris, and Anthony Freitas (New York: New York University Press, 2007), 219.
87. Ibid., 220.
88. Caldwell, 68.
89. John Dempsey, "DirecTV Bows PPV Service for Gay Auds," *Daily Variety*, July 8, 2003.
90. Ibid.
91. Moss, "Pushing the Boundaries."
92. Cited in Tim Clark, "Here, Logo Grow as Their Ranks Shrink," *Multichannel News*, July 10, 2006.
93. Linda Moss, "Gay-Aimed 'Here! TV' Goes Premium," *Multichannel News*, October 4, 2004.
94. Cited in Moss, "Pushing the Boundaries."
95. Cited in Lawrence Christon, "The Revolution Has Been Televised: Gay Images on TV Not Always Politically Correct, nor Uniform, but Isn't That the Point?," *Daily Variety*, April 28, 2005.
96. Stuart Levine, "Cablers Step up to the Plate with Original Gay Programming," *Daily Variety*, April 7, 2006.
97. Zara Taylor, *Dante's Cove*: Season 1 Backlot, DVD, n.d.
98. Tracy Scoggins, Charlie David, and Josh Berresford, *Dante's Cove*: Season 1 Backlot, DVD, n.d.
99. Tracy Scoggins, *Dante's Cove*: Season 1 Backlot, DVD, n.d.
100. Darren Elliott-Smith, "'Blood, Sugar, Sex, Magik': Unearthing Gay Male Anxieties in Queer Gothic Soaps *Dante's Cove* (2005–2007) and *The Lair* (2007–2009)" in *Melodrama in Contemporary Film and Television*, ed. Michael Stewart (New York: Palgrave Macmillan, 2014), 96.

101. Amanda D. Lotz, *Cable Guys: Television and Masculinities in the Twenty-First Century* (New York: New York University Press, 2014), 49.
102. Elliott-Smith, 99.
103. Walters, *All the Rage: The Story of Gay Visibility in America*, 121.
104. Jowett and Abbott, 46–47.
105. Charlie David, *Dante's Cove*: Season 2 Backlot, DVD, n.d.
106. Sam Irvin, *Dante's Cove*: Season 3 Backlot, DVD, n.d.
107. Gabriel Romero, The Men of *Dante's Cove*, DVD, n.d.
108. Paul Colichman, *Dante's Cove*: Season 1 Backlot, DVD, n.d.
109. Cited in Dempsey.
110. Cited in Moss, "Gay-Aimed 'Here! TV' Goes Premium."
111. Cited in Moss, "Pushing the Boundaries."
112. Thomas Waugh, *Hard to Imagine: Gay Male Eroticism in Photography and Film from Their Beginnings to Stonewall* (New York: Columbia University Press, 1996), 5.
113. Ibid., 12.
114. Colichman.
115. McCabe and Akass, 75.
116. F. Hollis Griffin, *Feeling Normal: Sexuality and Media Criticism in the Digital Age* (Bloomington: Indiana University Press, 2017), 4.
117. Elliott-Smith, 104–5.
118. Irvin.
119. Nguyen Tan Hoang, *A View from the Bottom: Asian American Masculinity and Sexual Representation* (Durham: Duke University Press, 2014), 6–7.
120. Leo Bersani, "Is the Rectum a Grave?," *October* 43 (Winter 1987): 216.
121. Ibid., 218.
122. See Lisa Duggan, *The Twilight of Equality?: Neoliberalism, Cultural Politics, and the Attack On Democracy* (Boston: Beacon, 2003).
123. Walters, 121.
124. Elliott-Smith, 101.
125. Chambers, 13.
126. Bersani, 215.
127. Ibid., 222.
128. Newman and Levine, 80–81.
129. Ibid., 81.
130. Ibid., 97–98.
131. Davis and Needham, 5.

EPILOGUE

On May 17, 2015, Showtime premiered the third episode in the second season of its hit supernatural drama *Penny Dreadful*. Imagining a fin de siècle London throughout which the lives of both original and adapted characters from nineteenth-century Gothic fiction collide, including Dr. Victor Frankenstein (Harry Treadaway) and Dorian Gray (Reeve Carney), this particular episode dedicates its narrative exclusively to the backstory of the series's central protagonist, Vanessa Ives (Eva Green). Haunted by demons, both literal and figurative, from her past, Vanessa confides in Ethan Chandler (Josh Hartnett), *Penny Dreadful*'s own bachelor-turned-werewolf whose influences from *Dark Shadows*' Quentin Collins are more than slight. "It all began several years ago," Vanessa's flashback commences, "and far from here."

Seeking answers to exactly who and what she is, Vanessa travels to the farthest reaches of the English highlands in search of a two-hundred-year-old witch known only as the Cut-Wife of Ballantrae Moor (Patti LuPone). Over several days of withstanding wind, rain, and lightning at the Cut-Wife's gate, Vanessa proves that she is more than a naïve village girl searching for a love potion or the witch's namesake specialty of abortion. Vanessa's merit is, moreover, proved through an introductory encounter most queer, as the Cut-Wife thrusts her hand up the young girl's skirt in order to "sense" her person via the most intimate areas of her body. "I am like no others," Vanessa confesses. "That's why I'm here."

"Leave everything you were outside this door," the Cut-Wife responds. "Everything you are, bring with you."

Once inside the Cut-Wife's cottage, what Vanessa is becomes increasingly clear: a tortured soul with magickal gifts who seeks redemption after failing to save her best friend Mina, whom she confesses to kissing and feeling romantic affection for, from capture by malevolent supernatural forces. As Vanessa discovers under the Cut-Wife's tutelage, however, magick is a fickle mistress that rarely rewards even the best of intentions. "I started thinking about themes," *Penny Dreadful* showrunner and head writer John

Logan told the *Hollywood Reporter*'s Lesley Goldberg in a January 2014 interview, "and why almost 200 years after [Mary Shelley's *Frankenstein*] was written, we're still reading *Frankenstein*. . . . I think it's because the monsters break my heart. Growing up as a gay man before it was socially acceptable, I knew what it was to feel different, alienated and not like everyone else."[1] If much of the affectively queer resonance of being a witch, a vampire, or any other supernatural entity resounds with a celebration of outlawry, secrecy, and living on the edge, then both the Cut-Wife and Vanessa exemplify this inclination. "Monsters all, are we not?" the Cut-Wife often reminds her protégé.

Upon *Penny Dreadful*'s premiere in May 2014, Tim Goodman, also of the *Hollywood Reporter*, began a review of the series's first episode by stating unequivocally that "the world doesn't need another psychosexual horror story."[2] Appearing on the crest of a media wave that included HBO's *True Blood*, F/X's *American Horror Story*, and the CW's *The Vampire Diaries*, *Penny Dreadful* struck Goodman as symptomatic of a genre that risked, quite literally, being done to death. Yet, as argued throughout this book, the cyclical recurrence of occult horror's deathly eroticism is exactly what the world, or at least a queer version of it, has proven itself to habitually require. Indeed, over the past sixty years, stories of the occultly marvelous have become some of the most fertile grounds for queer genders, sexualities, and sexual practices to make their mark upon Euro-American visual culture.

When asked why he chose to write *Penny Dreadful* as a period drama, Logan responded in revealing fashion: "I chose to set the show [in 1891] not because it would be cool visually but because the Victorian era reminds me of right now. . . . They were on the cusp of the modern world . . . grappling with the very elemental question of what it means to be human."[3] What's more, occult horror has thrived and will likely continue to thrive in both film and television precisely because its "always already queer"-ness has proven particularly portable not just in envisioning what it means to be human or even a human sexual subject but especially what it means to be queer.

Indeed, the queerness of contemporary occult media has constituted a robust constellation of media texts and sociocultural contexts that have coalesced into one of film and television horror's most enduring genres over the past sixty years. Yet the journey this book traces from *Dark Shadows* to *Dante's Cove* is far from comprehensive. Nor would I wish it to be. Following Noël Carroll, we would do well as media scholars not only to ask why particular genres persist but also why genre studies as a field of enquiry continues to endure. One answer may be found within the continuously shifting horizons of both past and present possibility that resist even our most emphatic urges to write the history of any given generic grouping. Indeed, it is only through the multiplicity of these generic histories that we can begin to grasp the dialectic between visual culture and particular forms of cultural production.

At the conclusion of the *Penny Dreadful* episode with which I began, Vanessa Ives watches in terrified anticipation while a mob of local villagers approaches to execute the Cut-Wife. Resigning herself to a death she believes to be long overdue, the Cut-Wife, now known more intimately to Vanessa as Joan Clayton, leaves her companion with a final aide-mémoire: "When Lucifer fell, he did not fall alone. They will hunt you until the end of days. Be true." The morning after Joan's execution, Vanessa takes up her mentor's charge as a new modus operandi. And while Vanessa's journey toward redemption may be just another psychosexual horror story to some, such narratives have and will continue to both hunt and haunt us for the foreseeable future. Indeed, the queer legibility that this genre authorizes may be the clearest avenue for both our screens and mediated selves to continue desiring after dark.

Notes

1. Cited in Lesley Goldberg, "Showtime's Monster Drama 'Penny Dreadful' Will Explore Modern Themes," Hollywood Reporter, January 16, 2014, http://www.hollywoodreporter.com/live-feed/showtimes-monster-drama-penny-dreadful-671676.

2. Tim Goodman, "Penny Dreadful: TV Review," Hollywood Reporter, May 8, 2014, http://www.hollywoodreporter.com/review/tv-review-showtimes-penny-dreadful-702313.

3. Cited in Goldberg.

INDEX

Aaron, Michele, 179
Abbott, Stacey, 32, 124, 161, 164, 174, 184
ABC: and counterculture programming, 27–28, 37, 42; and *Dark Shadows*, 24–25, 52n32, 167; Department of Broadcast Standards and Practices, 37; and *Ellen*, 163, 178–79; and family programming, 161; and fin-syn, 166; prime-time audience, 193n10; public availability, 168
abjection: and barebacking, 132–34; and HIV/AIDS, 109, 117–18; and menstruation, 116; and nonnormative sexuality, 85; as site of pleasure, 6; vampiric, 119, 121, 125, 134
Ackerman, Forrest J., 69
Addams Family, The, 18, 28
Adler, Margot, 146
AIDS: and barebacking, 130–34; beginning of epidemic, 101–2; in cultural imagination, 107, 109; mentioned, 2; and urbanism, 110–12, 114–15; and vampirism, 103–4, 112–20, 123–24, 130–33
Akass, Kim, 187
Allen, Robert, 33
Allied Artists, 4
American Horror Story, 2, 199
American International Pictures, 18, 55n114, 78, 84
American Underground, the: crossover success of, 71; history of, 63–64; and sexuality, 58, 62, 66, 68, 76, 95
And God Created Woman, 83
Andrews, David, 173
Anger, Kenneth: biography, 65–66, 69; films, 66–68, 71–74; mentioned, 57–58, 64, 92, 93. See also *Fireworks*, *Scorpio Rising*
Animals, the, 74
Aquarius Releasing, Inc., 84
Arnold, Catharine, 39
art cinema, 58, 83–86, 90

As the World Turns, 25–26. See also soap opera
astrology. See divination
Auerbach, Nina, 126

Bad Girls Go to Hell, 62
Banet-Weiser, Sarah, 153–54
Barebackula, 133
Barnouw, Erik, 165
Bataille, Georges: *The Accursed Share*, 16; theory of eroticism, 6, 137n85
Batman (television), 29
BBC, 2, 42
BDSM. See sadomasochism
Beatles, the, 42
Becker, Ron, 163, 169
Being Human, 2
Bennett, Jeffrey, 103
Benshoff, Harry, 5, 12, 27, 34, 60, 122
Berger, Helen, 147, 149
Bergier, Jacques, 16–19, 22, 29, 40–41
Bersani, Leo, 133, 189, 192
bestiality, 19, 82, 91
Beverly Hills Bordello, 173
Bewitched, 27–29
Bibby, Michael, 115
Black Sabbath (film), 18, 84
Black Sunday (film), 18, 84
Blavatsky, Helena Petrovna, 18. See also Theosophical Society
Blood and Roses, 44, 84
Bloom, Harold, 1–2
body genres: definition of, 96n17; and exploitation film, 62–63, 84
Bolte, Caralyn, 154
Bradbury, Ray: *Something Wicked This Way Comes*, 18
Brakhage, Stan, 64
Bravmann, Scott, 22, 50
Breaking Bad, 164

201

Bride of Frankenstein, The, 27, 66
Brides of Dracula, The, 43
British Board of Film Classification, 43–46, 48, 58. *See also* obscenity
British Witchcraft Act of 1736, 145
Bronski, Michael, 8
Brotherhood, The, 185–86
Buffy the Vampire Slayer, 2, 12, 160, 182
Byron, Lord, 39

Cabinet of Dr. Caligari, The, 105
Caged Virgins, 93
Caldwell, Joseph, 32, 37, 162
camp: as reading strategy, 64; sitcoms and, 29; types of, 50
cannibalism, 7
Carmilla (J. Sheridan Le Fanu), 12, 48–49; film adaptation of, 44
Carroll, Noël, 11, 199
Castle of Blood, 84
Catholicism, 89, 145, 150, 154–55. *See also* Christianity
CBS: family programming, 161; and fin-syn, 166; popularity of, 25–26; and prime-time, 193n10; public availability, 168
CBS Gold Classic, The, 23
censorship. *See* obscenity
de Certeau, Michel, 104, 110
Chambers, Samuel, 169, 178, 191
Chant D'Amour, Un, 57
Charmed, 2
Chauncey, George, 60, 110, 115
Cho, Alexander, 140–41
Christianity: and gothic subculture, 115; and heteronormativity, 21–22; sexual repression, 73; and Wiccan principles, 143–44, 146
Church of Satan. *See* Satanism
Cinemation, 78
Cinerama, 78
civil rights movement, 26, 32
Clark, Lynn Schofield, 141, 146, 152
Classification and Ratings System. *See* Motion Picture Association of America
Clover, Carol, 11, 92–93
Columbia Pictures, 86, 148–49

Communications Decency Act, 170–71. *See also* Federal Communications Commission, obscenity
Corman, Roger, 18, 185
Council of American Witches, 143
counterculture: 1960s, 18–21, 26–29, 31–32, 36, 43, 47, 50, 58, 74, 76, 148; British, 42; and fashion, 88; gothic, 114–15; occult, 19, 25, 29, 69, 79; queer, 22, 50
Covenant, The, 2
Craft, The, 2, 149–57
creature feature, 3–4
Creed, Barbara, 116, 118–19
Crimp, Douglas, 109, 132
Crimson Cult, 18
Crowley, Aleister, 18, 39–42, 48, 65, 67, 70. *See also* Hermetic Order of the Golden Dawn, Thelema
culture wars, 100–1
Curse of Frankenstein, The, 42–43
Curtis, Dan, 23–29, 31

Dallas, 162
Dante's Cove, 164, 182–93, 199
Dark Shadows: camp and, 50; development, 23–27; fan cultures of, 35–37; mentioned, 18; queerness in, 31–32, 35, 37, 42–43; reception, 29–30; as soap opera, 33–34; syndication of, 35
Davis, Glyn, 179, 187, 192
Dean, Tim, 131–32, 134
Deep Throat, 79, 93
DeGeneres, Ellen, 163, 178–79
Delany, Samuel R., 111, 115
Deren, Maya, 64–65
Devil in Miss Jones, The: critical reception, 80; mentioned, 94; premiere of, 79; queerness in, 81–83
Devil Rides Out, The, 42
Diamond, Lisa M., 142
Dick Cavett Show, 20
DirecTV, 181
Dish Network, 181
divination, 18
doppelgänger, 174–75, 177–78
Doty, Alexander, 4–5, 13, 37

Douglas, Susan, 28
Dracula (1931 film), 27, 100
Dracula (Bram Stoker), 12, 37, 39, 69, 105
Dracula Has Risen from the Grave, 43
Dracula: Prince of Darkness, 43
Dracula's Daughter, 44
drama: anthology, 179; melodrama, 29, 33, 72, 85, 96n17; period, 199; serialized, 192; suspense, 24
Duggan, Lisa, 189
Dunlop v. United States, 68. See also obscenity
Dyer, Richard, 12, 67, 73, 107, 132
Dynasty, 162

Ebert, Roger, 79, 150, 152
Edge of Night, The, 23
Elliot-Smith, Darren, 183, 188, 191
Ellis, Havelock, 7
Emmanuelle, 86
eroticism: occult, 66; queer, 71–72; terror and, 84; theories of, 6–7. See also homoeroticism
Evans, Arthur, 21–23, 29, 41, 61, 147. See also Radical Faeries
Evil of Frankenstein, The, 43
exploitation film, 62–63, 68, 81, 83–84, 93
extrasensory perception (ESP), 18
Ezzy, Douglas, 147, 149

fan: cultures, 2, 24, 26, 35–37; studies, 3–4
Fantastic Beasts, 2
Federal Communications Commission, 163–64, 166–68. See also Prime Time Access Rule, fin-syn
feminism: and goddess worship, 142; pro-sex, 82; and witchcraft, 147. See also women's movement
Feuer, Jane, 26, 162
Le Films de Saturne, 85
fin-syn (Financial Interest and Syndication), 166–67
Fireworks, 65–68, 71, 93. See also Anger, Kenneth
Flaming Creatures, 57–58
Foltz, Tanice, 149, 157

Forster, E. M., 38
Foucault, Michel, 7–8, 171
Frankenstein (1931 film), 27, 66
Frankenstein (novel), 69, 199
Frankenstein Created Woman, 43
Frankenstein Must Be Destroyed, 43
Freud, Sigmund, 7, 16. See also psychoanalysis
Friedman, Elisabeth, 140
Le Frisson des Vampires, 87–90. See also Rollin, Jean

Gardner, Gerald, 21, 145. See also Wicca
Gay Activists Alliance, 20
gay liberation, 21, 26, 48, 32, 58–61, 132. See also Stonewall rebellion
gender: difference, 11–12, 172–73; and Gothic fiction, 7; and horror, 3; nonnormative, 13, 21, 27, 48, 61, 115; postwar conventions of, 28–29; spectatorship and, 92–93, 175; television storytelling and, 175, 192; trans*, 135n22; vampires and, 106, 108, 111, 119, 128, 174, 183; witchcraft and, 72, 140–41, 149, 150, 160, 187–89
genre: and cultural hierarchies, 9–10, 66, 84–85; studies, 199–200; theories of, 2, 63. See also body genres
ghosts: and the closet, 178; in *Dante's Cove*, 185; in *Dark Shadows*, 25, 30, 36; esotericism and, 21, 69; in *Hamlet*, 1; mentioned, 36; and possession, 178; queer, 47
giallo film, 3
Gilmore, Peter H., 69
Ginsberg, Allen, 60
goddess worship, 142–43, 154
Gods and Monsters, 181
Golem, The, 105
Goodlad, Lauren, 115
Gothic: conventions of the, 5–6, 32–33, 46; erotics, 34, 133, 185; occultism, 70; revival of the, 18, 23–25; sexuality and gender in the, 7–9; subculture, 114–15; tropes, 174–75; Victorian, 39, 198
Griffin, F. Hollis, 188
Grunenberg, Christoph, 164–65
Guiding Light, 25. See also soap opera

Index

Haggard, Rider, 39
Halberstam, Judith, 7
Hamlet. See Shakespeare, William
Hammer Studios, 18, 37, 42–50, 58, 86–87, 160
Hanson, Ellis, 6, 12, 47, 109, 117, 119, 122, 163
Harner, Michael, 69
Harry Potter, 2
Haunted Castle, The, 105
Hawkins, Joan, 84
Heffernan, Kevin, 27, 148
Heilman, Robert B., 5
here!, 164, 172, 180–82, 184–87
Hermetic Order of the Golden Dawn, 18, 40, 145. *See also* Crowley, Aleister
heroin. *See* opiates
Herring, Scott, 120, 127
heteronormativity, 28, 128; anti-, 19–20, 22, 29, 34–35, 115, 183; and Christianity, 73; definition of, 169; and gender, 49, 60, 126; hegemony of, 5, 32, 109; in horror, 129, 156; and reproduction, 8–9, 50
High Priestess of Sexual Witchcraft, 94–95
Hill, Annette, 151
Hills Have Eyes, The, 168
Hill Street Blues, 161
Hirsch, Paul M., 169
HIV. *See* AIDS
Hoberman, J., 65, 66
Hoffman, Abbie, 19
Hoggart, Richard, 38
Holmes, Trevor M., 115
homonormativity, 12, 112, 189–91
homophile movement, 60
homophobia, 9, 45, 109, 120–21, 123, 140, 184
homosexuality: and the closet, 11–12; and the counterculture, 74; as magickal practice, 41, 82; and perversion, 58; mentioned, 22; and sexual liberalization, 61; and vampirism, 12, 35, 37, 44–45; Victorian ideas of, 8, 41. *See also* lesbianism
homosociality, 150–51
horror: and cultural hierarchies, 6, 9–10, 66, 84–85; and gendered spectatorship, 46–47; genre, 3, 9–10, 155; film, 27, 34, 42–43, 66, 72, 76–77, 93, 103, 153; Gothic, 5, 7, 70, 175; occult, 12, 37, 46–47, 117–18, 127, 186–87, 199; queerness and, 3–4, 11–13, 57, 60–61, 104, 116, 119, 177, 185–86; and sexuality, 10, 45–46, 62–63, 79, 83–84, 86, 93, 96n17, 129, 132, 189; television, 37, 161, 164, 184–85
Horror of Dracula, 42–43
Hot Springs Hotel, 173
House of Dracula, 27
Hunger, The (film), 112–20, 125, 165
Hunger, The (television), 164, 174–79

I Am Curious (Yellow), 84
I Ching, 33
I Drink Your Blood, 63
Immoral Mr. Teas, The, 62
incest, 5, 7, 29–30, 48, 50, 61, 89. *See also* perversity
Interview with the Vampire (film), 2
Interview with the Vampire (novel), 12
Invisible Man, The, 66
Invisible Man Returns, The, 27
Invocation of my Demon Brother, 74. *See also* Anger, Kenneth

Jackson, Shirley: *We Have Always Lived in the Castle*, 18
Jagose, Annamarie, 4, 146
Jarvis, Christine, 155
Jenkins, Henry, 36
Jowett, Lorna, 32, 161, 164, 174, 184
Joyce, James, 57
Joyrich, Lynne, 164–65, 176–77, 178
Jung, Carl, 16
Jungle Jim, 85

Kerr, Paul, 26
Killing of Sister George, The, 45
Kinsella, James, 102
Kinsey, Alfred, 67–68
Kinsey Reports, the, 19–20
Kipnis, Laura, 82
Kiss of the Vampire, The, 43
Klein, Marty, 83
von Krafft-Ebing, Richard, 7

Lachman, Gary Valentine, 17, 19
Lair, The, 183, 185, 193
Lavey, Anton, 19, 80, 81; biography, 68–71; in film, 74, 77. *See also* Satanism
Lawrence, D. H., 37–38, 44, 57
Leary, Timothy, 19

Legacies, 2
Leiber, Fritz, 69
lesbianism: in pornography, 81; and vampirism, 43–50, 85, 88, 90–91, 116–19; and witchcraft, 156, 198
Levin, Ira: *Rosemary's Baby*, 18
Levine, Elana, 26, 61, 162, 192
Lewis, Jon, 77
Lewis, Matthew: *The Monk*, 7
Little Witches, 154
London, England, 38–39
Lost Boys, 121–26
Lost in Space, 29
Lotz, Amanda, 166, 168, 183
Louv, Jason, 147
Lovers, The, 83
Love Street, 173
Love Witch, The, 2
Lucifer, 2
Lupton, Deborah, 102
Lust at First Bite/Dracula Sucks, 95
Lust Boys, The, 133
Lust for a Vampire, 46–50
lycanthrope. *See* werewolf

Mad Men, 164
Magicians, The, 2
magick: black, 49–50, 71–72, 143, 145; commodification of, 148; definition of, 5, 14n15, 17; gender and, 187–89; individualism and, 40–41; maternal, 29; mentioned, 16–17, 20, 33, 88; as narrative force, 28; necromancy, 87; pornography, 79, 81–82, 89–90; practitioners of, 19, 21–22, 39–40, 139–47; as queer practice, 21–22, 61, 156, 190, 192; rituals, 47, 49–50; Satanic, 69–71, 81, 87; sexual, 41–42, 48, 145, 191; and teenage rebellion, 148–49, 152, 157; and transgression, 19, 30, 73, 155. *See also Craft, The*; Crowley, Aleister; LaVey, Anton; occult; Satanism; witchcraft
Man and a Woman, A, 85
Manson, Charles, 19, 74–75
Martin, Nina K., 173
masochism. *See* sadomasochism
masturbation, 19, 41, 72, 81, 94, 154, 171, 188
Mattachine Society, the. *See* homophile movement

McCabe, Janet, 187
McCarthy, Anna, 163, 178
McCarthy, Joseph, 19
Mekas, Jonas, 57–58, 75–76. *See also* American Underground
Miller, Cynthia, 129
Miller v. California, 93–94. *See also* obscenity
miscegenation, 7
Modleski, Tania, 33, 34
Mod Squad, The, 20
Monogram, 4
moral panic, 9, 110. *See also* homophobia
Morrissey, Paul, 64
Motion Picture Association of America, 43, 76–78, 84, 167. *See also* obscenity
Motion Picture Production Code, 43, 76
MTV, 165, 174, 180
Munsters, The, 18, 27
Mysterious Dr. Satan, The, 85

National Association of Broadcasters, 37, 42, 162; 167–68. *See also* Television Code
National Association of Theatre Owners, 78
Near Dark, 126–30
Needham, Gary, 179, 187, 192
Newcomb, Horace, 169
Newman, Michael, 162, 192
Nguyen, Tan Hoang, 189
Nielson ratings, 25
Night of Submission, 95
Night of the Living Dead, 77
Nixon, Dr. Cecil E., 69
Nosferatu: Eine Symphonie des Grauens, 105–07
nostalgia, 39
Nurses, The, 24

obscenity: definition of, 20; prosecution, 37–38, 57–58, 68, 93–95, 167; regulation of, 37, 42–43, 163–71, 82, 89–90
occult. *See* magick, queer occultism, witchcraft
Olney, Ian, 84, 90, 93
Only Lovers Left Alive, 2
Opening of Misty Beethoven, The, 62
Originals, The, 2
Outer Limits, The, 18, 174

paganism, 22, 85, 89, 115, 140, 145–46, 153.
    See also under magick, Wicca, witchcraft
Palmer, Paulina, 30, 49
Paramount Decision, 84
Paris Adult Theatre I v. Slaton, 94. *See also* obscenity
Passions, 183
Pauwels, Louis, 16–19, 22, 29, 40–41
Penny Dreadful, 198–200
perversity: and gender deviance, 182; implantations of, 8–9; and media culture, 109, 114; mentioned, 22, 31, 32, 34, 65, 119; necrophilia, 7; occult, 48, 70, 73, 81, 84; pleasurable, 6, 49, 91; polymorphous, 8, 22, 62, 115, 121, 187; and pornography, 68, 82, 86; queer, 41–42, 58, 130, 133, 175; rural, 127–28, 130; viral, 120, 165. *See also* incest, sadomasochism
Playboy (magazine), 20
Playboy Channel, 186
Poe, Edgar Allen, 18
Polanski, Roman, 18, 77
Poltergeist, 174
pornography, 38–39, 46–47, 61–64, 68, 78–84, 89–90, 170; bareback, 133; generic conventions of, 67, 91; Satanism and, 81–82, 91. *See also* obscenity
poststructuralism, 17
Prime Time Access Rule, 166–67
Process Church of the Final Judgment, 71. *See also* Satanism
psychadelia, 20, 26–27, 39, 74
Psycho, 77
psychoanalysis: death drive, 9, 73; and film theory, 47; mentioned, 8, 10; subconscious, 10, 13, 46. *See also* death drive; Freud, Sigmund
Psych-Out, 20
pulp: magazines, 23; fiction, 174

Quartermass Xperiment, The, 42
queer: anti-urbanism, 120–23, 126–28; coming out, 11, 21, 61–62, 140–42, 145, 157; definitions of, 4–5; histories, 22, 30, 44, 47–50; identity, 22–23; urbanism, 110–12, 119–20

queer occultism: definition of, 4–6; in film, 11, 47–48, 64, 74; and sex, 73, 83, 85–86, 100, 117–18; in television, 183, 185; and transgression, 41. *See also* magick, witchcraft

Rabid, 107–9
Radcliffe, Ann: *Mysteries of Udolpho*, 7
Radical Faeries, 147
Radner, Hilary, 41
Real Sex, 170
Red Shoe Diaries, 170, 172–73
Reich, Wilhelm, 19
reproductive futurism, 34, 8–9, 34, 42
Requiem pour un Vampire, 87, 90–93. *See also* Rollin, Jean
respectability politics, 12, 133
RKO Pictures, 4
rock and roll, 18, 74, 121, 148, 153, 165
Rollin, Jean: biography, 85; influences, 88, 95; mentioned, 112, 134; occult films of, 84–87, 89–93
Rolling Stones, the, 74
Rosemary's Baby (film), 18, 77
Rosenbaum, Jonathan, 65, 66
Ross, Sharon, 157
Roszak, Theodore, 19
Roth v. United States, 38, 57, 93, 167. *See also* obscenity
Rowan and Martin's Laugh-In, 20
Rubin, Jerry, 19
Russo, Arlene, 100
R v. Penguin Books Ltd., 37–38. *See also* obscenity

sadomasochism, 7, 19, 58, 66–67, 92, 185
Satanis: The Devil's Mass, 70
Satanism, 19, 39, 62, 68, 69, 79, 87, 143–44; in film, 72–75, 77, 79–83, 84, 88–92, 95; history of, 70–71
Savin-Williams, Ritch C., 142
Scahill, Andrew, 153
Sci-Fi Channel, 35
Sconce, Jeffrey, 71, 79, 81, 175, 178
Scorpio Rising, 71–74, 76, 81. *See also* Anger, Kenneth

Screen Gems, 27
Search for Tomorrow, 26. *See also* soap opera
Secret Circle, 2
Secret Storm, The, 24
Sedgwick, Eve, 5–6, 175, 178
Sender, Katherine, 179
Le sexe qui parle, 62
sexology, 7–8
Sexorcist Devil, 95
sexploitation. *See* exploitation
sexuality. *See* homosexuality, lesbianism, pornography, queer
sexual revolution, 19–21, 23, 61: British, 38
Shadow, The, 85
Shadowhunters, 2
Shakespeare, William: *Hamlet*, 1–2; *Macbeth*, 2
shamanism, 22, 146
Shaw, Adrienne, 140
Shelley, Percy, 39
Shilts, Randy, 131
Shipka, Danny, 88
Showtime, 164, 168, 170–74, 179–80, 182, 187, 198
Silverman, David, 171
Skal, David, 103, 123
Skull of the Marquis de Sade, The, 18
slash fiction, 36
Smith, Andrew, 6
Smith, Jack, 57, 64. *See also* Flaming Creatures
Smith, Patricia Julia, 22
Smothers Brothers Comedy Hour, The, 20
soap opera, 24, 192; conventions of, 33–34, 53n68, 178; and eroticism, 52n29; and fan culture, 36; gay and lesbian, 182–84; syndication of, 35. *See also* drama
Sontag, Susan, 50, 103
Sopranos, The, 164
sorcerer. *See* witches
spectatorship: gendered, 46–47, 92–93; queer, 66–67
Spigel, Lynn, 28
St. Elsewhere, 162
Staiger, Janet, 64–65
Stanley v. Georgia, 94. *See also* obscenity

Stein, Louisa, 157
Stonewall riots, 20, 58–61. *See also* gay liberation
Strieber, Whitley: *The Hunger*, 112–16, 118
Studio One, 24
Summer with Monika, 83
Symonds, John Addington, 7

television: adult content and, 37, 163, 165–73; cable, 165–79, 180–81; and counterculture, 20, 26–27, 42, 50; daytime, 24–26; deregulation of, 166–67; domestic installation of, 19; and LGBTQ+ programming, 161, 163–65, 169, 182, 184, 187–88, 190, 192; narrowcasting, 168; occult, 2–6, 8, 12–13, 27, 157, 164; pay-per-view, 180–82; quality, 161–64, 192, 187; queer potential of, 175–79, 183, 199; ratings, 25–26; serial, 33–34; and youth programming, 141, 148–49. *See also* soap opera
Television Code, 167
Texas Chainsaw Massacre, 128
theatre, movie: adult, 78, 94; Coronet Theater, 68; New Bowery Theatre, 57
Thelema, 66, 69. *See also* Crowley, Aleister
Theosophical Society, 18. *See also* Blavatsky, Helena Petrovna
Thirst, 133
thirtysomething, 162
Thriller, 18
Times Films, 78
Todorov, Tzvetan, 63, 87
Tohill, Cathal, 85, 93
Tombs, Pete, 85, 93
Trans American Films, 84
Trans-Lux, 78
Trip, The, 20
True Blood, 2, 12, 199
Tudor, Andrew, 9
Tumblr, 139–41
Twilight, 2
Twilight Zone, The, 18, 161
Twink Blood, 133
Twinklight, 133
Twin Peaks, 160

Twins of Evil, 46–48
Two Moon Junction, 173
Tyler, Parker, 64–65, 66

Universal-International, 27, 66, 72, 160
Urban, Hugh, 6, 41

Vahimagi, Tise, 26
Vampire, The, 105
Vampire Diaries, The, 2, 12, 199
Vampire Lovers, The, 44–48, 58, 92
vampirism: and AIDS, 102, 130–31; and barebacking, 130–34; Dracula (character), 42–44; and eroticism, 34–35, 107; and folklore, 105; gay male, 122–26, 193; heteronormativity and, 126–29; lesbian, 6, 44–50, 84–88, 90–91, 116–19, 163; as metaphor for homosexuality, 109, 111; as perversion, 31–32, 50; as queer, 2, 12, 37, 100, 110–11; as romantic tragedy, 25, 30–32; as sexual disease, 103–04, 106, 112–21, 123–30, 133–34; on television, 26, 33–34; vampire hunter, 89, 124
Vampyr, 44
Vampyre, The (novel), 12
Victorian: era, 199, 39; literature, 12, 23, 43, 105; sexuality, 7–8, 41
Vietnam War, 26
Villarejo, Amy, 165, 175
Le Viol du Vampire, 85–87. See also Rollin, Jean
V is for Vampire, 103
voyeurism. See spectatorship

Wald, Priscilla, 110, 113, 119
Walpole, Horace: *Castle of Otranto*, 7
Walpurgisnacht, 72–73
Walters, Suzanna Danuta, 184, 190
warlock. See witch
Warner, Michael, 132
Watney, Simon, 109, 117, 132
Waugh, Thomas, 187
WB, the, 148, 160

Web, The, 24
Wee, Valerie, 148
Weeks, Jeffrey, 38
Weird Sisters Partnership, 22
Weiss, Andrea, 46, 119
werewolf, 25, 29, 198
Wheatley, Helen, 165, 186
When Did You Last See My Mother?, 58
Where the Action Is, 24
White, Hayden, 50
Wicca, 22, 139, 142–48, 149, 151–52
Wilde, Oscar, 39, 41
Wild in the Streets, 20
Wild Orchid, 173
Williams, Linda, 20, 64, 67, 82, 91–92
Williams, Raymond, 38
Wisker, Gina, 49
Witch, The, 2
witchcraft: alterity and, 34; commodification of, 153–54, 157; as countercultural form, 30; erotics of, 41, 79, 84; in film, 84, 87, 94–95, 150–56; and gender, 27–30, 72–73, 140, 149, 188–89; history of, 18, 21, 105, 142–46; as liberatory practice, 21, 50, 149; online, 139–41; and popular culture, 18–19; in print, 90; queerness of, 12, 37, 141, 146–47; teen, 130–40, 149; on television, 25–28, 33, 36, 185–86, 199–200. See also magick, occult, witch, Wicca
WNBC-TV, 35
Wolf Man, The, 27
Women: Stories of Passion, 173
women's liberation, 26, 32, 76, 142
Wood, Robin, 9–10, 177

X-Files, The, 160

youth: and consumerism, 148; culture, 153–54
Yurguis, Katia, 124

Zimmerman, Bonnie, 46
Ziplow, Stephen, 81

ANDREW J. OWENS is a Lecturer in the Department of Cinematic Arts at the University of Iowa.

www.ingramcontent.com/pod-product-compliance
Lightning Source LLC
Chambersburg PA
CBHW031816220426
43662CB00007B/670